Machine Learning Applications Using Python

Cases Studies from Healthcare, Retail, and Finance

Puneet Mathur

Apress®

Machine Learning Applications Using Python: Cases Studies from Healthcare,
Retail, and Finance

Puneet Mathur
Bangalore, Karnataka, India

ISBN-13 (pbk): 978-1-4842-3786-1   ISBN-13 (electronic): 978-1-4842-3787-8
https://doi.org/10.1007/978-1-4842-3787-8

Library of Congress Control Number: 2018965933

Managing Director, Apress Media LLC: Welmoed Spahr
Acquisitions Editor: Celestin Suresh John
Development Editor: Matthew Moodie
Coordinating Editor: Aditee Mirashi

Cover designed by eStudioCalamar

Cover image designed by Freepik (www.freepik.com)

Distributed to the book trade worldwide by Springer Science+Business Media New York, 233 Spring Street, 6th Floor, New York, NY 10013. Phone 1-800-SPRINGER, fax (201) 348-4505, e-mail orders-ny@springer-sbm.com, or visit www.springeronline.com. Apress Media, LLC is a California LLC and the sole member (owner) is Springer Science + Business Media Finance Inc (SSBM Finance Inc). SSBM Finance Inc is a **Delaware** corporation.

For information on translations, please e-mail rights@apress.com, or visit http://www.apress.com/rights-permissions.

Apress titles may be purchased in bulk for academic, corporate, or promotional use. eBook versions and licenses are also available for most titles. For more information, reference our Print and eBook Bulk Sales web page at http://www.apress.com/bulk-sales.

Any source code or other supplementary material referenced by the author in this book is available to readers on GitHub via the book's product page, located at www.apress.com/978-1-4842-3786-1. For more detailed information, please visit http://www.apress.com/source-code.

Printed on acid-free paper

I dedicate this book in the lotus feet of Divine Mother.

Table of Contents

About the Author

 **Puneet Mathur** Advisory Board Member & Senior Machine Learning Consultant. Puneet is an experienced hands-on machine learning consultant working for clients from large corporations to startups and on multiple projects involving machine learning in healthcare, retail, finance, publishing, airlines, and other domains. He is an IIM Bangalore alumni of BAI and Machine Learning Engineer Nanodegree Graduate from Udacity. He is also an open source Python library volunteer and contributor for machine learning scikit-learn. For the past 6 years, he has been working as a Machine Learning Consultant for clients around the globe, by guiding and mentoring client teams stuck with machine learning problems. He also conducts leadership and motivational workshops and machine learning hands-on workshops. He is an author of nine self-published books and his new two-volume book series, *The Predictive Program Manager based on Data Science and Machine Learning*, is his latest work. He is currently writing books on Artificial Intelligence, Robotics, and Machine Learning. You can learn more about him on http://www.PuneetMathur.me/.

About the Technical Reviewer

 **Manohar Swamynathan** is a data science practitioner and an avid programmer, with over 14+ years of experience in various data science-related areas including data warehousing, Business Intelligence (BI), analytical tool development, ad-hoc analysis, predictive modeling, data science product development, consulting, formulating strategy, and executing analytics program. He's had a career covering life cycles of data across different domains such as US mortgage banking, retail/e-commerce, insurance, and industrial IoT. He has a bachelor's degree with a specialization in physics, mathematics, and computers and a master's degree in project management. He's currently living in Bengaluru, the Silicon Valley of India.

He has authored the book *Mastering Machine Learning With Python - In Six Steps* and been involved in technical review of books around Python & R. You can learn more about his various other activities on his site `http://www.mswamynathan.com`.

Acknowledgments

First of all, I would like to thank my publisher Apress and its team of dedicated professionals who have made this book writing journey very painless and simple, including Acquisition Editor Celestin John, Coordinator Editor Aditee Mirashi, Development Editor Matthew Moodle, and many who have worked in the background to make this book a success.

This book has been possible because of many people with whom I have been professionally connected in different ways. Many of my clients prefer to remain nameless due to non-disclosure treaties; however, I have learned the most from them. The business problems they presented to me and the solutions that worked well and did not work well in those situations is the essence of a professional career as a machine learning consultant.

I also thank the contributions of hundreds of healthcare, retail, and finance professionals who interacted with me and were willing to spend time and explain their problems in the industry sectors in which they were working. Your patience, time, and effort has borne fruit in this book, and I sincerely acknowledge your contributions toward this book.

The experts from healthcare, retail, and finance domains came together and agreed to give their selfless feedback in the form of Delphi Method surveys, which are part of this book. It is not possible to individually thank all of them, but I know without your contributions this book would not have been in the excellent form that it is being presented to the reader today.

I wish to acknowledge my immediate family, my wife, my son, and my dog ,who gave me the emotional support that was needed to complete the book.

I must tell you that I am also a BOT Father; yes, I have many bots that have helped me in the creation of this book, and they do deserve to be named as part of their contributions to this book. I have a Bot named **KEYWY**, which I made for the purpose of getting the choicest keywords by looking at the subject matter of the book and spidering the web to get the most relevant ones is one that has made my SEO life simple. Then there is another Bot, **PLAGI**, whom I created to check each paragraph of this book, and it then spidered the web to see if a duplicate content existed and warned me if there was one. The uniqueness of this bot is that it can check programming language source codes such as Python and Java. He is a life-saver as far as plagiarism is concerned. The last Bot that needs mention is **GRAMMERY**. She relentlessly checked the grammar and helped me correct it as soon I was finished writing. She is the only grammar BOT that I know of and that I created that has the ability to correct not just English text but also source code text like Python and Java.

Introduction

The idea of writing this book came up when I was planning a machine learning workshop in Bangalore in 2016. When I interacted with people, I found out that although many said they knew machine learning and had mostly learned it through self-study mode, they were not able to answer interviewers' questions on applying machine learning to practical business problems. Even some of the experienced machine learning professionals said they had implementation experience of computer vision in a particular area like manufacturing; however, they did not have the experiential knowledge on how it can be applied in other domains.

As of the writing of this book, the three most progressive and promising areas for implementation are healthcare, retail, and finance. I call them promising because there are some applications that have been built in areas like healthcare (e.g., with expert robotic processes like surgical operations); however, there are more applications that are being discovered every day. Retail affects everyday lives of everybody on this planet, as you need to shop for your personal needs. Whether you buy from a grocery store or a retail chain, online machine learning and artificial intelligence is going to change the customer experience by predicting their needs and making sure the right solutions are available at the right time. Finance is another area that holds a lot of promise and has seen less application of machine learning and artificial intelligence in comparison to the other sectors. The primary reason for that is because it is the sector with the maximum regulations and law enforcement taking place heavily here. It is also the sector which forms the backbone of the economy. Without finance, there is no other sector that can operate.

Readers, be they those who are just starting off with machine learning or with experience in Python and machine learning implementation in projects other than these sectors, will definitely gain an experiential knowledge that I share with you the through the case studies presented in this book. The reader will get motivation from my famous quote on artificial intelligence and machine learning it is not the Artificial Intelligence but the Human Intelligence behind the Artificial Intelligence that is going to change the way we live our lives in the future.

There are three sections in this book, and I think each of these could have been printed as separate books in themselves. The good thing that the reader will find is that the structure of these three sections is identical. Each section starts off with an overview section where you will understand the current scenarios for that segment, such as healthcare, retail, or finance. Then there is the technological advancement chapter common to all the three segments, where the state of machine learning has been discussed in detail. It is also the section where I present to you the results of the Delphi Method expert survey for each of those domains. Then there is a chapter on how to implement machine learning in that particular domain. This is where you will learn how to use an industry-emulated or modeled data set and how to implement it using Python code, step-by-step. Some of this code and approach you will be able to directly apply in your project implementations. In each section, you will find two case studies taken from practical business problems, again modeled on some of the practical business problems that are commonly faced by businesses in that industry segment. Each case study is unique and has its own questions that you must carefully study and try to answer independently. I have given the solution for only one of the case studies using Python code, and I have let the second case study in each section be a discussion-only solution. The reason for doing this is because I want you to apply your own mind to solve them after looking at how I have solved the first one. Please remember each business is different, and each solution has to also be different. However, the machine learning approach does not differ much.

I know for sure that many of you who read this book are highly experienced machine learning professionals in your field and that is why you are looking for expert advice on how to avoid common gotchas or pitfalls during machine learning in that domain, such as healthcare or retail or finance. Each sector has its own set of pitfalls, as the nature of the business is very different.

There could be many readers who could belong to the startup eco-system and would like to get new ideas on implementation of machine learning and artificial intelligence in these areas. In each of the three sections, you will find three innovative ideas that I present to you that you could immediately take and start implementing.

If you are looking for a book that gives you experiential and practical knowledge of how to use Python and solve some of the problems in the real world, then you will be highly satisfied.

All the Python code and the data sets in the book are available on my website URL: `http://www.PuneetMathur.me/Book009/`. You will need to register there using your e-mail ID and the link to download the code, and data sets will be sent to you as part of the registration process.

## CHAPTER 1

Overview of Machine Learning in Healthcare

In late January 2018, I sat in a plush downtown hotel in Bangalore with one of the fine minds in healthcare, as well as a renowned international doctor and a Python programmer. The discussion was around how to apply machine learning in healthcare and finance. Being one of my clients, he wanted to not just get ideas but to see in practical Python code terms how data could be put to use in some of the work that was done in his large hospital chains as well as his investments in the areas of the stock market, commodities investments, etc. My discussions during the 4 days of meetings were not just intense but deep into the business domain of the healthcare industry. After having studied such similar patterns in many of my healthcare projects with my clients, in this book I present to you fine practical examples of implementation that are not just workable but also make a lot of business sense. While most of the work I do falls under non-disclosure agreements, thus not allowing me to reveal the confidential stuff, in this book you will find many examples of implementation of ideas that are from the real world. The real data has not been used. Most of the data I present in this book is from the public domain. I shall be using Python version 3.x compatible code throughout this book.

Note **Python version 3.x** has been used throughout the book. If you have an older version of Python, the code examples may not work. You need a version of Python 3.x or later to be able to run them successfully.

© Puneet Mathur 2019
P. Mathur, *Machine Learning Applications Using Python*, https://doi.org/10.1007/978-1-4842-3787-8_1

Installing Python for the Exercises

For running the exercises in this book, you will need Python 3.x. I recommend you use WinPython for this purpose. WinPython is a simple Python distribution, and it does not require any installation whatsoever like Anaconda. You can just copy it in a folder in Windows, change your $PYTHONPATH to the folder where you copied WinPython, and you are done. WinPython has pre-installed all the major packages that we need in this book. So you'll save time if you use WinPython. You can download WinPython from `https://winpython.github.io/` on github. Choose from 64-bit or 32-bit versions of the distribution, as per your computer requirement. As of the writing of this book, the WinPython website has a release of WinPython 3.5.4 1Qt-64bit. All the code exercises in this book work on this version of WinPython. If, however, you want to work on Windows, I would recommend you go with Anaconda for Python on Linux installers, given here: `https://anaconda.org/anaconda/python`.

Process of Technology Adoption

Before we begin to look at how machine learning is transforming healthcare, let us look at machine learning technology and the process of its adoption. This process is common to all sectors and industries. I will also explain this with examples as to how the adoption process has worked in some of the areas of healthcare, retail, and finance.

As per the definition of machine learning, it is a field of computer science that gives computer systems the ability to "learn" (i.e., progressively improve performance on a specific task) with data, without being explicitly programmed [5]. The later part of the definition, "without being explicitly programmed," is controversial, as there are hardly any computers that do not require programming to learn. But what this could mean for applying machine learning in business is the use of supervised and unsupervised machine learning techniques. Supervised learning techniques are the ones where the computer needs references of past data and explicit categorization and explanation of patterns, trends, and facts from it. However, for unsupervised learning this is not a requirement; we let the computer learn on its own to find the patterns, trends, and facts. This is also known as auto-discovery or auto-data-mining.

So when we use unsupervised learning, you can say that the computer program is not being explicitly programmed to learn. It is learning on its own by discovering the facts, patterns, and trends. But we do program it by selecting the algorithms it will use to discover them. It does not select the algorithms by itself. To give you an example of how this happens, let us say we want to develop a machine learning algorithm for developing and finding out if hospital consumer data has any given patterns for predicting whether a particular outpatient would be admitted to the hospital or not. Simply put, are there any hidden patterns in the data to find out the profile of a patient? This can be done in two ways: the first uses a human machine learning engineer who can start to look at the hospital outpatient and in-patient data sets and then see if there are any patterns; the second uses unsupervised learning and lets the computer select clustering algorithms to find out if there are any clusters in both the outpatient and in-patient data sets. We will look at this example with code and how to implement this in Chapter 3. Now we look at Figure 1-1 Machine learning technology adoption process below.

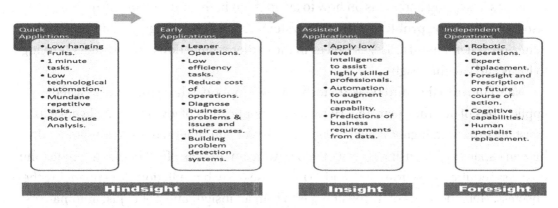

Figure 1-1. *Machine learning technology adoption process*

Now let us look at how this machine learning technology adoption takes place in the industry. I am outlining here the process that is common to all sectors, regardless of their technological complexity. In the technology adoption diagram in Figure 1-1, you will find four phases of the technology adoption that takes place in any sector. The first phase is quick applications. This phase is marked with certain characteristics. This is the stage where the **business tries to apply machine learning technology on the low-hanging fruits**. As an example, a company may want to automate its social media analysis or sentiment analysis. It would also look to automate some of the less-than-**1-minute tasks performed by its employees**. This task would be **low on technological complexity**. It would also like its employees to list the repetitive tasks and to do things like **root cause analysis** for any failures or issues in the business systems. The focus here would be **hindsight**. This means that the business is trying to focus on such issues or problems and trying to address those that have **caused failures in the past**. As an early adopter of the technology, the business is still trying to understand how machine learning is going to help them advance their **applications for business growth**.

The next stage is that of early applications of machine learning, where the business will try to create learning operations. This means that they are trying to look at the past data and find out what can be learned from it. The business is also trying to address the low-efficiency test so it may carry out an efficiency audit in its operations to help find out identify those areas where it can learn and be more efficient in its business operations. In early applications of machine learning, the business could also think of reducing the cost of its existing operations. And in this it could also carry out cost audit for its various business operations carried out by its employees. It could, as an early adopter, target those operations that are high cost and high growth in nature. It is also to diagnose clearly the business, which would look at the business problems and the reasons for the issues it is facing and focus on how to avoid them in the future. The business would also look at building **problem detection systems,** such as building a credit card fraud detection system. In this case, as well as in the earlier applications, the business is trying to focus and gain hindsight.

Now I move to the third phase of technology adoption, where there are assisted applications of machine learning. Here there is application of low-level intelligence to assist the experts in highly skilled tasks. The focus of automation here is to augment the human capability for business growth and advancement. The effort here is to predict the business requirements from data and to make use of such predictions for enhancing the business. Here the focus of the business is to gain an insight and not to just automate its operations but also to gain from the hidden patterns, facts, or trends that may have been lying hidden in its data. In this stage, the organization is discovering about its customers, its employees, and also its operations and, as a result, trying to understand the things that have been troubling it in the form of business issues or problems. This is actually where the business organization will start to look to apply machine learning-supervised techniques with the unsupervised techniques.

Now we move on to the fourth and the last phase of technology adoption, which is independent applications of operations using machine learning. This is a stage where the automation of a company has reached its fullest capability. Most of its operations are robotic in nature. This is also the stage where there is an expert human replacement happening. In this stage, there is also foresight and prescription on a future course of action for a particular business strategy or vision or mission. As I said before, this is the stage where the human specialist is being looked at being replaced or assisted at a high level. So here the machine learning is being used at a level where the learning by the machine is at its fullest extent. The machine is capable of learning from the huge data generation happening inside the business operations. It has also developed skills for finding out hidden patterns, facts, and trends to prescribe to its business leaders the future course correction or actions that need to take place in order for the business to grow. This machine learning capability can also be used for averting any kind of debacle, such as financial crisis or scams that may happen in the future or may be reflected in the current data of the business organization. In this stage, the **business is using foresight**, and it is this foresight that actually gives its operations the **course correction capability**. This is the maximum extent that a business operation can use machine learning to **gain advantage in the market against its competitors**. I am not suggesting that the entire company operations be run in an **auto-mode**. That is not what this phase represents. This state is that of an organization that has intelligent automation in place. By intelligent automation, I mean that the key business functions, such as finance marketing purchase, are sufficiently automated to provide foresight about the business operations. The company also has the ability to gather data from its business environment and to avoid any tragic incidents that may occur not due to the company's fault but due to the nature of the business environment, such as recession, market crashes, etc.

I now present in tabular format the characteristic feature of each phase so that you gain a clear understanding of the entire process.

Table 1-1. *Phases of Technological Adoption and Advancement*

Phase	Characteristics	Focus	Analytics used	Level of prediction	Technological complexity
Quick applications	1) Low technological complexity 2) Replacement of repetitive and mundane tasks 3) Solutions for common issues and problems	Problem-solving of day-to-day issues faced in its operations	Descriptive analytics	Hindsight	Low

(continued)

5

Table 1-1. (*continued*)

Phase	Characteristics	Focus	Analytics used	Level of prediction	Technological complexity
Early applications	1) Improve efficiency and productivity 2) Reduce cost of operations 3) Diagnosing business problems and issues faced in the past 4) Building problem detection systems	Learning from the problems faced in its operations	Diagnostic analytics	Hindsight	Medium
Assisted applications	1) Assist highly skilled professionals in business operations 2) Augment human specialist capabilities 3) Predictions of business requirements	Automation	Predictive analytics	Insight	Medium to Complex
Independent operations	1) Robotic operations 2) Robots gain specialist capabilities after learning from the human specialists. 3) Prediction on future events and capability to course correct in advance 4) Cognitive capability building	Cognition	Prescriptive analytics	Foresight	Highly complex

From Table 1-1 we can clearly see what I have described in Figure 1-1 and also understand a few more aspects of the process of technology adoption. I will also explain this table in detail by taking examples in healthcare where some organizations have used these capabilities. I have added the aspect of analytics in Table 1-1, which I have not discussed in this book so far, so let's look at what these forms of analytics are and how they can be used by healthcare organizations.

I have explained these analytics types in my book *The Predictive Program Manager Volume 1* (Chapter 2, page 17) and I take the definitions of analytics from there [6].

Descriptive Analytics: This field of analytics is invoked to know about the answers to questions for projects that have already happened, such as "What is the status of X Project?"

Diagnostic Analytics: This field of analytics is used to know the root cause of a phenomenon, such as a project's success or failure. Why did the X Project fail? What are the positive lessons we can learn from this project's success? All such questions can be answered using diagnostic analytics.

Predictive Analytics: This type of analytics is used for determining the outcome of an event in the future, such as project success or failure, project budget overrun, or a schedule slippage for an ongoing project.

Prescriptive Analytics: In this field of analytics the maximum value of analytics is achieved as it builds upon the prediction made based on predictive analytics, and it prescribes actions that should be taken for the future.

I have used descriptive analytics for a client in the US for detecting whether a healthcare institution was using racial discrimination practices in its operations. I was given data on the patient records and their backgrounds. Patient data was given with their racial orientation, such as Asian, Native American, etc., along with data on admissions to the ICU, operations, and admissions to hospital wards and private rooms. I had to analyze and give conclusive evidence using statistical techniques as to whether there was any racial bias. By using descriptive analytics and looking at the patient records, I was able to say with confidence that there was not much evidence of such acts in the data. My findings were later used for evidence in legal proceedings as well. So I had to be careful to analyze data from all angles to confirm that there was no such pattern present in the data set.

Diagnostic analytics is used in the life of every healthcare professional. The industry is very diagnostic-driven, as it tries to diagnose the disease based on symptoms. So building systems that diagnose issues and problems is not very difficult. Genomics is a field where much diagnostic research is taking place at IBM Watson project for

Genomics is at the forefront in such research [1]. IBM Watson is an analytics engine built by IBM for use in machine learning and artificial intelligence. The machine learning engine IBM Watson is helping find solutions for individual treatment of cancer patients using its huge data sets comprised of medical literature, clinical study results, pharmacopeia, etc., to find cures for cancer patients. This is public research available to oncologists worldwide and is helping unearth possible new cures for various forms of cancer [1].

Predictive analytics is the next level of implementation of machine learning in the healthcare industry. In such an implementation, for example, the focus would be on predicting the likely group of people who could develop cancer. A system so developed would be able to predict accurately the age and type of people who are likely to develop a particular type of cancer. It would have the ability to create a profile of cancer patients, and as such a person comes in contact with this type of analytical system, it would throw up an alarm on the likely case of developing cancer.

Prescriptive analytics is being used by an IBM Watson for Genomics project, where it not just diagnoses the disease but also gives a prediction and then a likely prescription for the type of cancer by looking at clinical drug trials and their results. Although this system is undergoing rigorous testing, it will yield significant results when it is able to increase its predictive and prescriptive accuracy.

How Machine Learning Is Transforming Healthcare

Let us now look at some of the ways that machine learning is transforming the healthcare segment of business. The healthcare industry is one of the most labor-intensive industries around the world. It requires the presence of humans to take care of people at various stages of their illnesses. I was at the AI Conclave held by Amazon in 2017 in Bangalore and was amazed to see how an acute problem of staff scarcity, which has been plaguing the healthcare industry in the United Kingdom, has been aptly solved by creating artificial tabletop bots that would take care of elderly patients needs **(1)**. The artificial tabletop bots remind elderly patients to take their pills, track their prescriptions, and track and suggest wakeup routines. At the heart of Echo Alexa (as it is known) is the machine learning developed by the Amazon team using its cloud infrastructure Amazon Web Services (AWS). At the heart of Alexa is the Python machine learning code that helps it to perform tasks and learn from them through a feedback mechanism. The wonderful part of this service is that Echo Alexa is available to a common Python developer to use and develop their own programs and products based on Amazon's infrastructure.

In another DataHack Summit in 2017, I had an opportunity to see the demo of IBM Watson for healthcare services. Developers built their own applications on top of this base analytics engine. IBM has proven to use its analytics engine in applications such as testing genetic results, drug discovery, oncology, and care management, to name just a few. One more area where not just IBM but other analytics engines are making headway is in diagnosing disease using imaging. In healthcare imaging, such as X-ray images or CAT scan images, all have traditionally been interpreted by humans. However, there are some reasons why we need machines to do this work more efficiently:

- High volume of imaging data with increased patients.

- Stress on doctors due to high volumes makes them more error-prone. Machines can handle large sets of imaging data with a lower error rate.

- Inability of healthcare professionals to link and see the big picture from imaging data. Machines can help them by assessing large numbers of image datasets and determine whether there are any patterns or any connections among groups of patients or groups of localities, for example.

- Replace doctors or specialist at times of their absence. This is a key operation that a machine can do—when a specialist is not available, it can replace the human specialist and provide diagnosis in even critical cases. In my opinion this function of a machine will be used more and more, and the day is not far when the entire area of image diagnosis will be done by machines with no human intervention.

- Drug discovery is a very key area for the healthcare industry. Research in the pharmaceutical companies for diseases like cancer or HIV is continuously happening. Machine learning is helping speed up drug discovery by analyzing medicinal data and providing prediction models on drug reactions even before they are injected into subjects in a controlled environment. This saves both time and money, as the simulation of drug reactions gives an estimate on likely cure patterns and reactions to the drug.

- Patient Research in difficult fields like Cancer, etc. There is a lot of data available in this field for both patient and clinical trials of medicines. Clinical trials are time-consuming and require collection of subject data on reactions in the body. This is either collected invasively, such as via a blood test, or non-invasively, such as through urine tests or putting probes on certain body parts of the subject.

One of the common fears that I hear with healthcare professionals is their fear that AI will replace them. The machines may make their jobs redundant. That fear is valid and is not without evidence. This report comes from The Sun [4] China where a Robot named "Xiao Yi" has passed China's National Medical Licensing Examination successfully and has achieved all the skills to practice medicine. Some people say this is a scary trend. Some say it is a clear sign that robots are going to rule the humans. However, I say this is just the tip of the iceberg. The following are some of the trends we are likely to see in the healthcare world as far as machines are concerned:

- Robots replace workers in low-paying jobs first, where humans do not want to do the mundane work, such as the case of Amazon's Echo Alexa replacing elderly healthcare due to staff shortage.

- Robots become assistants to senior specialists, like neurosurgeons, and learn the skills for diagnosis and surgery.

- Robots will replace senior specialists in diagnosis, as it requires more analysis and processing. Humans can't process large information and spot patterns in big data sets. This is where robots will score significantly higher in accuracy of diagnosis than a human specialist.

- Surgery will be done by humans with assistance from robots. This has already been demonstrated by the University of Oxford Surgeons [7]. So in my view, it is possible as more and more robots are built to do precision operations on humans and are successful, they will work jointly with human specialists to carry out complex, precision-based surgeries. This trend will start to emerge in the next 2 to 3 years. They may be termed as **Auto-doctors and Guided-doctors**.

Auto-doctors would use unsupervised learning techniques to treat a patient for new discovery diseases.

Guided-doctors would use supervised learning techniques. They would work for known diseases on known lines of treatments. We will be looking at an in-depth example of a Python program for supervised learning in Chapter 3, "How to Implement Machine Learning in Healthcare."

End Notes

[1]   IBM Watson Genomics, https://www.mskcc.org/ibm-watson-and-quest-diagnostics-launch-genomic-sequencing-service-using-data-msk

[2]   https://www.portsmouth.co.uk/news/hampshire-council-to-use-amazon-echo-technology-for-elderly-social-care-patients-1-8122146

[3]   For the First Time, a Robot Passed a Medical Licensing Exam, Dom Galeon, https://futurism.com/first-time-robot-passed-medical-licensing-exam/

[4]   Robot Passed a Medical Licensing Exam: https://www.thesun.co.uk/tech/4943624/robot-doctor-medical-exam-china-beijing/

[5]   Definition of Machine Learning, https://en.wikipedia.org/wiki/Machine_learning

[6]   Page 17, Chapter 2, The Predictive Program Manager Volume 1, Puneet Mathur

[7]   World first for robot eye operation, http://www.ox.ac.uk/news/2016-09-12-world-first-robot-eye-operation#

Key Technological advancements in Healthcare

Scenario 2025

In the not so distant future in the year 2025, one fine morning an old lady receives an alert on her personal home management device that she is going to develop cancer in the near future. This report has been sent by her robot doctor, after her visit last week for a checkup. She is mildly shocked to hear such news. She then decides to get a second opinion from a human doctor. The human doctors are very few in numbers now in her city and are more expensive than the robot doctors. So she decides to visit the human doctor nearest to her home. She visits the doctor and shows him her report, which was sent to her by the robot doctor this morning. The human doctor carefully looks at the report and finds that the robot had mentioned a clinical study that was done in the year 2019 where it was proven that people with a sleeping disorder lasting more than 3 weeks in a row had a 90 percent chance of getting a certain type of cancer. Using its probe sensors installed in the patient's house, the robot doctor had detected that she had experienced a disturbed sleeping pattern for more than 6 weeks in continuation. Based on this fact, the robot doctor had looked at her vital statistics data, such as her heart rate, blood pressure, breathing patterns, etc., and had reached the conclusion that she was on the path to get cancer. The human doctor, on the other hand, checks her vital statistics again and asks her to conduct some blood tests and other required tests for determining her current medical condition. After a few days, when her medical reports arrive, the human doctor declares that she does not have any signs of cancer.

Does this sound far-fetched and something too distant?

© Puneet Mathur 2019
P. Mathur, *Machine Learning Applications Using Python*, https://doi.org/10.1007/978-1-4842-3787-8_2

This is not an unlikely scenario but something that we may witness once the robot doctors become a reality. We have seen in Chapter 1 that there is a robot in China that has already successfully passed the medical examination and has attained the medical degree of a doctor. What questions arise in your mind once you read the situation? What would you do if something like this happened to you? Would you trust the robot doctor? Would you trust the human doctor more? Would you dismiss the report by the robot doctor as false and ignore it after the human doctor gave you a clean chit on your current medical condition? These are some of the questions that the future society is going to have to deal with once we accept robots as specialists in the healthcare industry.

If you noticed, this is a scenario where the human expert does not have the ability to prescribe any medicine based on the patterns that it is observing in a human being. In this case, the robot doctor is better prepared to predict and prescribe course-corrective medication to a human being based on the data that it gets from its connected probes or sensors.

The healthcare industry in particular deals with human beings and their lives. This is one of those industries where a simple judgmental error could cause death to a patient. However, when we talk about building prediction models based on machine learning (ML), which is the brain behind any robot, we know that no matter what algorithm is selected for predicting the outcome from any data set, there is going to be a percentage of errors in the final prediction by the model. In the case of human beings, a human being or a human doctor or a healthcare professional is also prone to errors. This is something that we know as human error. A recent research by Hopkins Medical Organization or the Johns Hopkins Medical Organization shows that 10 percent of all the U.S. states happened due to medical errors by the doctor and it is the third highest cause of death in the US [1]. So if we were to build and create a replacement or a competitor for a human doctor, we know that it would have to do better than this error rate. It can only survive if it gives predictive diagnosis at a lower error rate than that of the human doctor. Since we are dealing with human life in the healthcare industry, we need a gradual and careful way of adopting technology, as a lot is at stake. The requirement is to build robust algorithms with prediction models with higher accuracy levels.

Narrow vs. Broad Machine Learning

Now let us understand the brain behind robotics, which is ML. There are two types of ML applications: one is narrow in nature, and the second is broad in nature. Narrow ML deals with creating programs algorithms and robotics software that caters to a narrow focused set of activities or skill set. Here, the narrow means that the area of application is a specialized skill. It relates to an expert and its purpose is to emulate and exceed the human expert in their specialized skill. Narrow ML works best when it has an expert to learn from and to copy. An example of narrow ML robots would be the robotic arms belt for doing heart operations, such as removing blood clots from arteries. This example is of a robot that requires assistance from a human being in order to carry out its operation. We can see this in Figure 2-1.

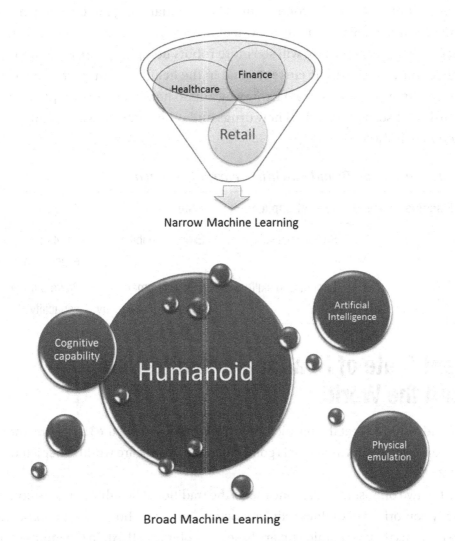

Figure 2-1. *Narrow versus broad ML*

In Figure 2-1, we can clearly see that narrow ML concentrates on things like healthcare, finance, and retail. In comparison, broad ML is about building a humanoid, giving it cognitive capabilities in artificial intelligence (AI) and the ability to emulate physical characteristics of human being.

Now let us look at the broad ML application. Here, we are talking about creating programs algorithms and Robotics software that caters to generalized skill as opposed to specialized skill. It emulates general human behavior, and the purpose is to prove robotic capability equal to that of a human being. A recent example of such broad application of ML is the robot named Sophia that has gained citizenship in the Kingdom of Saudi Arabia due to its proven ability to emulate human conversation. As the technology advances we will see more robots being developed on broad ML applications. However, the current trend in the healthcare industry is to adopt robotics and its applications in a narrow way and to help emulate or replace experts in diagnosis of disease research of new drugs and other such areas. We can look at the difference in Table 2-1.

Table 2-1. *Narrow vs. Broad Machine Learning Application*

Applied Machine Learning	Area of Application	Focus	Purpose
Narrow	Specialized skill	Expert capability	Emulate & exceed expert performance
Broad	Generalized skill	General human behavioral capability	Prove human-like capability

Current State of Healthcare Institutions Around the World

Now I would like to look at the big picture of the current state of the healthcare industry around the world. The turmoil that is going on in the healthcare world is depicted Figure 2-2.

Note the two opposing forces: one that is the traditional healthcare institution that is generally comprised of wellness clinics, doctor clinics, and hospitals. A another new set of institutions that are coming up are based on robotics ML AI. In the international conference on best practices in healthcare management held in Bangalore in March 2018 at XIME, where I participated, this trend was clearly brought out. You can read more about the conference in the following url: `http://xime.org/Health%20care%20 conference%20report`.

The traditional healthcare system derives its values from empathy, human touch, and healing through the doctor. As opposed to this, there is another set of institutions that are coming up rapidly. The values that these institutions bring forward are those of efficiency and accuracy of healthcare operations, better management of resources, and minimal human touch to avoid spread of communicable diseases. Both the systems target giving better care to the patient. In the traditional view the doctor is irreplacable and is the center of the healthcare institution. However, the new and modern view is that the doctor has a limited capacity of analysis and cannot analyze the big picture—hence, such machine algorithms and robots, which can do a better job. I have already discussed the narrow versus broad ML applications in this chapter. The reader should take note that institutions based on robotic ML and AI are trying to make headway into replacing the traditional healthcare system by targeting narrow ML applications first. Here the attempt is not to replace the doctor as a whole but to replace or emulate and then replace certain specialized functions of a doctor or healthcare professional.

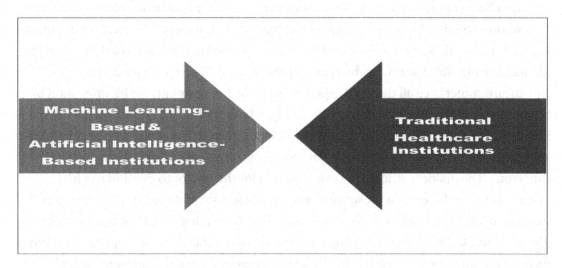

Figure 2-2. *Opposing forces in the global healthcare industry*

One example of ML being used for narrow healthcare tasks comes from Siemens Company from the division healthineers. They have computer vision imaging on computer tomography and look at what the brain wiring looks like through an MRI scan. They have brain anatomy machines known as Tesla machines, which I used to do this task. The other application of ML by the same company is the CT scanner, which is used for parametric imaging or molecular imaging, and healthcare workers have applied it to show whether a tumor is benign or malignant. This research has been done based on applying AI to 250 curated images for the path lab machine. They have developed precise algorithms for positioning the patient using 3D cameras inside the Tesla machine, as this used to be a human-aided task, and every human had their different way of positioning the patient inside the machine, sometimes leading to poor quality of images. The ML algorithm has now enabled positioning of patients as quickly as possible to get better images. They have also developed deep learning algorithms for reading chest X-rays and to detect abnormality in the X-ray machine. This is an attempt to replace the specialized role of radiologist with numerous hours of expertise with all X-rays that are thrown before them, including an MRI and CT scan. On the same line, Siemens has developed an MRI image fingerprinting technique using deep learning to emulate what a radiologist does. It is also a pioneer in the field of lab robotic automation, using an electromagnetic levitation technique, which is used in speed trains around the world [3].

I now bring to the reader another example of an organization using ML applications to develop a solution for overcoming a social barrier in an innovative way. This company is a startup in India known as **Niramai [4]**; it was conceptualized by two women, Geetha Manjunath and Nidhi Mathur, who founded this startup. Nidhi presented in the XIME Healthcare conference all the solutions developed by her company for identification of breast cancer in women. In a country like India, where traditional beliefs are prevalent in the rural regions, the major hindrance to detecting breast cancer is that the traditional system requires a doctor to touch the patient's breast to detect a lump that may become cancerous. The major method used even today is for the doctor to feel and use his/ her hands to see if there is a presence of a lump in the region of the body. To overcome this drawback, Manjunath and Nidhi looked at how technology could be used to help diagnose breast cancer without using touch or invasive procedures or applying pressure through mammography, which is painful. So they looked at a solution by using high-resolution, full-sensing thermal image with ML and use images to detect prevalence of cancer [4]. By using a high-resolution thermal sensing device and artificial intelligence and ML, they are able to develop API, which is non-invasive, does not require any test, and does not cause any pain to the patient. They require permission to take off the patient's clothes while the machine detects for the prevalence of cancer and whether it is malignant or benign, which matches any mammography test done manually. Over time I am sure that the algorithm will learn and improve by itself. Such innovative use of technology that focuses on overcoming social issues in healthcare are going to be adopted faster in countries where the population is high and there are social stigmas against medical help that are preventing it from spreading as a method of cure with the common population.

Importance of Machine Learning in Healthcare

The fact that sets healthcare apart from other fields like finance and retail is that healthcare deals with human life, and when we apply ML we need to have a gradual and careful way of adopting technology, as a lot is at stake here. Robust algorithms with prediction models with higher accuracy levels are required. This can be changed from a very simple example where we build a prediction model that predicts a particular type of cancer with an accuracy of 95 percent. In this case the prediction model will predict accurately for 25 patients and predict incorrectly for the other 5 patients. So the incorrectly predicted patients will still think they do not have cancer. This is the reason why application of ML in healthcare requires more testing before a model is deployed in production.

Some of the key areas where healthcare has machine learning applications are:

1. **Disease identification**

2. **Personalized medicine**

3. **Drug discovery**

4. **Drug manufacturing**

5. **Clinical trial research**

6. **Radiology**

7. **Digital health records**

8. **Epidemic outbreak prediction**

9. **Surgical robotics**

All of these areas in healthcare are core to the healthcare industry. Now we are going to look at the aforementioned areas of the healthcare industry and do the ML technology adoption process that I discussed in Figure 1-1 of Chapter 1. This mapping is going to help us in understanding where these areas stand with regard to the technology adoption process in the current scenario. By doing this we further look at what kind of advancement can happen in each of these particular areas. For an example on how to use this mapping information, let's say that your hospital has implemented surgical robotics in the field of heart surgery. By knowing from this chart how advanced the robotic surgeries are with respect to the technology adoption process, we can look at what kind of technological advancement could come in the future for this surgical application.

In order to have a current view of the global healthcare industry in the year 2018, I carried out a research study using the Delphi Method with 18 healthcare professionals. This is an independent study done by me and is not sponsored by any institution. I am also not directly connected with any healthcare institution on a regular basis, given to study a more independent perspective. The purpose of the study was to take expert opinion and to find out the current state of artificial intelligence and ML in the healthcare industry. I used the Delphi Method in research. We need to understand what the Delphi Method is and how it has helped us in this study. Let's first look at the research methodology used in this study.

Research Objective: The primary objective of this research is to use expert opinion in finding out and mapping two parameters of AI and ML: (1) the current technology maturity level of AI and ML in the key areas of the healthcare industry, and (2) the parameter of the technology adoption process inside the healthcare industry.

There were initially 12 key areas identified by the expert groups in the first iteration. These areas were then reiterated with the expert group to find out the most important areas that would evolve in the future. The expert group was able to identify nine areas in healthcare that would be important for the healthcare industry to advance further. The research study does not provide the results of this iterative selection of the key areas, but it starts from the point where the experts have selected these nine key areas. I have already discussed in this chapter those nine areas, starting from disease identification to surgical robotics.

Research sample: The group of experts that was selected was from a total population of 232 experts. The expert group was comprised of healthcare professionals who had worked in the industry for more than 20 years at positions including patient care, a management expert in a healthcare institution as a director, chief executive officer of a major healthcare facility, and academic professors who had worked on research in the healthcare industry with accepted and published papers. I have covered all the experts from each of the areas in healthcare, such as patient management, drug research, surgeons, CEOs, and AI experts—to name just a few. A total of 18 such professionals were shortlisted for this study. There were no absentees or attrition in this study.

Information needed: In order to make decisions and to support them, various secondary data like published papers on the state of ML and AI in healthcare were provided. An example is that of Siemens healthineer Emma Watson's research in genome study and cancer detection. The required information in order to create a map between the two parameters mentioned earlier was based on the experts' understanding of the current state of technology implementation in the nine areas, starting from disease diagnosis to clinical trial research. The decision making of the expert explanations on the levels of technological maturity and the phase-wise identification of technology was provided to them. Beyond that there was no other information provided, so care was taken not to create a bias in the minds of the experts. The information needed for this study included contextual, theoretical, and expert knowledge. The research also required for the experts to use their tacit or inherent knowledge, which they possess from being associated with the healthcare industry for so long.

Research Design overview:

The primary steps involved in this research are the following:

1. Define the objectives of the research.

2. Find experts who are willing to help in this research study.

3. Design questionnaires that gather information and involve less writing effort by the experts.

4. Administer the questionnaires to the experts.

5. Gather responses to the questionnaires and analyze them to see if consensus was achieved.

6. Iterate and administer more questionnaires until the experts reach a consensus on a particular key area.

7. Once a consensus is reached, move on to the next key area and iterate the questionnaire until consensus is reached. Until the time consensus is reached, provide more information based on the previous responses provided by the experts.

8. Analyze and create a map of the technical maturity levels and phases of adoption of AI and ML.

Data Collection methods:

Literature regarding healthcare was not data to be collected for this study. The test study that was conducted, which I mentioned earlier, was that of taking expert help in narrowing down from 12 to 8 key areas that are going to be important for the future of healthcare industry. This is important because in our study we are using expert judgment on what is going to be the focus of the healthcare industry based on their past experience. We have used the Delphi Method of study from a paper by Chittu Okoli and Suzanne De Poweski named "The Delphi Method" as a research tool and example of design considerations and applications [6].

The questionnaire method was used for data collection from the experts through e-mail online administration of surveys and personally giving the questionnaire in the paper mode.

Data analysis:

During a particular iteration, when the data was collected, Microsoft Excel was used to record the experts' responses in a tabular format. For any given key area a graph was made to check whether there was a consensus reached and if the graph sufficiently showed The Expert's consensus. Then the iteration was stopped. So the data analysis was done manually with the help of computer software. The mapping of technology maturity and phases of technology adoption waere undertaken using Excel software to create a technology map graph.

Ethical considerations:

It is possible that bias could have slipped into the study had we not made sure that the results were the responses of the experts and were kept anonymous, not affecting the outcome of this study. So due care was taken in order to ensure that the experts were not known among each other. As I have already mentioned, there is in the healthcare industry two groups of people: one group whose members like technology and the other group whose members do not like technology. We did not do an expert selection based on these specific criteria so this study could very well be biased on such grounds, and we have not tested for this.

Limitations of the study:

Qualitative research has as its biggest limitation that of not being able to exactly quantify the outcome of the future, and this is very much applicable to our study as well. However, by using categorical variables in our questionnaires we have tried to take the quantitative analysis of our outcome as well. Mapping of the technological adoption and understanding of the technological maturity is not something that a normal human being can do unless they have been associated with the industry, and that is why we chose experts to carry out the study. However, it is possible that some of the experts may not have had sufficient knowledge or exposure to the advances in AI and ML. We acknowledge that this could be a limitation to the study.

We already know from Figure 1-1 in Chapter 1 that there are four phases of technology adoption. In Figure 2-3 we look at this mapping.

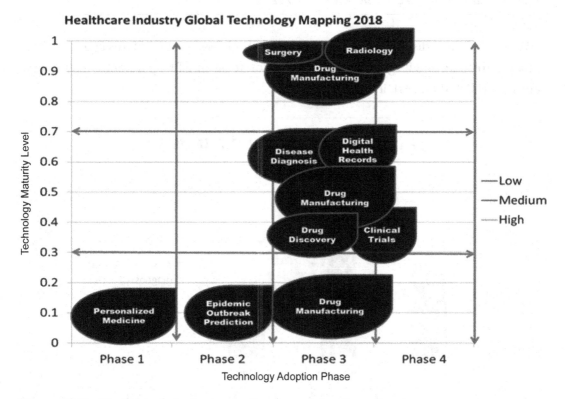

Figure 2-3. *Healthcare industry technology adoption phases*

In Figure 2-3 there are two axes. The x-axis represents the technology adoption phase as outlined in Figure 1-1, and the y-axis shows the technology maturity level. The technology maturity application level. The maturity application level is divided into Low,

Medium, and High. Low means the technology is at a research stage and is not in production yet. Medium means the technology has been implemented in production with some hits and misses and needs more research to move mainstream production. High means the technology is well-researched and is ready to move into production or is being used in the production environment, such as hospitals, etc.

Table 2-2 and Figure 2-4 present data with its analysis from the Delphi Method of research.

Table 2-2. *Data on the Delphi Method of Research Used in the Study*

Topic	No of Healthcare Experts		No of Iterations
Delphi Method	Invited	Shortlisted	
Current Application of AI & ML in Healthcare	232	18	4

We have already discussed this data in the methodology section of this chapter. Now we look at the data and its graphical representation regarding first parameter technology maturity level of AI and ML in healthcare.

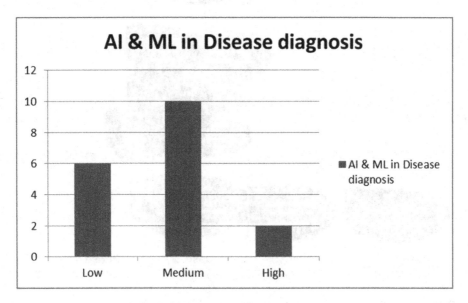

Figure 2-4. *State of AI and ML in disease diagnosis*

In the area of disease diagnosis with regards to the first parameter of technology maturity levels of AI and ML in the healthcare industry, 56 percent of the experts felt that disease diagnosis had a medium level of maturity. The identification of disease diagnosis as a medium level of maturity means that the technology has been implemented in this area of disease diagnosis in production, but there are hits and misses and it needs more research to move in to mainstream production. A good example of this area would be Google's deep learning for detection of diabetic eye disease [5].

In this use of AI for disease detection in the traditional way, ophthalmologists use pictures of the back of the eye and also the computer vision retinopathy (CVR) to detect if there is a hint of a diabetic eye disease. CVR determines the types of lesions that are present in the image that show if there is any fluid leakage or if there is bleeding in the eye. In such a complicated analysis that is done by a retinopathy by an ophthalmologist, Google's diabetic eye detector is able to create an AI-based system by the use of development data sets of 100 and 28,000 images given by 327 ophthalmologist [5]. The deep neural network trained on these images of diabetic retinopathy, and when it was applied on more than 12,000 images it was able to match the majority decision of the panel of 728 US-board certified ophthalmologists. The algorithm's AP scores compared to those scores done for disease detection manually by the ophthalmologist were identical, at a score of 9.5.

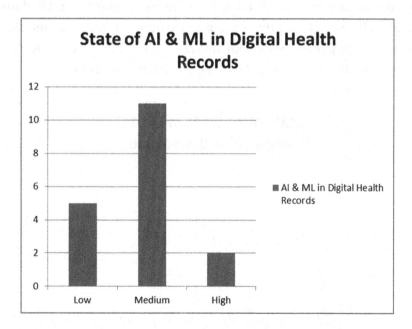

Figure 2-5. *State of AI and ML in digital health records*

Now let us look at another area: digital health records. Our experts conclude that this is at a medium state of technological maturity, with 61 percent of our experts in agreement of this opinion. We can see in Figure 2-5 that some of them (about 28 percent) also feel that the level of maturity is at a low level. Medium means that the technology is not being moved into mainstream production and has a few hits and misses here and there. However, a low state means that the research has not yet moved into production. To give you an application of use of AI in electronic health records, there is a company known as Savana (Madrid, Spain) that has successfully developed an application to re-use electronic health records with AI [7].

The most notable feature of this system is that it uses the natural language in the form of free text written by medical practitioners in the electronic health records or in the digital health records to analyze real-time information that is generated by a doctor. The Savannah system performs immediate statistical analysis of all patients seen in the records of its software and offers results relevant to the input variable provided by the user. It uses natural language processing to accomplish this goal in the background. It uses supervised ML in classifying a written text by a doctor into background information or diagnosis information. The unsupervised ML techniques use cases for determining the semantic content of words as the algorithm learns autonomously without any predefined semantic or grammar relations. For example, engineers and Parkinson's have similar meaning or different meaning of an example naproxen oh and Ibuprofen or asymmetrical is similar to just give you an idea of how it is done practically. Now let us look at the Figure 2-6 the state of AI & ML in Digital Personalized Medicine.

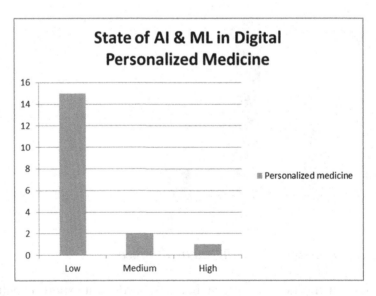

Figure 2-6. *State of AI and ML in personalized medicine*

Now we look at the state of AI and ML in the area of personalized medicine. After the four iterations our experts have told us that the technology adoption maturity is at a very low level. Eighty-three percent of our experts tell us with certainty that this is the case. The area of personalized medicine is also known as precision medicine. Here the treatment of disease, and its prevention for a patient is based on their personal variability in genes, the environment in which they live, and the lifestyle that each person follows. It is like building your own custom treatment. It is clear that this profession is not possible without the use of AI, which runs on super computers in order to learn using deep learning and to develop cognitively. It is similar to that of physicians—the computers need high processing power. They use deep learning algorithms and they need the specialized diagnosis knowledge in the area that they wish to do diagnosis, such as physicians in cardiology, dermatology, and oncology—to name just a few.

Now we look at another key area that of epidemic outbreak prediction in Figure 2-7.

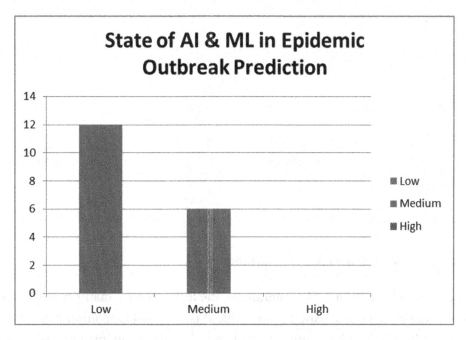

Figure 2-7. *State of AI and ML in epidemic outbreak prediction*

In Figure 2-7 we can clearly see that our experts tell us that the technology maturity is at a low level. Sixty-seven percent of our experts feel this after three rounds of iteration, when a consensus was reached. One good example of this is the Google flu trends [2], where Google was able to predict the spread of flu across many countries; however, it is no longer publishing the results. The way it used to work is that Google would analyze search queries to identify the world regions from which such large numbers of queries were coming, and it would automatically predict that those regions were going to be affected by flu. This project was started in 2008, and it was shut down over concerns of privacy issues raised by various agencies. However, in the background, Google is going to provide such data to different public health institutions to help them see and analyze the trends. This technology exists, but it needs to take care of the privacy issues before it can become mainstream.

We now look at an interesting application of AI and ML in the area of radiology in Figure 2-8.

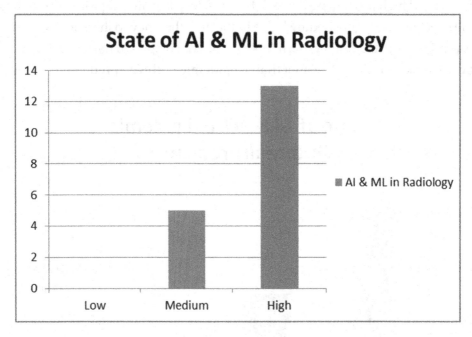

Figure 2-8. *State of AI and ML in radiology*

Our experts tell us that after four iterations, the technological maturity in this area is high, and 72 percent of our experts concluded this. A notable accomplishment by the Siemens healthineers involved application of neural networks on imaging like X-rays and converting such images into data and then analyzing them like a radiologist does. This uses deep learning and, more specifically, artificial neural networks (ANNS), which replicate the human neurons. They are reported to have detected through chest radiographs with 97 percent sensitivity and the results of cases of lung tuberculosis with 100 percent specificity [3] (https://www.healthcare.siemens.com/magazine/mso-artificial-intelligence-in-radiology.html).

More and more such applications are going to arise that may be integrated into the medical devices, making them automated independent robotic functions. This is the future of radiology as it stands today. We now look at Figure 2-9 for state of AI & ML in surgery below.

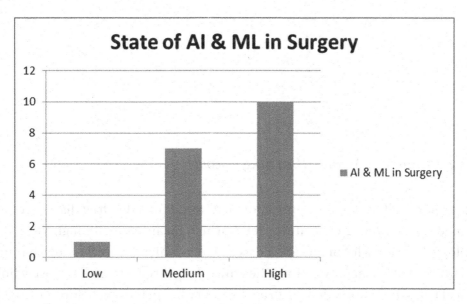

Figure 2-9. *State of AI and ML in surgery*

As we can see in Figure 2-9, in the field of surgery our experts see that use of AI and ML is at a very high maturity level, and 56 percent of the experts shared this opinion after our iterations. In the task of flesh cutting, which is a basic skill for a surgeon, a robot is able to make precise cuts with much less tissue damage as compared to human surgeons [8; `https://spectrum.ieee.org/the-human-os/biomedical/devices/in-fleshcutting-task-autonomous-robot-surgeon-beats-human-surgeons`].

There is a robot named STAR (Smart Tissue Autonomous Robot) that hovers over a patient and then, based on the algorithm, makes precise cuts that expert surgeons make, but STAR makes less damage by surrounding the flesh. This STAR system is able to sew back flesh that has been cut in surgery, and such stitches have been found to be more regular and leak-resistant than those of experienced surgeons. So this clearly shows that the use of robots in the field of surgery is indeed at an advanced stage. In Figure 2-10 we look at the State of AI & ML in Drug Discovery.

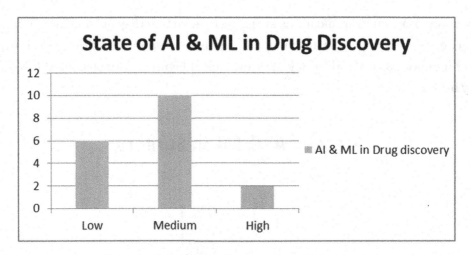

Figure 2-10. *State of AI and ML in drug discovery*

Our experts tell us that the application of AI and ML in the drug discovery area is at a medium technological maturity level, which means that although there is technology there are a lot of hits and misses, due to which this technology has not moved into mainstream production. The entire drug discovery area is closely linked to clinical trials, but in practice the drug discovery happens long before a clinical trial happens for any drugs. The drug discovery process requires pharmaceutical many tests to check and it is carried on many different drug compounds, which could help in eliminating or limiting the spread of a particular disease. So this discovery shows a particular compound works on this disease in the lab for the tests done for toxicity and other things such as the absorption in the human body, the motor metabolism rate, and so on. Once the compounds show results in these early lab tests, then they are moved to clinical trials to get government approvals. The largest pharmaceutical companies are using AI. Companies like 50 Shades SK are using AI and ML to find new compounds for potential drugs. They are also building models to predict how well potential drugs are going to do in the testing phase. Discovery drugs and their combinations are being developed using AI for combinational treatments and AI is creating personalized medicine based on genetic codes of the patients [9; https://emerj.com/ai-sector-overviews/machine-learning-drug-discovery-applications-pfizer-roche-gsk/]. In the Figure 2-11 below we look at State of AI & ML in Drug Manufacturing.

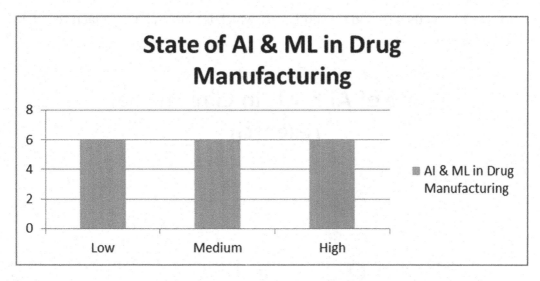

Figure 2-11. *State of AI and ML in drug manufacturing*

Now we look at the state of AI and ML in the area of drug manufacturing. This is an interesting case where our experts, at the end of four iterations, were able to conclusively tell us that drug manufacturing was at all three levels of maturity (i.e., low, medium, and high). So this means that in the area of drug manufacturing, the technology is at research stage and some of it has not moved into production. There is also technology that has been implemented to be tested in production but it has not yet moved into mainstream production environment, such as hospitals. And the experts also tell us that there is technology in drug manufacturing that is well-researched and is ready to move into production or it is already being used in a production environment. In truck manufacturing, robots and AI are being used in the pharmaceutical factories for automated inspection and packaging, leading to efficiency and saving workers from hazardous and repetitive tasks. The robots used in pharmaceutical manufacturing facilities are Cartesian Parallel and Selective Compliance Assembly Robot Arm (SCARA) [10; http://www.pharmtech.com/using-robotics-pharmaceutical-manufacturing].

Merck is using a robot in its bottling line to place dispenser caps onto bottled allergy medications, and this is providing efficiency to its operations. Robots at Enclave are increasingly being used for vial-filling applications, inspections, and packaging and in various kinds of drug assemblies' inspections—to name just a few applications.

Now we look at the last and the ninth area, which is that of clinical trial research in Figure 2-12 below.

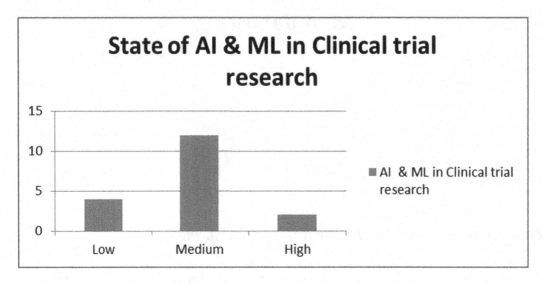

Figure 2-12. *State of AI and ML in clinical trial research*

From Figure 2-12, we can see that our experts tell us that it is at a stage of medium technological maturity and the AI and ML state is at that level. After four iterations, 67 percent of the experts in this group were able to conclude this. So this means that there is lot of research happening in this field; however, there are hits and misses, and it needs more careful research in order to move technology into mainstream production. There is research by an MIT robot laboratory that was performed in September 2014 [11; https://news.mit.edu/2014/mit-robot-may-accelerate-trials-for-stroke-medications-0211].

There has also been research done by KPMG voice in 2016 [12; https://www.forbes.com/sites/kpmg/2016/12/21/using-smart-robots-to-run-clinical-drug-trials/#749ef31f36d2].

This promises to implement automated clinical trials in order to demonstrate the effectiveness of drug treatment in hundreds of patients. Since the laboratories are still working on this technology, there is little application of it in the real world, but there are lot of experiments ongoing to see how it can help minimize the clinical trials stage of drug discovery. If this technology moves into production, then it will reduce the cost of drug discovery and clinical trials, which can take up to 2 million dollars and is an extremely costly and time-consuming affair.

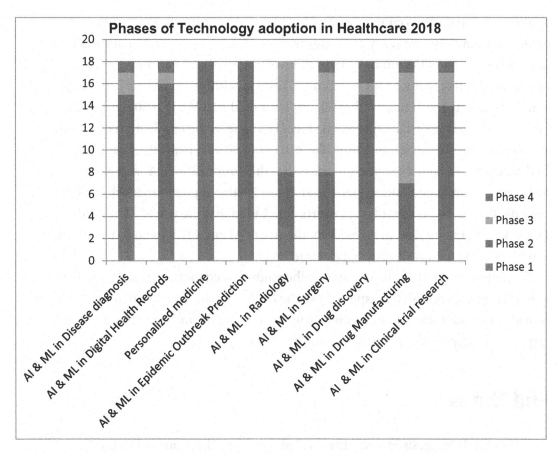

Figure 2-13. *Phases of technology adoption in the healthcare industry, 2018 gives us a quick view of the technology adoption process as reported by the healthcare survey in this book.*

Now we move on to the second parameter of our research study, which is that of phases of technology adoption in healthcare, which we have already discussed in Chapter 1 Figure 1-1 Machine Learning Technology Adoption Process. As you will recall from the previous chapter that there are four phases Phase 1: Quick Applications phase, Phase 2: Early Applications phase, Phase 3: Assisted Applications phase and Phase 4: Independant Operations. Here we have the quick applications in Phase 2 the independent operations in Phase 4 analysis. We can see from Figure 2-13 that the disease diagnosis is at an early application Phase 2 status, as told to us by our expert group. The digital health records are at Phase 2 status, with 56 percent of our experts concluding this after three iterations. Personalized medicine is at Phase 1, which is quick application status, and 83 percent of our experts concluded this after four iterations. The epidemic outbreak prediction area is at Phase 2 for AI and ML applications, and this is concluded by 67 percent of our experts. Our experts also concluded that 56 percent say radiology is at a Phase 3 assisted application stage, and we have seen in technology maturity level that there are various applications by companies like Siemens for use in their Tesla machines. For surgery, our experts conclude after three iterations that 50 percent say AI and ML is at 50 percent for Phase 3, which is assisted application stage. I have seen the application of robotic surgery in mainstream applications like surgery to correct heart disease; it's a trap. In drug discovery, our experts concluded that the application of AI and ML is and 56 percent of them concluded that it is at Phase 2 early application level. For drug manufacturing, 56 percent of our experts concluded that the use of AI and ML is at a Phase 3 level. For clinical trial research, the use of AI and ML was concluded by our experts to be at a Phase 2 early application level.

With this, we end the presentation of the study, which took me more than 3 months to implement along with the experts from the healthcare industry. I do hope that it will provide the reader with a concise view of where the healthcare industry stands with respect to its applications and adaptation of AI and ML.

End Notes

[1] Study Suggests Medical Errors Now Third Leading Cause of Death in the U.S., May 3 2016, https://www.hopkinsmedicine.org/news/media/releases/study_suggests_medical_errors_now_third_leading_cause_of_death_in_the_us

[2] Google Flu Public Data: https://www.google.com/publicdata/explore?ds=z3bsqef7ki44ac_#!ctype=m&strail=false&bcs=d&nselm=s&met_s=flu_index&scale_s=lin&ind_s=false&ifdim=region&hl=en_US&dl=en_US&ind=false

[3] Siemens Healthineers: https://www.healthcare.siemens.com/about

[4] Niramai: http://niramai.com/

[5] "Google's AI program can detect diabetic eye disease," Jul 17
     2017, https://research.googleblog.com/2016/11/deep-
     learningfor-detection-of-diabetic.html. Chapter 2 Key
     Technological advancements in Healthcare 35

[6] The Delphi Method, https://www.academia.edu/399894/
     The_Delphi_Method_As_a_Research_Tool_An_Example_Design_
     Considerations_and_Applications

[7] Medrano, I. H., J. T. Guijarro, C. Belda, A. Ureña, I. Salcedo,
     L. Espinosa-Anke, and H. Saggion "Savana: Re-using Electronic
     Health Records with Artificial Intelligence," 27 March 2017,
     International Journal of Interactive Multimedia and Artificial
     Intelligence 4(7):8-12. http://www.ijimai.org/journal/sites/
     default/files/files/2017/03/ijimai_4_7_1_pdf_22755.pdf

[8] Eliza Strickland, 13 Oct 2017, 19:30 GMT, Robot named STAR
     (Smart Tissue Autonomous Robot), https://spectrum.ieee.
     org/the-human-os/biomedical/devices/in-fleshcutting-task-
     autonomous-robot-surgeon-beats-human-surgeons

[9] Machine Learning Drug Discovery Applications – Pfizer, Roche,
     GSK, and More, Last updated on November 29, 2018, published
     on October 12, 2017 by Jon Walker, https://emerj.com/
     ai-sector-overviews/machine-learning-drug-discovery-
     applications-pfizer-roche-gsk/

[10] Cartesian Parallel and Selective Compliance Assembly Robot
     Arm (SCARA), By Jennifer Markarian, Nov 19, 2014, http://
     www.pharmtech.com/using-robotics-pharmaceutical-
     manufacturing

[11] https://news.mit.edu/2014/mit-robot-may-accelerate-
     trials-for-strokemedications-0211

[12] Using Smart Robots to Run Clinical Drug Trials, Ashraf Shehata,
     Dec 21, 2016, 11:45 am, https://www.forbes.com/sites/
     kpmg/2016/12/21/using-smart-robots-to-run-clinical-drug-
     trials/#3d61d05336d2

## CHAPTER 3

How to Implement Machine Learning in Healthcare

We now look at the areas of healthcare areas that hold huge potential. For this we need to carefully examine the technology mapping graph in Figure 2-2 of Chapter 2. There are certain areas in the graph that lie in Phase 1 and are low in technological maturity level. Although these hold potential, they do not give us a huge area of opportunity, as the technology is not currently supporting developments in these areas. For example, personalized medicine is very new and there is huge amount of research that must happen, including use of AI, to enable it to move to the next phase. Such research must be linked to the healthcare industry very closely so that the adoption happens faster. Next is the Phase 2 area of epidemic outbreak prediction, which has a few hits and misses and needs to address privacy issues in order to move to Phase 3. The real potential lies in the Phase 3 column of areas, where the technology has moved into the assisted applications stage.

Areas of Healthcare Research Where There is Huge Potential

I am not going to discuss all the technology used in the Phase 3 column of Figure 2-2, but I am going to discuss the ones that hold huge potential. The three most promising areas in healthcare are:

1. **Digital health records**

2. **Disease diagnosis**

3. **Radiology**

© Puneet Mathur 2019
P. Mathur, *Machine Learning Applications Using Python*, https://doi.org/10.1007/978-1-4842-3787-8_3

Digital health records hold huge potential for three reasons: first is that the number of patients for a doctor goes up as the population around the world increases; second, the amount of data per patient is also going to go up; and finally doctors can make good decisions for treatment only if they have the complete case history of the patient. There is another reason why digital health records hold huge potential. The advancement of machine learning and artificial intelligence allows analysis of data in a quick and efficient manner. The hospital or healthcare facility of the future will access digital health records or patient records that will be digitized and accessible to all the healthcare facilities when a patient has authorized the facilities to see its records. In essence, we would have **connected hospitals,** which would access common electronic patient health records in addition to storing private data of its patients. In the US, there are electronic medical records that are mandatorily maintained by any practicing doctor. However, this data is not available and shared among hospitals, the government, or any other agency or individual who wants to treat the patient. So in the future there is going to be a change to a universal database of patients, which will enable any healthcare facility authorized by the patient and the government of the country to access common case records. The major challenge that could stand in the way of such a data-sharing mechanism involves concerns around data privacy. However, if proper authorization and security of data can be guaranteed by the central nodal agencies and governments, then it would be possible very soon to house such a case history database, and it could lead to building global digital health record systems.

In the near future we could see better record-sharing mechanisms being developed in technology, leaving concerns such as data privacy and security behind. As a result, instead of hospitals working in silos, they would start to work in a connected manner. In a hypothetical scenario, there could be a patient who, after being treated by a particular hospital and not being satisfied with the line of treatment given, would like to change their hospital or healthcare facility. In such a case, they would just have to give their consent to sharing all the healthcare diagnostic reports with the new hospital, and once this is done, the data would automatically be accessible by the new hospital to which the patient is about to be admitted. There is another challenge that currently does not allow the concept of connected hospitals, and that is of disconnected diagnostic centers. The diagnostic centers are the labs that cater to the patients' needs of getting their lab tests done, such as blood or urine tests. They give out reports based on their findings from the lab tests. So they generate a lot of data after the lab tests are done, in the form of measures in the values in the reports. This data that is generated in each of the reports for the patient is currently done by printing the reports in the form of PDF files or through printing reports on paper. There is no central mechanism where the diagnostic centers can upload the patient reports, and there is no current benchmark in place in the healthcare industry that can enable them to use the same standards for publishing their reports. All this will have to be standardized, including the format of the lab test reports and the central database where the electronic record of the patient will get updated. In order to move from Phase 3 to Phase 4 or to even move from a medium technological maturity to high technological maturity, digital health records will need to standardize all of the aforementioned things.

Now let us look at disease diagnosis. This area has huge potential, given the fact that we have doctors but their availability in certain areas is low. Some people treat the development of chatbots in the healthcare sector as different from disease diagnosis. However, when I spoke to our experts, they confirmed that chatbots will be a part of disease diagnosis and patient care systems.

Any disease diagnosis system that is developed using machine learning or artificial intelligence needs to have the same capability as that of a human doctor. This is a narrow application of technology and is also a quick win. I now quote Dr. Devi Shetty, the Chairman of Narayana Health in Bangalore, from the conference at XIME Bangalore I mentioned earlier in this book, "Smart Software is smarter than the doctors. There are only **6,000 diseases,** out of which there are 1,000 that are common. There are **about 50,000 signs and symptoms of these diseases**. There are **100,000 types of lab reports**. Matching these to diagnose a disease can be done by **any software very easily, which takes a doctor years to practice.**" In addition to what Dr. Devi Shetty said, any robotics software will need to understand how doctors work. It could also involve studying the surgeon's logbook, etc., in order to gain such expertise. Key reasons why we need disease diagnosis to be done by machines are:

1. Every year 195,000 patients in the **US die of medical diagnostic error [7].**

2. **Inability of a human being to process huge amounts of information, analyze it, and apply it to a particular disease diagnosis**

3. **Cloning of an expert robot is cheap and fast compared to a doctor, where cloning of expert human doctors is forbidden by law in many countries.**

4. **Accuracy in diagnosis is critical, as an incorrect diagnosis increases the cost of healthcare for the patient. Using machine learning, we can track, measure, optimize, learn, and improve based on feedback on the accuracy of diagnosis by a robot or a machine.**

5. **To increase the value of healthcare to its patients, it is an absolute must to decrease the cost of diagnosis given to a patient.**

6. **Value = Patient health outcome per dollar spent on the treatment.**

If the patient health outcome is bad due to bad diagnosis, then the value of healthcare goes down. If the patient health outcome is good, then the value of healthcare provided goes up. So it is extremely important that we use machine learning to increase the value of healthcare for the patient.

Now let us look at radiology and the potential it holds in healthcare advancement.

Common Machine Learning Applications in Radiology

Here is a list:

1. **Medical image segmentation**

2. **Registration**

3. **Computer-aided detection and diagnosis**

4. **Brain function or activity analysis**

5. **Neurological disease diagnosis from FMR images**

6. **Content-based image retrieval systems for CT or MRI images and text analysis of radiology reports using natural language processing (NLP)**

The primary purpose of machine learning is to help radiologists make intelligent decisions on radiology data, such as conventional **radiographs, CT, MRI, and PET images and radiology reports**.

In my opinion, we are going to see the emergence of the fourth phase of application machine learning and artificial intelligence. There will be rapid advancement in machine learning-based automatic radiology disease detection and diagnosis systems. This technology exists in the labs and has shown comparable test results to those of a trained and experienced radiologist, and hence it should just take a few years for this technology to move into production, creating robotic radiologist [1].

Working with a Healthcare Data Set

Now we will be looking at a very small python code implementation with a healthcare data set. This will enable the reader to understand how machine learning is being applied in the healthcare domain in practical terms. I have used Python 3.x to run this code, and the procedure to install some of the required Python libraries is given in the following exercises. All the exercises that I have shown here have been run using spyder 3.x IDE and have been tested to run on the iPython kernel, and all source code can be downloaded from my github profile (`https://github.com/puneetmathurDS/`).

Before we start to look at machine learning and applying prediction models to the various data sets, I would like to bring a disclaimer to the reader's attention that none of the data that is being used in the exercises belongs to any of my clients or from real patients in the real world. Any resemblance to any data set around the world is merely a coincidence. Neither the author nor the publisher of this book takes any responsibility of the authenticity or privacy of this data set. The purpose of publishing this medical data set is to make The Reader understand how to apply machine learning on a healthcare data set in the production environment. This data set cannot be used for any other purpose, such as clinical trials or any production or commercial-related activities electronically or otherwise.

Life Cycle of Machine Learning Development

Before proceeding to look at data sets and building machine learning models, let us first look at what a typical machine learning life cycle is and learn its implementation within our short applications. This is a generic life cycle model that I am presenting to the reader; this can be applied to any machine learning application development and not just in the healthcare industry but also in retail, finance, or other sectors. Following a step-by-step approach ensures that the person carrying out machine learning in their applications does not get lost or miss any important parts of the process and are able to complete their application as per professional standards. This model does not have any reference; because it is based on my experiential knowledge with years of working on machine learning applications for my clients, I am giving out this life cycle process.

In Figure 3-1 we can see that the machine learning life cycle starts with the identification of a business need.

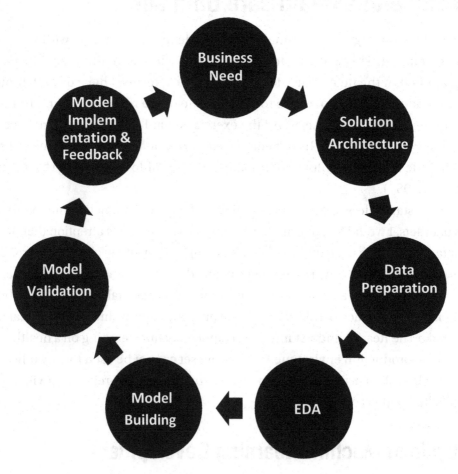

Figure 3-1. *Machine learning life cycle universal framework*

This business need is key to any machine learning application, as it provides the justification for need for resources during the life cycle development. The business need also is something that we go back to during various stages of the life cycle so that the team implementing the project does not lose sight of the original goal.

The next step is creating the machine learning solution architecture. During this process it is the machine learning engineers and the data science team that set out to create a template, based on which the machine learning application would be created. It is during this stage that the conceptualization of the business need and translation of the business need into technical architecture takes place. It is also the part of life cycle where the architects of the machine learning application go back to the business in order to understand their need better and to start translating it into an implementable solution.

The next stage is that of data preparation, and this is a very important phase because right from data we need to identify what kind of data is required to identifying the sources from where it will come. Once we know what data is required to build this machine learning solution, we can see if such data exists within the organization where the application is being built or it needs to come from outside of the organization. The next stage in data preparation is acquisition of the data, where the team that is building the machine learning solution acquires it. If the whole data set is big, then at least a sample data set can be used, based on which it will build the solution. Data acquisition needs to happen both from internal and external sources. The most important task here is to determine what kind of format the data is available in, such as flat files like csv, XML, or JSON or Oracle database or DB2 database, etc. Classification is made by the implementation team regarding what is the source of structured data and what is the source of unstructured data. The treatment of unstructured data and structured data in machine learning are very different, hence its identification is equally important.In the next step of data preparation, we perform data wrangling, which largely deals with cleaning up data. Here all such data that does not add any value to our business solution need is eliminated and only that data required for solving the business need is kept.

Once the data cleaning happens we do the next step of the machine learning cycle, which is exploratory data analysis. In exploratory data analysis, we look at the basic statistics of data such as its mean, median, and mode and its correlation between the different labels, and we identify whether the data is comprised of numerical or categorical variables, etc. This exploratory data analysis gives direction to the model building. For example, the choice of algorithm would depend on the kind of variables that we have.

In the sample we may have data sets with categorical variables such as gender (male or female) to be predicted based on other labels. In such a case we may have to use non-quantitative algorithms for our model building. Model building is the next step and is closely tied with exploratory data analysis. In this process we do the analysis of descriptive statistics, we identify which modeling technique we are going to use, and then we build a benchmark predictive model. We use other methods and algorithms on the data set, and we try to interpret and find the best algorithm for creating the predictive model. Once the identification of the model is done, the next step is to create model validation. We use staging data sets that are closer to production and see how our model behaves; if it gives good results, then the model is deployed and it is implemented. After this the feedback is taken to see if it has met the business need for which it was built. If there is a new business need or the model needs to take care of some things that the business requires, then again we go back to the process of solution architecture data preparation, EDA model and building model, and then we do model validation. In essence, this is a cyclic process that goes on until the machine learning application is terminated.

Implementing a Patient Electronic Health Record Data Set

We have looked at the entire machine learning application development life cycle, now let us implement it in a patient electronic health record data set. This data set is in the form of a flat file, which is available at the following URL: http://www.PuneetMathur.me/Book009/ Diabetes_Dataset.csv. We are now going to look at the code from Listing 3-1 onwards for the python code on loading and analyzing the electronic health record dataset.

Listing 3-1. Code for Loading Electornic Health Record Data Set

```
# -*- coding: utf-8 -*-
"""
Created on Thu Mar 15 23:46:06 2018

@author: PUNEETMATHUR
"""

#Importing python libraries
import pandas as pd
import os
os.getcwd()
```

```
#Reading dataset from flat file
fname="Diabetes_Dataset.csv"
patients= pd.read_csv(fname, low_memory=False)
df= pd.DataFrame(patients)

#Look at the first record
print(df.head(1))
```

In the Python code given in Listing 3-1, I have loaded the required Python libraries. First, I have loaded the Pandas library to load the csv flat file. This is the most efficient library for handling csv and JSON flat files. Next I have loaded the os library to identify the current working directory. If you have started Python from the directory where the data set and your Python script ElectronicHealthRecord.py reside, then you do not need to change directories; otherwise you can change it using curdir() function from the os package. You can download this from my github profile (http://www.PuneetMathur.me/Book009/).

Table 3-1. *Exploring the Data Set*

Patient ID	Gender	Age	Type of diabetes	Diabetes status	A1cTEST	BPSystolic	BPDiastolic
5.557686412	Female	29	Type 2	1	8.81	147	93

Now we move to the next step: data preparation. For this we need to explore and see the shape and size of data in Figure 3-2 Below().

Listing 3-2. Exploring the Shape and Size of Data Set

```
print(df.size)
8632
print(df.shape)
(664, 13)
print(df.columns)
Index(['Patient ID', 'Gender', 'Age', 'Type of diabetes', 'Diabetes status',
       'A1cTEST', 'BPSystolic', 'BPDiastolic', 'HeartRateBPM', 'BMI',
       'FrozenShoulder', 'CarpalTunnelSynd', 'DupuytrensCont'],
      dtype='object')
```

In Listing 3-2 we can see that there are a total of 8,632 cells in the data set given by df.size statement. We have a total of 664 rows and 13 columns given by df.shape statement. Listed by df.columns statement, we see various columns starting from Gender, Age, Type of Diabetes, Diabetes Status, A1cTest, etc. Let us now look at the data dictionary, which describes each of the columns and its values.

'Patient ID': This is a unique Patient ide which is represented by a decimal value.

'Gender': Male or Female.

'Age': In years, this gives the total age of a patient at the time of commencing treatment.

'Type of diabetes': Type 1 or Type 2 are the two types of diabetes that we are tracking.

'Diabetes status': This is the predictor column that declares whether a person has diabetes. 0 means no diabetes and 1 means patient has diabetes.

'A1cTEST': Test result is in percentage. NORMAL: normal range for the hemoglobin A1c level is between 4 percent and 5.6 percent. PREDIABETIC: Hemoglobin A1c levels between 5.7 percent and 6.4 percent mean you have a higher change of getting of diabetes. DIABETIC: Levels of 6.5 percent or higher mean you have diabetes.

'BPSystolic': Normal blood pressure in adults is below 140 mmHg for systolic and below 90 mmHg for diastolic.

'BPDiastolic': Normal blood pressure in adults is below 140 mmHg for systolic and below 90 mmHg for diastolic.

'HeartRateBPM': A normal resting heart rate for adults ranges from 60 to 100 beats per minute.

'BMI': A BMI of less than 18.5 kg/m2 indicates you are underweight. You may need to gain weight. If your BMI is 19 to 24.9 kg/m2, you're a healthy weight and should aim to stay that way. A BMI of 25 to 29 kg/m2 is defined as overweight. It's a good idea to lose some weight for your health's sake, or at least aim to prevent further weight gain. A BMI of over 30 kg/m2 is defined as obese and means your health is at risk. Losing weight will improve your health.

'FrozenShoulder': Yes/No is determined by doctor on physical examination of patient.

'CarpalTunnelSynd': Yes/No after physical examination doctor determines the result. Google [1] dictionary defines Carpal Tunnel Syndrome as:

Carpal tunnel syndrome

Noun

A painful condition of the hand and fingers caused by compression of a major nerve where it passes over the carpal bones through a passage at the front of the wrist. It may be caused by continual repetitive movements or by fluid retention.

'DupuytrensCont': Yes/No Doctor determines after physical examination and tests of the result.

The affected fingers can't be straightened completely, which can complicate everyday activities such as placing your hands in your pockets, putting on gloves, or shaking hands. Dupuytren's contracture mainly affects the ring finger and pinky and occurs most often in older men of Northern European descent [2].

Now that we understand the data dictionary of this data set let us now look at the data closely and clean it and then explore it in Listing 3-3 below. For doing this we will be using Python libraries and functions. These are commonly used with machine learning algorithms so you must familiarize yourself with them and understand them in more detail.

Listing 3-3. Code for Checking Missing Values

```
#You can use the Describe method to see; however, since our columns are more
#We will use individual functions to do EDA
print(dfworking.describe)
df.info()
<class 'pandas.core.frame.DataFrame'>
RangeIndex: 664 entries, 0 to 663
Data columns (total 13 columns):
Patient ID        664 non-null float64
Gender            664 non-null object
Age               664 non-null int64
Type of diabetes  664 non-null object
Diabetes status   664 non-null int64
A1cTEST           664 non-null float64
BPSystolic        663 non-null float64
BPDiastolic       663 non-null float64
HeartRateBPM      663 non-null float64
BMI               663 non-null float64
FrozenShoulder    664 non-null object
```

```
CarpalTunnelSynd       664 non-null object
DupuytrensCont          664 non-null object
dtypes: float64(6), int64(2), object(5)
memory usage: 67.5+ KB
```

We notice in Listing 3-3 that none of the columns have null or empty values. In the real world, however, you may find this to be true very rarely. There would definitely be a need to clean up the data. There are three things that you can do with each of the column empty values. Number one is to delete the entire row. Number 2 is to replace the row with average values. Number 3 is to leave the rows unchanged. Whatever you decide with your data, you need to carefully analyze and see how it's going to affect your overall result. Deleting rows or columns leads to losing precious information from columns that do not have missing values. It also helps to know how much percentage of values in a given column are missing. This helps us make a well-calculated decision. We will now proceed to the next step of exploratory data analysis. You will notice I have used df.working dataframe by dropping PatientID column in Listing 3-4. This is a good practice, as it retains the original Pandas dataframe and does not delete it. For example, you could have written the lines as: df- df.drop("Patiend ID", axis=1). It is easier to implement; however when you find during your code execution that the code execution path you have taken does not work or give any meaningful results, then you will need to turn back and take the original dataframe df and then do another round of code execution. But you would have already lost the original value in df.dataframe. So I advise you to use another dataframe, which will be the working dataframe, and not to touch the original dataframe as a coding best practice in machine learning applications. In fact you should use an alternate dataframe name in your code wherever you may need to come back to the dataframe state in order to see if the results are meaningful for meeting the business objectives or not. Let us now do some Exploratory data analysis on the dataset which is shown in code Listing 3-4 below.

Listing 3-4. Code and Results of EDA

```
#Now using a dfworking dataframe to maintain original data in df pandas
dataframe
dfworking=df.drop('Patient ID',axis=1)
dfworking.mean()
Out[146]:
```

```
Age                  38.899096
Diabetes status       0.240964
A1cTEST               5.890858
BPSystolic          116.278522
BPDiastolic          93.130680
HeartRateBPM         91.812971
BMI                  23.870348
dfworking.median()
Out[148]:
Age                  30.000000
Diabetes status       0.000000
A1cTEST               5.600000
BPSystolic          100.720000
BPDiastolic          91.539001
HeartRateBPM         91.000000
BMI                  24.000000
```

Now that we have the code and results of EDA, we need to interpret and see what our data tells us. In our data set the average age of a person is 39 years. The average patient has an A1ac Test percentage of **5.89 percent, which means the sample of patients is prediabetic**. The average BP systolic is 116. 8, which means the average patient has normal blood pressure. The BP diastolic is 93. On average this means it is slightly higher than the benchmark BP diastolic level of about 90 mmHG for diastolic standard in our data set. The average heartrate beats per minute (bpm) is 91.8, which is within the range of 60 to 100 bpm standard. The average BMI is 23. This indicates that an average patient has a healthy weight. So these are important findings from studying the statistical moments of our data set. After having looked at statistics from our data set, we now look at another statistical measure that defines relationships between the variables in the data set. Please note that our predictor is diabetes status, which is either 0 for no diabetes and 1 if the patient has diabetes. Median is also an important status to look for, and it is generally used when there are outliers in the data. If there is a huge difference between the median and mean values of a column or variable, then it confirms the presence of outliers in the data. However, in our data set, when we compare the variable values between the mean and median given in Listing 3-5, we find age as having a difference from mean of 30 years, and for rest of the columns the difference can be ignored.

Now we will be checking our data set for the presence of outliers. We will first look at how the data in each of these columns is distributed. This will give us an idea on the spread of data. In code Listing 3-5 I now show you the spread of data using standard deviation.

Listing 3-5. Spread of Data

```
dfworking.std()
Out[160]:
Age                 19.109127
Diabetes status      0.427991
A1cTEST              1.833379
BPSystolic          27.826840
BPDiastolic          5.112349
HeartRateBPM         3.649444
BMI                  1.990809
```

We know that the standard deviation is a summary measure of the differences of each observation from the mean [3].

In our data we can see standard deviation for age at 19 years, which means there is a spread of about 19 years from the mean age of 39 years. We will ignore the diabetes status number because it does not have any meaning, as it is a binary value of 0 or 1, and this value is 0.4, which is in between 0 and 1. We will look at the A1c test standard deviation, which is at 1.8 percent from the mean value. Similarly the BP systolic is 27. This means that the high BP has more variation, and this is where the problem lies for our sample patients. BP diastolic has a standard deviation of 5, which does not seem to be very high when we compare it to the standard deviation of BP systolic. The heartrate bpm standard deviation is 3.64, which is also negligible, and the BMI of 2 is of concern, and it also means that we have patients with higher variations in their body mass index. Now let us go deeper into our data and look at it more closely with regards to how it is spread and what we can interpret from it. For this we will be using the max/min, the quantile kurtosis, and skewness functions, which are part of a pandas data frame. In code Listing 3-6 we look at the Max values of the numerical variables in the dataset.

Listing 3-6. Checking Spread of Variables in Data Set

```
dfworking.max()
Out[167]:
Gender              Male
```

```
Age                           79
Type of diabetes          Type 2
Diabetes status                1
A1cTEST                    10.99
BPSystolic                   212
BPDiastolic                  126
HeartRateBPM                 113
BMI                      30.9951
FrozenShoulder               Yes
CarpalTunnelSynd             Yes
DupuytrensCont               Yes
dtype: object
dfworking.min()
Out[168]:
Gender                    Female
Age                           10
Type of diabetes            None
Diabetes status                0
A1cTEST                     2.02
BPSystolic                100.01
BPDiastolic                   87
HeartRateBPM                  88
BMI                      17.1278
FrozenShoulder                No
CarpalTunnelSynd              No
DupuytrensCont                No
```

The maximum value for age is 79, which means the oldest patient in this sample is 79 years old. The most common diabetes type is Type 1, diabetes status is 1, and the a1c test percentage maximum value is 10, which is very high. The BP systolic value is 212, which is also very high, and the diastolic value is 126, which are also very high. The heartrate bpm maximum value is 113, which is also on the higher side. The BMI maximum value is 31, which is overweight, and the rest of the items have categorical values. Similarly to the max values, we have the minimum values. The minimum age of a patient in this sample data set is 10 years. The minimum diabetes status is 0, which means the patient does not have diabetes. The minimum value for a 100 test is 2. This is below the normal hemoglobin A1c level. The BP systolic minimum value is 100. This is below 140 mmHg and is considered normal for adults. The BP diastolic minimum value is 87, which is also considered normal if it is below 90 mmHg for a patient. The heartrate bpm is considered normal if it is within the range of 60 to 100 bpm, and here we have the minimum of 88, which is in the normal range. The BMI value minimum is 17. This means the patient is underweight because it is below 18.4. The rest of the column values are categorical.

Detecting Outliers

Now we get into the task of detecting outliers. Any serious data analysis cannot happen unless we know for each variable or column if there are any outliers in the data set. In order to detect outliers we need to first define what it is. It is a matter of debate on the method of computation of outliers; however, I go with the commonly used cut-off of 1.5 x interquartile range. The range of our data set for any column can be known by using the max and min functions from the Pandas data frame. For calculating the outliers I will first take the maximum and minimum values of the numeric columns in Listing 3-7 and 3-8 below.

Listing 3-7. Calculating Maximum Values

```
dfworking.max()
Out[203]:
Gender               Male
Age                    79
Type of diabetes   Type 2
Diabetes status         1
A1cTEST             10.99
BPSystolic            212
BPDiastolic           126
HeartRateBPM          113
BMI               30.9951
FrozenShoulder        Yes
CarpalTunnelSynd      Yes
DupuytrensCont        Yes
dtype: object
```

We see in Listing 3-7 that the maximum value for age is 79, the percentage maximum of a 100 test is 10.9, BP systolic is 212, BP diastolic is 126, heartrate bpm is 113, and BMI is 30.99. Similarly we see in Listing 3-8 that the minimum value for age is 10, and for a 100 test percentage it is 2.2. BP systolic is 100.0, BP diastolic is 87, heartrate bpm is 88, and the BMI is 17.12.

Listing 3-8. Calculating Minimum Values

```
dfworking.min()
Gender              Female
Age                     10
Type of diabetes      None
Diabetes status          0
A1cTEST               2.02
BPSystolic          100.01
BPDiastolic             87
HeartRateBPM            88
BMI               17.1278
FrozenShoulder          No
CarpalTunnelSynd        No
DupuytrensCont          No
```

Let's pick up the age column to help understand the range of this column. We have seen that for age, the max value is 79 and the minimum value is 10. So in our patients, the youngest is 10 years old and the oldest is 79 years old. So our range is 79 minus 10, which is 69 years. So we are measuring patient health records for patients who have 69 years of range as far as age is concerned.

Now that we know our maximum and minimum values and we have calculated the range of our data, we need to look at interquartile ranges for this age column. Interquartile range is the difference between the first quartile and third quartile of a data set. It is used to describe the spread of data inside the data set [4]. In code Listing 3-9 we now look at 1st Quartile of our numeric dataset.

Listing 3-9. Measuring 1st Quartile of Our Data Set

```
dfworking.quantile(0.25)
Out[206]:
Age                29.000000
Diabetes status     0.000000
A1cTEST             5.177500
```

```
BPSystolic          100.375000
BPDiastolic          91.107946
HeartRateBPM         91.000000
BMI                  23.000000
```

Listings 3-9 and 3-10 show you a quick way of calculating the first quartile and the third quartile in our data set. We see that in the first quartile, the age is 29, A1c test is 5.1, the BP systolic is 100, the BP diastolic is 91.2, heartrate bpm is 91, and the BMI is 23. In Listing 3-10 we now look at the 3rd Quartile of our dataset.

Listing 3-10. Measuring 3rd Quartile of Our Data Set

```
dfworking.quantile(0.75)
Out[210]:
Age                  49.000000
Diabetes status       0.000000
A1cTEST               6.000000
BPSystolic          122.355000
BPDiastolic          92.070602
HeartRateBPM         92.000000
BMI                  24.441247
```

In order to determine the threshold values of outliers for each of the variables in our data set, in Listing 3-11, I show the code for calculating these threshold values.

Listing 3-11. Measuring Outlier Threshold Values of Our Data Set

```
dfworking.quantile(0.25)*1.5
Out[214]:
Age                  43.500000
Diabetes status       0.000000
A1cTEST               7.766250
BPSystolic          150.562500
BPDiastolic         136.661919
HeartRateBPM        136.500000
BMI                  34.500000
Name: 0.25, dtype: float64
```

```
dfworking.quantile(0.75)*1.5
Out[215]:
Age                  73.500000
Diabetes status       0.000000
A1cTEST               9.000000
BPSystolic          183.532500
BPDiastolic         138.105902
HeartRateBPM        138.000000
BMI                  36.661871
```

In Listing 3-11, the first quantile multiplied by 1.5 threshold values for each column is given. For the Age column, the lower threshold is 43.5 and the third quantile is 73.5.We can see that the data shows us in practical terms that any age below the first quantile value for age 43.5 is an outlier. Similarly any value for the age column that is above 73.5 is also an outlier. Similarly for A1c test the lower threshold limit for the outlier is 7.7, and the upper threshold limit for A1c test is 9. Any values in our sample that are below the lower threshold value of 7.7 or above the upper threshold value of 9.4 are outliers. Similarly for BP systolic, any value that is less than 150.5 and above 183 is an outlier. For BP diastolic we know that this range is much less than the lower threshold, being 136 points, and the upper diastolic limit, being 138. Similarly we have heartrate bpm whose lower threshold is 136.5 and upper threshold is 138. Even for BMI, the value follows diastolic and heartrate bpm, with a lower range between its thresholds, as the lower threshold is 34 and the upper threshold for BMI is 36.6. To understand this spread in data set better, I now show you a graphical representation using box plots for our variables in Listing 3-12. In code Listing 3-12 I now show you how to look at the visualization of the spread of data for each of our 6 columns.

Listing 3-12. Visualization of the spread of data for each of our 6 columns.

```
#Horizontal default boxplot chart
dfworking.boxplot(figsize=(10, 6))
#Vertical Boxplot chart
dfworking.plot.box(vert=False)
#Boxplot by selecting only the required columns
dfworking.boxplot(column=['A1cTEST','BPSystolic','BPDiastolic','HeartRateBPM',
'BMI','Age'],figsize=(10, 6))
```

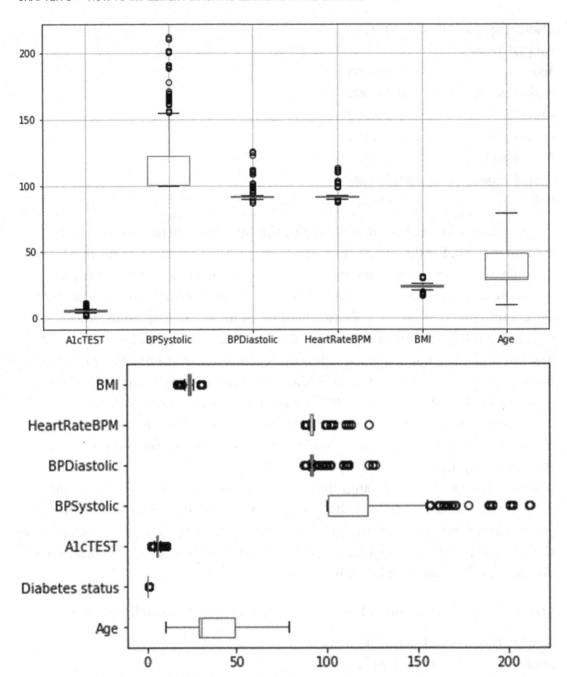

Figure 3-2. *Box plots of electronic patient health records data set*

Visually Figure 3-2 shows us a box plot of our variables. Age shows an even spread, and it does not show any outlier visually; however, for A1c test we can see that the percentage is lying in very narrow range. On both the lower threshold and upper threshold, we can see some outliers splattered on the graph. For BP systolic, we can see that the outliers lie in the range of 150+. For BP diastolic, we can see some outliers in the lower threshold range, but most of them lie in the upper threshold range. This is similar for the heartrate bpm and BMI columns. The common spread between BP diastolic and heartrate bpm, and BMI, which can be seen visually, shows that they have a narrow range. However, for BP systolic, this range is very high, and hence it is evident in the function quantile that is used to calculate the interquartile range and then calculate the outlier threshold values. I make the decision to retain the outlier values based on the fact that in a column variable like BP systolic, which is one of the key variables in this study, if I delete the values above the outlier then I will be left with much less meaningful data to analyze. By using the code dfworking['BPSystolic'].loc[df['BPSystolic'] >=183.562500]. count(), we get a value of 35, which shows that we have 5.3 percent outliers in this column variable, and this is quite significant. Hence we will retain the outlier data for our analysis. However, we will need to select a classifier algorithm that is robust to outliers, such as decision trees [5].

So now we understand the spread of our data and have seen visually and otherwise through commands how our data is spread. Let us look at another two measures for our column variables: skew and kurtosis. This will give us specific information on the shape and size of the curve of data. In Listing 3-13 we can see the values for skew and kurtosis.

Listing 3-13. Skew and Kurtosis Values of Our Variables in Our Data Set

```
dfworking.skew()
Age                0.878405
A1cTEST            0.344770
BPSystolic         1.720338
BPDiastolic        3.693222
HeartRateBPM       3.327100
BMI                1.098987
dfworking.kurtosis()
Age               -0.286342
A1cTEST            0.461561
BPSystolic         1.948725
```

```
BPDiastolic        15.712615
HeartRateBPM       13.172057
BMI                 5.468543
```

Before we look into skew and kurtosis, I would like to remind the readers of the normal distribution curve that has a property of mean = mode = median. However, by looking at the skew and kurtosis of our data set variables, we are trying to see how close or how different they are from the normal curve. This can also be visually seen through plots, which we will be doing later; however, skew and kurtosis numeric values also help us understand the distribution of our data set. I will not go into the formula for calculating skew and kurtosis because I expect the reader to know this or to refer to some good references on the Internet. Skew (or skewness) is calculated mathematically and the result of the number that we get first. If skew is greater than 0, then we say the distribution is positively skewed; however, if the number that we calculate for skew is less than 0, then we say that the distribution is negatively skewed. If the number of skew is equal to 0, then the distribution is said to be symmetric. Negatively skewed distributions have a long left tail, and positively skewed distributions have a long right tail. With this knowledge we now get into the task of interpreting the results of each column in our data set. The age column has a value of 0.8, which means that this variable age is positively skewed and tethers along the right tail. We will verify our numerical data analysis on the variables with visualizations later. For A1c test skewness, we have a value of 0.34, which means it is closer to a normal curve; however, it is slightly positively skewed. For BP systolic we have a value of 1.2 and this clearly means that the data is positively skewed. BP diastolic also has a very high positive value of 3.9, which shows it is also highly positively skewed. Heartrate bpm is also a value of 3.3 and it also means it is highly positively skewed. BMI is also positively skewed.

Next we move to kurtosis, which shows the thickness in a distribution. If a data distribution has more peaks, then it is said to be left or leptokurtic and the distribution is said to have fatter tails. In such a distribution, there are more chances of extreme outcomes as compared to a normal distribution. The kurtosis formula calculates the degree of wickedness to a normal distribution with a value equal to 3. Excess kurtosis would mean the value of the distribution of the variable would be above 3, and less kurtosis would mean it would be below 3. If the value of kurtosis is less than 3, then it also denotes a type of distribution that is known as mesokurtic; however, the range for mesokurtic distribution is a kurtosis value between 0 and 3.

If the value of kurtosis is less than 0, then it is called platykurtic. The tales of a platykurtic distribution are shorter and thinner and the central peak is lower and broader. The kurtosis for age is a negative value of 0.2. A1c test is a positive value of 0.4, but it is below the value of 3. BP systolic is a value of 1.9, but it is below 3 and greater than 0. BP diastolic is 15.1 and heartrate bpm is 13.1. BMI is 5.4. We have already noted that if the value of kurtosis number is less than 0 then such a distribution is platykurtic, which means its tails are shorter and thinner and often its central peak is lower and broader. We have the variables A1c test and BP systolic lying between the value of 0 and 3, indicating that the distribution in these variables is mesokurtic. Three variables in our data set, BP diastolic, heartrate bpm, and BMI, have kurtosis values of more than 3, indicating that the data distribution in these variables is leptokurtic. The tails are longer and fatter and its central peak is higher and sharper.

In Figure 3-3 you can see the visual output of our variables in the data set using the highest method of Pandas dataframe.

```
dfworking.hist(figsize=(10, 6))
```

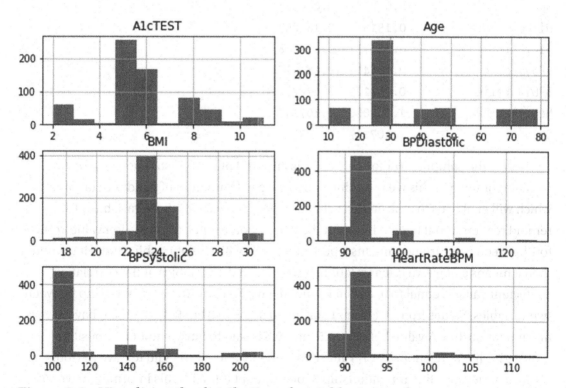

Figure 3-3. *Visualizing the distribution of variables in our data set*

We can confirm the skewness and kurtosis numerical interpretations with the visualization in Figure 3-3. In code Listing 3-14 below, using the corr() function of the dataframe dfworking we look at the correlation coefficient results.

Listing 3-14. Correlation Coefficient Results

```
dfworking.corr()
```

	Age	Diabetes status	A1cTEST	BPSystolic	BPDiastolic \
Age	1.000000	-0.006059	0.011436	0.013097	0.028190
Diabetes status	-0.006059	1.000000	0.816808	0.902857	0.560962
A1cTEST	0.011436	0.816808	1.000000	0.827919	0.591827
BPSystolic	0.013097	0.902857	0.827919	1.000000	0.735363
BPDiastolic	0.028190	0.560962	0.591827	0.735363	1.000000
HeartRateBPM	-0.052383	0.151831	0.147737	0.168413	0.058129
BMI	0.027911	0.181897	0.167908	0.181927	0.130275

	HeartRateBPM	BMI
Age	-0.052383	0.027911
Diabetes status	0.151831	0.181897
A1cTEST	0.147737	0.167908
BPSystolic	0.168413	0.181927
BPDiastolic	0.058129	0.130275
HeartRateBPM	1.000000	0.107147
BMI	0.107147	1.000000

Next is the computation to see if there is any kind of relationship between our variables or not. For this we are going to use the corr() function of Pandas dataframe, which will enable us to look at the correlation between each of these variables. To remind readers about how to interpret the correlation results, a correlation value equal to 1 between two variables means a perfect linear positive relationship, and if it is minus then it means a negative linear relationship between the variables. If the correlation coefficient value is equal to 0, then it is said to have no really linear relationship between two variables. Values from 0 to 1 or -1 staggered across 0.34 to 0.3 are said to have a weak linear relationship. A value between 0.5 and -0.5 is said to have a moderate positive or negative linear relationship. A value between -0.7 and +0.7 is said to have a strong positive or negative linear relationship to our data set [6]. With this information we can now quickly analyze the results of applying correlation function to our data set.

When we look at Listing 3-14 our main motive is to take out those variables that have at least moderate to strong and, if possible, a perfect linear relationship. So we are looking for variables that are starting from plus minus 0.5 to 0.12 as close to 1 or −1 as possible in their correlation coefficient. We can see that the age variable does not have any significant relationship linear relationship with other variables; however, when we look at the predictor variable for diabetes status, it does seem to have a positive correlation of 0.8 with A1c test and value of 0.9 with BP systolic. It has a moderate relationship with BP diastolic (0.5). The A1c test has an understandably strong relationship with the predictor variable diabetes status, which is 0.8, and with BP systolic (0.83) and with BP diastolic (0.59). BP systolic and BP diastolic have a positive correlation of 0.74. BP diastolic has a positive correlation with the moderate relationship with diabetes status the predictor variable of 0.5. The heartrate bpm does not seem to have any significant correlation with any of the variables in our data set. This is also the case with the BMI, which also does not seem to have any correlation with any of our data set.

Now we are in a position to look at the significant variables that seem to have some kind of relationship between them and look at them visually and understand how they are placed. To give you an example, in Figure 3-4 presents a scatter plot showing the visual relationship between the column variables A1c test and BP systolic.

```
dfworking.plot.scatter(x='A1cTEST', y='BPSystolic',s=dfworking['A1cTEST']*2)
```

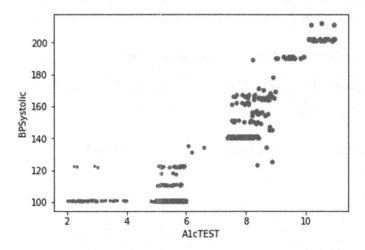

Figure 3-4. *Scatter plot between A1cTest and BPSystolic variables*

In Figure 3-4 we see some kind of a pattern between the two variables. We see that there are groups of clusters that are placed for A1c test; as the results go up, the patients are grouped into certain cluster patterns that show ladder-like upward movement. It starts from 100 BP systolic and goes beyond 200 BP systolic and from A1c test value of 2 more than the percentage. Detecting such patterns early through visualization is very important in machine learning. We could try implementing certain classification techniques to classify patients in these groups that are visually appealing to us.

The last step in our exploratory data analysis is to look at the columns that have categorical variables including the predictor variable diabetes status. We have six categorical variable columns in our data set. The first is gender, which categorizes our data set into male or female. The next categorical column is type of diabetes. In our data set, there are no patients with Type 1 Diabetes; however we have patients who either do not have diabetes or have Type 2 diabetes. The diabetes status column is the predictor variable whose value is also categorical, where 0 means no diabetes, and 1 means the patient has diabetes. Frozen shoulder, which is determined by the doctor by manual examination, has value of yes or no: yes means the patient has frozen shoulder and no means the patient does not have frozen shoulder. In carpal tunnel syndrome, it is same as frozen shoulder, where yes means the patient has carpal tunnel syndrome and no means the patient does not have this disease. For loop Dupuytren's contracture, it is also a yes and no column where yes means the patient has the disease no means the patient does not have this disease. Now I am going to use cross-tabulation based on these categorical variables to have a look at how our data set is categorized for these columns. In code Listing 3-15 we look at the Gender classification in the dataset.

Listing 3-15. Gender Classification in the Data Set

```
my_tab = pd.crosstab(index=df["Gender"], columns="Count")
# Name the count column

my_tab=my_tab.sort_values('Count', ascending=[False])
print(my_tab)
col_0    Count
Gender
Female    351
Male      313
```

In Listing 3-15, we can see that in our data set the number of females are 351 out of a total of 664 and the male patients are 313, so 53 percent of our patients are female by gender. This can be seen visually as well in the graph given in Figure 3-5.

```
data_counts = pd.DataFrame(my_tab)
pd.DataFrame(data_counts).transpose().plot(kind='bar', stacked=False)
```

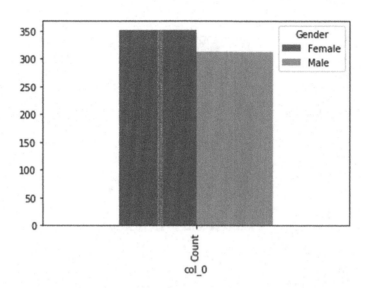

Figure 3-5. *Gender classification data visualization*

Now we look at the next column, which is type of diabetes, in Listing 3-16.

Listing 3-16. Type of Diabetes Classification

```
my_tab = pd.crosstab(index=df["Type of diabetes"], columns="Count")
# Name the count column

my_tab=my_tab.sort_values('Count', ascending=[False])
print(my_tab)
col_0           Count
Type of diabetes
None            504
Type 2          160
```

We can see that 24 percent of the patients in a data set have Type 2 diabetes, and 504 do not have diabetes. The reason for calculating percentage is important for any of the categorical columns because we need to determine if we are dealing with a rare event. In case we are dealing with a rare event, we need to deal with the model building by using univariate analysis. The visual representation of the type of diabetes column is given in Figure 3-6.

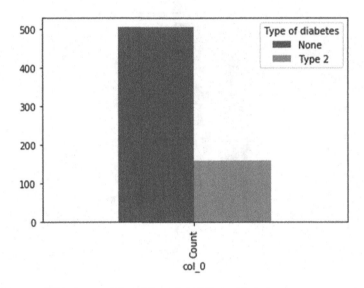

Figure 3-6. *Type of Diabetes Classification Visualization*

Next we look at the column frozen shoulder in Listing 3-17.

Listing 3-17. Classification of Frozen Shoulder Disease in Our Data Set

```
my_tab = pd.crosstab(index=df["FrozenShoulder"], columns="Count")
# Name the count column

my_tab=my_tab.sort_values('Count', ascending=[False])
print(my_tab)
col_0           Count
FrozenShoulder
No              533
Yes             131
```

In Listing 3-17 we can see that 19.1 percent of the patients in our data set have frozen shoulder and 533 patients do not have frozen shoulder. Since this percentage is above 10 percent, we can now be sure that with frozen shoulder we are not dealing with a rare event for our prediction. The data visualization for frozen shoulder is given in Figure 3-7.

```
data_counts = pd.DataFrame(my_tab)
pd.DataFrame(data_counts).transpose().plot(kind='bar', stacked=False)
Out[316]: <matplotlib.axes._subplots.AxesSubplot at 0x243ae851278>
```

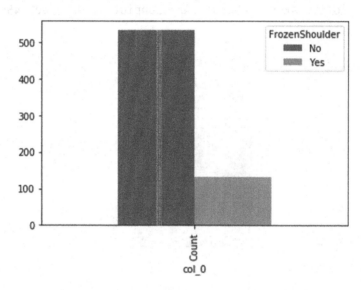

Figure 3-7. *Frozen shoulder disease classification visualization*

Listing 3-18. Carpal Tunnel Syndrome Classification

```
my_tab = pd.crosstab(index=df["CarpalTunnelSynd"], columns="Count")
# Name the count column

my_tab=my_tab.sort_values('Count', ascending=[False])
print(my_tab)
col_0            Count
CarpalTunnelSynd
No                 546
Yes                118
```

Now let us look at the carpal tunnel syndrome. In Figure 3-8 we can see the code for cross-tabulation and the count of people who said they had carpal tunnel syndrome and people who were not diagnosed as having carpal tunnel syndrome. Seventeen percent of our samples were diagnosed to have this disease. This was a total of 118 people, and 546 did not have this syndrome.

```
data_counts = pd.DataFrame(my_tab)
pd.DataFrame(data_counts).transpose().plot(kind='bar', stacked=False)
Out[319]: <matplotlib.axes._subplots.AxesSubplot at 0x243ae6a45c0>
```

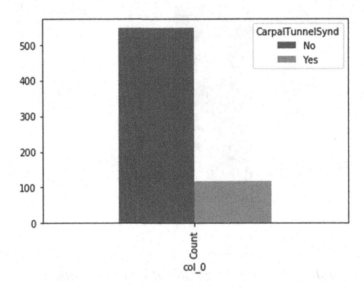

Figure 3-8. *Carpal Tunnel Syndrome visualization*

The visualization of this classification is given in Figure 3-8.

Now let us look at the disease of Dupuytren's Contracture and its classification, which is given in Figure 3-8. In code Listing 3-19 we use cross tabulation to see the classification of people with Dupuytren's contracture disease.

Listing 3-19. Dupuytren's Contracture Classification

```
my_tab = pd.crosstab(index=df["DupuytrensCont"], columns="Count")
# Name the count column

my_tab=my_tab.sort_values('Count', ascending=[False])
print(my_tab)
col_0           Count
DupuytrensCont
No               544
Yes              120
```

Patients who have been diagnosed with Dupuytren's Contracture form 18 percent of our data set, and 544 patients did not have this disease. I end my analysis of all the categorical columns as we have explored our data set and analyzed it sufficiently to start building a predictive model.

Data Preparation

Now we have completed our exploratory data analysis and we move on to the actual data preparation before building the model. I gave some of the steps that we need to do and their purpose in the Table 3-2. We see in the table that there are four steps. The first is to divide data into target variables and features; we do this in order to avoid counting the target variable with the features. This is common in machine learning and needs to be avoided. The second step is standardizing data, and this is done to create uniformity or a standardized scale for measuring all the variables in our data set. The next step is creation of dummy variables, and the main purpose is to convert all the categorical variables into dummy variables, such as gender (male or female). We could say gender of 0 is equal to male and gender of 1 is equal to female. Twenty represents male and 1 represents female so numerical encoding is what we need to do in this particular step. The last step for data preparation is the shuffle and split of data, and both are done in order to add some degree of randomness and to remove any virus that is there in the data. Once we have completed these four steps, we will be able to start building our prediction model. For each of the steps I will be showing you the code for our data set and the result as well as how to carry out data preparation.

The code for Step 1 is given in Listing 3-20.

Table 3-2. *Steps for Data Preparation*

Data Preparation Steps		
No#	Task	Description
1	Divide data into target variables and features.	We need to split the data into features and target variables in order to ensure that we do not count the target variable as a feature; otherwise, our prediction model will give wrong results.
2	Standardize data.	We need to standardize data since this brings all the variables to a common scale. As the common saying goes, you cannot compare oranges with apples. So also is the case with our variables. They are different measures with different scales of measures such as BP systolic is different from the scale of heartrate bpm.
3	Dummy Variables	A limitation with Scikit library in Python is that it can only work with numeric data and does not work with categorical data. A way to remove this limitation is to convert categorical variables in our data set, such as Frozen shoulder columns, to a numerical encoding format.
4	Shuffle and split data.	We now shuffle data to introduce an element of randomness and then split it into train and test in order to remove bias from data.

Listing 3-20. Step 1 of Data Preparation

```
#Data Preparation Steps
#Step 1 Split data into features and target variable
# Split the data into features and target label
diabetics = pd.DataFrame(dfworking['Diabetes status'])
features = pd.DataFrame(dfworking.drop('Diabetes status', axis = 1))
diabetics.columns
features.columns
features.columns
Out[352]:
Index(['Gender', 'Age', 'Type of diabetes', 'A1cTEST', 'BPSystolic',
       'BPDiastolic', 'HeartRateBPM', 'BMI', 'FrozenShoulder',
       'CarpalTunnelSynd', 'DupuytrensCont'],
     dtype='object')
```

In Listing 3-20, while implementing the code for step 1, we see that features dataframe does not have the column diabetes status, which is our target variable. I have created two data frames: diabetics, which is the predictor or the target variable Pandas dataframe, and features data frame, which does not have the column diabetes status. I've used the Drop method of Pandas dataframe to remove diabetes status column. Now we move on to step 2: standardizing the data. This can be seen in Listing 3-22. For implementing this, I will be using sklearn.preprocessing library and importing MinMaxScaler from it to standardize our data set. Please note that this standardization should happen for only the numeric variables and not the categorical or dummy variables.

Listing 3-21. Numerical Columns in Our Working Data Set

```
dfworking.dtypes
dfworking.dtypes
Out[355]:
Gender            object
Age                int64
Type of diabetes  object
Diabetes status    int64
A1cTEST          float64
BPSystolic       float64
BPDiastolic      float64
HeartRateBPM       int64
BMI              float64
FrozenShoulder    object
CarpalTunnelSynd  object
DupuytrensCont    object
```

We can see in Listing 3-21 that age A1c test, BP systolic, BP diastolic, heartrate bpm, and BMI columns are numeric. We are going to ignore diabetes status column because it is a categorical variable for a patient, where 0 means no diabetes and 1 means the patient has diabetes. In Listing 3-22, I have provided the code to extract these numerical features and then to apply the standardized scalar on them.

Listing 3-22. Step 2 of Data Preparation

```
# Import sklearn.preprocessing.StandardScaler
from sklearn.preprocessing import MinMaxScaler

# Initialize a scaler, then apply it to the features
scaler = MinMaxScaler()
numerical = ['age', 'education-num', 'capital-gain', 'capital-loss',
'hours-per-week']
features_raw[numerical] = scaler.fit_transform(dfworking[numerical])

# Show an example of a record with scaling applied
display(features_raw[numerical].head(n = 1))
        Age    A1cTEST  BPSystolic  BPDiastolic  HeartRateBPM        BMI
0  0.275362  0.756968    0.419591     0.153846      0.028571   0.545713 No
Yes           Yes
```

In Listing 3-22, we can see an example record of features that have been scaled. Please notice that I have not yet transformed the categorical variables into dummy variables, and this is the next step given in Listing 3-23.

Listing 3-23. Step 3: Dummy variables

```
# Step 3 One-hot encode the 'features_raw' data using pandas.get_dummies()
features = pd.get_dummies(features_raw)

#Checking output
display(features.head(1),diabetics.head(1))

# Print the number of features after one-hot encoding
encoded = list(features.columns)
print("{} total features after one-hot encoding.".format(len(encoded)))

# See the encoded feature names
print(encoded)
display(features.head(1),diabetics.head(1))
        Age    A1cTEST  BPSystolic  BPDiastolic  HeartRateBPM        BMI  \
0  0.275362  0.756968    0.419591     0.153846      0.028571   0.545713

   Gender_Female  Gender_Male  Type of diabetes_None  Type of diabetes_Type 2  \
0              1            0                      0                        1
```

```
    FrozenShoulder_No      FrozenShoulder_Yes  CarpalTunnelSynd_No  \
0                  1                       0                      0

    CarpalTunnelSynd_Yes  DupuytrensCont_No      DupuytrensCont_YEs  \
0                     1                  0                        0

    DupuytrensCont_Yes
0                    1
    Diabetes status
0                  1
encoding.".format(len(encoded)))
17 total features after one-hot encoding.
print(encoded)
['Age', 'A1cTEST', 'BPSystolic', 'BPDiastolic', 'HeartRateBPM', 'BMI',
'Gender_Female', 'Gender_Male', 'Type of diabetes_None', 'Type of diabetes_
Type 2', 'FrozenShoulder_No', 'FrozenShoulder_Yes', 'CarpalTunnelSynd_
No', 'CarpalTunnelSynd_Yes', 'DupuytrensCont_No', 'DupuytrensCont_YEs',
'DupuytrensCont_Yes']
```

From Figure 3-3 we see the code for hot encoding. I have used the get_dummies()
function from Pandas library to convert raw features into final dummy-based features.
You can then see the output of how the dummy variables have been automatically
created by the get_dummies function; for example, it has created one with gender female
and one with gender male. After this is done, we look at a summary of how many total
features have been hot encoded and find that there were 17. Finally with print encoded,
we take a look at all the columns in the data set. The next step and the fourth and final
step are to shuffle and split the data. In Listing 3-24 we can see the code to generate first
shuffle and split and then the train and test split.

Listing 3-24. Step 4 of Data Preparation

```
#Step 4 Shuffle & Split Final Dataset
# Import train_test_split
from sklearn.cross_validation import train_test_split
from sklearn.utils import shuffle

# Shuffle and split the data into training and testing subsets
features=shuffle(features,  random_state=0)
```

```
diabetics=shuffle(diabetics,  random_state=0)
# Split the 'features' and 'income' data into training and testing sets
X_train, X_test, y_train, y_test = train_test_split(features, diabetics,
test_size = 0.2, random_state = 0)
print("Training set has {} samples.".format(X_train.shape[0]))
print("Testing set has {} samples.".format(X_test.shape[0]))
Training set has 531 samples.
Testing set has 133 samples.
```

Listing 3-24 shows the code and the result of first randomly shuffling features and the target variable and then splitting it into train and test data sets. We can see that there are 531 created for the training set and 133 were created for the testing set, for a total of 664. With this our steps for data preparation are now complete. We now move into model building validation and implementation phases of our machine learning life cycle. In code Listing 3-25 I now show you how to build a model using 7 classifier algorithms.

Listing 3-25. Model Building Initializing the Classifier Algorithms

```
#Loading model Libraries
from sklearn import model_selection
from sklearn.linear_model import LogisticRegression
from sklearn.tree import DecisionTreeClassifier
from sklearn.neighbors import KNeighborsClassifier
from sklearn.discriminant_analysis import LinearDiscriminantAnalysis
from sklearn.naive_bayes import GaussianNB
from sklearn.svm import SVC
from sklearn.ensemble import RandomForestClassifier

# prepare models
#Using seed to maintain reproducability and consistent results
seed = 7
models = []
models.append(('LR', LogisticRegression()))
models.append(('LDA', LinearDiscriminantAnalysis()))
models.append(('KNN', KNeighborsClassifier()))
models.append(('CART', DecisionTreeClassifier()))
```

```
models.append(('NB', GaussianNB()))
models.append(('SVM', SVC()))
models.append(('RFC', RandomForestClassifier()))
```

Listing 3-25 shows algorithms for model building initialization of the classifier. I have initialized seven common classed. I'm going to use logistic regression, decision tree classifier, k neighbors classifier, linear discriminant analysis cause, naive Bayes classifier, SVC, and random forest classifier. In Listing 3-26 you can see that I have loaded these algorithms from the Python library SKlearn and then I have prepared these models by initializing them one by one. Now the next step is to run a loop for all the models' dictionary, run kfold cross-validation, and then load the results into the results data dictionary and show the mean and standard deviation for each of the algorithms or classifiers. Next I show in graphical format the algorithm comparison results for each of the algorithms. This is shown using the matplot library.

Listing 3-26. *Model Evaluation*

```
# evaluate each model in turn
results = []
names = []
scoring = 'accuracy'

import warnings
warnings.filterwarnings("ignore")

for name, model in models:
    kfold = model_selection.KFold(n_splits=10, random_state=seed)
    cv_results = model_selection.cross_val_score(model, X_train, y_train,
    cv=kfold, scoring=scoring)
    results.append(cv_results)
    names.append(name)
    msg = "%s: %f (%f)" % (name, cv_results.mean(), cv_results.std())
    print(msg)
```

Table 3-3. *Classifier Algorithm Accuracy*

Classifier Algorithm	Accuracy	STD
LR	1.000	0.000
LDA	1.000	0.000
KNN	1.000	0.000
CART	0.998	0.006
NB	0.998	0.006
SVM	1.000	0.000
RFC	0.998	0.006

In Table 3-3 we can have a look at the classifier algorithms accuracy from the accuracy column, and we see that three algorithms have not done well in comparison to others with accuracy score less than 1 for naive Bayes and random forest classifier. With this, I end the chapter on how to implement machine learning in healthcare. I have tried to take up a data set that pertains to the healthcare electronic patient records and that in my opinion is very common to find in the healthcare world. I am pretty sure that you, The Reader, will find the complete application in this chapter very helpful when you try to implement the code and its results. You can also do a comparision of the algorithms using the AUC values or the RoC metrics, a task that I leave up to the reader to compute and verify. You can learn more about the Scikit learn libraries auc metrics from the following web url: sklearn.metrics.auc(x, y, reorder=False [8]). You can also look at the quick method to calculate AUC and RoC score metrics from the official Scikit learn library web url [9].

End Notes

[1]   ShijunWangRonald M.Summe, Medical Image Analysis, Volume 16, Issue 5, July 2012, pp. 933-951 https://www.sciencedirect.com/science/article/pii/S1361841512000333

[2]   Dupuytren's contracture, By Mayo Clinic Staff, https://www.mayoclinic.org/diseases-conditions/dupuytrens-contracture/symptoms-causes/syc-20371943

[3]   Mean and standard deviation. http://www.bmj.com/about-bmj/resources-readers/publications/statistics-square-one/2-mean-and-standard-deviation

[4]   Interquartile Range IQR http://www.mathwords.com/i/interquartile_range.htm

[5]   Why are tree-based models robust to outliers? https://www.quora.com/Why-are-tree-based-models-robust-to-outliers

[6]   https://www.dummies.com/education/math/statistics/how-to-interpret-a-correlation-coefficient-r/

[7]   https://www.medicalnewstoday.com/releases/11856.php

[8]   Scikit Learn Auc metrics: http://scikit-learn.org/stable/modules/generated/sklearn.metrics.auc.html

[9]   Scikit Learn Library RoC and AUC scores: http://scikit-learn.org/stable/modules/generated/sklearn.metrics.roc_auc_score.html

## CHAPTER 4

Case Studies in Healthcare AI

Disclaimer: The case studies in this book have been taken from real-life organizations. Care has been taken to ensure that the names of the organizations and the names of their employees are changed and do not resemble my clients in any way. The reader familiar with the healthcare industry will definitely find these situations very practical and insightful.

Before we move into looking at our case studies let us look at the case study methodology and its advantages. One can argue that case study methodology is used mainly by MBA programs, especially Harvard Business School [`https://www.hbs.edu/mba/blog/post/3-benefits-of-the-case-method`], where this methodology originated. Here, we are talking about machine learning applications with Python and how this methodology is used with solutions involves programming code. Before I step into answering the specific issue, let us look at the three advantages that case study method brings today and the other benefits we acquire through the use of case studies in our business situations.

The first benefit that we derive out of case study methodology is that the person who is going to give a solution for the case study is supposed to prepare not just by reading the case and the questions that the case study poses but also by doing some background work on the business problem at hand and available to the problem solver that can be used to solve it. This information stays with the person and learning continues in an informal manner after the case study solution is complete. There is no need to cram any reticular curriculum for answering the case studies as they are unique business situations and may not necessarily have theories supporting their solution.

The second advantage of using case study methodology is that while giving a solution for case study business problem, the person is supposed to contribute their own independent views to the case questions. This is the practice of applying machine

© Puneet Mathur 2019

P. Mathur, *Machine Learning Applications Using Python*, https://doi.org/10.1007/978-1-4842-3787-8_4

learning and Python code to a business situation and then when you look at it closely and try to prepare yourself for giving solutions for them, by writing code that would solve that particular business problem. It is important to note that in the case study method there is no absolute right or wrong because a particular business problem can be solved in many ways. The practice here is to come out with as many solutions to the business problem and explore the most rewarding one in the given situation. So the third advantage of using case study method problem solving is it matters in the business environment and it is the most sought-after skill for an applied machine learning engineer.

I have chosen these case studies carefully from real-life examples and I am pretty sure that the reader will find them useful. I would advise you to read the case study at least two times before attempting to answer the questions given in each case study. In my opinion, what you should do is to first read and understand the business situation given in the case study text, and then look at each question and then go back to the case study text to understand the situation again. Once you have looked at the case study with respect to each question you should start formulating solutions in your mind as to what you would do if you were facing this scenario in the healthcare industry. Think back to the process of machine learning applications that I showed you in Chapter 3. Take care not to miss any steps while formulating your solution.

Once you have a rough sketch of the solution you think is most appropriate in the given business situation, then you should proceed to looking at the proposed solution along with the code for a given case study. Please remember that in case study method, different people can come up with different solutions, and there is no right or wrong solution. However, the criteria that this follows is that the solution should answer all the needs of the business problem, and it should also be acceptable to the business. In the case study solutions given in this book, I have given solutions that were acceptable to the business and hence can be taken as a benchmark by The Reader to judge the solution that they have proposed for the case study. The objective is to first create your own solution without looking at the solution that I have given in this book to make you start thinking independently and to start applying machine learning in healthcare business situations.

CASE STUDY 1: Lab Coordinator Problem

Dr. Deshmukh was sitting in his office on a Monday morning, and he had in front of him on his laptop screen a report from the financial department about the financial situation of his healthcare organization, DIRECTPyth diagnostic centers global chain, which was comprised of more than 250 diagnostic centers around the world.

The core business of DIRECTPyth was diagnostic centers for diabetes. The sudden growth of DIRECTPyth diagnostic centers has occurred in the last 5 years. DIRECTPyth started as a homegrown diagnostic company, with just four centers in India. In the last 10 years of its operations, it had expanded its diagnostic centers to all major cities in not just India but also in Southeast Asia, the Middle East, and Canada. Most of it overseas centers had turned up in the last 5 years as diagnostic companies had seen rapid growth in the need for people to get diagnosed for diabetes.

The World Health Organization report on diabetes (`http://www.who.int/diabetes/global-report/en/`) shows that diabetes has now become an epidemic around the world. In 2012 diabetes caused 1.5 million deaths due to heart attack, stroke, blindness, kidney failure, and lower limb amputation. Various governments around the world have been spreading awareness by running information programs in the media about the epidemic of diabetes. Delhi Ford also highlights that since 1980 there has been an increase in patients with Type 2 diabetes, which has quadrupled sense then. In order to control this epidemic, the governments around the world in the last 5 years have stepped up prevention and treatment of diabetes programs. The DIRECTPyth diabetes diagnostic healthcare chain is right in the middle of this epidemic and offers tests for any person to diagnose whether they have diabetes.

The report that Dr. Deshmukh was looking at pointed out financial losses in the past 2 years to the tune of 200 million US dollars. The financial position of the company is given in Table 4-1.

Table 4-1. *Two-Year Financial Synopsis Report*

Financial Synopsis ($US million)	Fiscal Year, 2015-2016	Fiscal Year, 2016-2017
Income from diagnostics	930	1221
Cost of operations	1031	1354
Average operational days for diagnostic centers	118	106
Loss due to non-operations	101	133

Let me briefly explain Table 4-1. The financials are given for two financial years: 2015-2016 and 2016-2017. The status given in columns 2 and 3 as the income from diagnostics has been given by the financial department, and you can see that that income for the DIRECTPyth organization has been growing on a yearly basis. Cost of operations was higher than the income from diagnostic in the first year as well as in the second year. The last row gives the loss due to non–operations, which is a DIRECTPyth subtraction of the cost of operations from income from diagnostics. The combined loss for both years stands at 234 million dollars. The third row provides the number of average operational days for all diagnostic centers of DIRECTPyth around the world. The average operational days for DIRECTPyth is 118, which is significantly lower than the benchmark number of 200, which DIRECTPyth follows internally to guage its performance. We can also see that in the year 2016 and 2017, the average operational days for diagnostic centers has gone down to 106 days. Loss due to non-operation has also gone up from 101 million dollars the first year to 133 million dollars the second year.

In order for DIRECTPyth to remain competitive in the market, it needs to decrease its cost of operations and loss due to non-operations, and it will need to take serious measures now.

The report clearly shows the loss due to human resource constraint. Dr. Deshmukh called for an early morning meeting with the human resource manager at DIRECTPyth. The purpose was to discuss the financial losses and to find out what the single-most cause of this problem. The human resource manager was Ms. Abbey, and she was to give a presentation to the Dr. Deshmukh regarding the cause for the financial losses DIRECTPyth and how to prevent them in the future. Dr. Deshmukh then got up, well-prepared for the 10 a.m. meeting. Ms. Abbey arrived at the meeting along with her staff. After the greetings were over, she started presenting the 2-year financial synopsis. She pointed out to Dr. Deshmukh that the cost of operations had gone up by 131 percent between years. The loss was also at the same percentage, as it was derived from cost of operations. She explained that the average operational days for diagnostic centers was calculated based on the number of days a diagnostic center remained open on any given business day throughout the year. The target average operational days for DIRECTPyth was 200 operational days. She presented the breakdown of the average operational diagnostic centers data given in Table 4-2.

Table 4-2. *Breakup of Average Operational Days (AOD) Data*

Average operational days	No. of centers meeting AOD benchmark	No. of centers not meeting AOD benchmark
India	32	234
Oversees	13	98
Consolidated	45	332
%AGE	11.9	88

The breakup of average operational days data shows that on an overall global basis, the percentage of diagnostic centers at DIRECTPyth that were meeting the benchmark of 200 days was only 11.9 percent and the percentage of centers not meeting the AOD benchmark was 88 percent. This shows the criticality and extent of the problem at DIRECTPyth. It also shows that there is acute loss of revenue happening because of the centers not meeting the AOD benchmark. In order to deep-dive into the problem further Ms. Abbey presented data relating to human resources at the lab diagnostic facilities for the DIRECTPyth organization. This data is given in Table 4-3.

Table 4-3. *Human Resources Data at DIRECTPyth Labs*

Human resources at DIRECTPyth Labs	Lab coordinator	Lab technician	Lab attendant
Average days present	88	97	194
Average days absent	26	15	8
Attrition rate (%)	12%	9%	6%

We can see from Table 4-3 that the highest absenteeism occurs with the lab coordinator and lab technician roles. The lab attendant has the highest average and lowest absenteeism. The best data has been pulled from the payroll systems of DIRECTPyth Labs, which records the daily attendance of each human resource in the lab. The total number of days present is taken as a benchmark value of 220 productive business days. The role of lab coordinator is one that interacts with the customer who walks into the diagnostic lab, taking them to the various diagnostic options available in the lab and then helping them find the most appropriate test for their diabetic condition. The lab coordinator checks whether the patient is already registered with the diagnostic center and then pulls up computer records and requests a new test. A technician at DIRECTPyth is the one who actually conducts the lab test for the patient who is waiting in the queue. The lab attendant is the person who takes the data from the lab technician for a particular patient, enters the data into the computer, and then produces a report that is to be presented to the patient. These three key positions are very important for the business operations of the diagnostic center at DIRECTPyth. Ms. Abbey presented in the meeting that the high absenteeism at the lab coordinator and lab technician roles was leading to the losses in revenue for DIRECTPyth. There was an urgent need for the organization to find out how to improve the productivity and decrease the absenteeism in this role. We can also see that the lab coordinator role has the highest attrition rate (12 percent) followed by the lab technician (9 percent). The lowest attrition (6 percent) showed the need for DIRECTPyth to find a way to decrease the absenteeism and attrition rates for the lab coordinator. The most important was the lab coordinator role, where the absenteeism and attrition rates were very high. The human resources department should try to look at ways to reduce the absenteeism and attrition rates. They had tried for five ways over the past 3 years but with very marginal success in finding a solution. So it was very clear that if DIRECTPyth wanted to increase its profitability and reduce its losses, it needed to urgently address the problem of absenteeism and attrition in the lab coordinator role.

The solution, which required an immediate implementation, should be to use technology to emulate the role of a lab coordinator. DIRECTPyth had received funding from foreign investors and was in a position to invest in technology in order to increase its efficiency, thereby increasing its revenue. You are required to use Python-based machine learning to address and answer the questions given in this case study.

1. What do you think is the reason for the losses at DIRECTPyth Diagnostic Centers?

2. What human issues are we dealing with and how do you think they can be addressed?

3. Do you think technology can help address the issues that you identified in Question 2?

4. Will a Python-based machine learning solution be able to address these issues at DIRECTPyth?

5. What is your proposed Python-based machine learning solution? Please use Python 3.x source code for your solution.

6. What business justification do you give for your solution that you think will be acceptable by the business leaders at DIRECTPyth?

I would suggest that you first try to independently answer these questions and then look at the solution given in this book. Please note the solution that I have given is one among many solutions that can be given in this business scenario. It is the business owners that ultimately decide if your solution is good and is able to address their business problem.

Pro Tip   In applied machine learning, we machine learning consultants work hand-in-hand with business leaders of an organization in order to determine what works for them. Always remember to circle back with them and to present even a small half-baked plan and get it vetted before converting it into a full-blown solution. This will save you a lot of wasted meetings and energy.

Now let me try to answer the questions in my own way, giving the solution I had proposed, which was accepted by the organization.

1. What do you think is the reason for the losses at DIRECTPyth Diagnostic Centers?

The reason for the losses of DIRECTPyth Diagnostic Centers was the high operational losses, with about 88 percent of the diagnostic centers not meeting the average operational-based benchmark. The real reason for this was attributed to high absenteeism and attrition rate by lab coordinators in the organization. Lab coordinator absenteeism was very high at 26 percent, and attrition rate was 12 percent, whereas for the lab technician the absenteeism was 15 percent, and the attrition rate was 9 percent. The human resources came up with five various techniques to stop attrition and absenteeism but with very marginal results.

2. What human issues are we dealing with and how do you think they can be addressed?

I think we are dealing with a work force with low morale, and that is the reason we are seeing high absenteeism and attrition rate.

3. Do you think technology can help address the issues that you identified in Question 2?

In my opinion using technology in areas where human beings fail to perform at an optimal level required by a business is an apt scenario for bringing in automation, machine learning, and artificial intelligence. The good point about technology is that it can do any given task repeatedly without getting bored or tired. It can also use intelligence on data and be trained to perform expert tasks very easily. In the case of DIRECTPyth Diagnostic Centers, we can use technology to replace the task of lab coordinator, putting an automated lab machine on its premises, thereby letting the customer choose the lab test that they want to perform. The automated lab machine can run Python-based machine learning programs that help the customer choose the best diagnostic test for their scenario.

4. Will a Python-based machine learning solution be able to address these issues at DIRECTPyth?

Yes, a Python-based machine learning system can be used to automate the entire process in the lab right from the time the customer comes in and selects the diagnostic package to generate the lab test to the next stage of generating the report with its meaningful interpretations for the customer. Python-based machine learning systems can be connected to any modern automated lab testing machine to get the output from it.

5. What is your proposed Python-based machine learning solution? Please use Python 3.x source code for your solution.

In this book, I am going to give a solution that is going to be short; however, it is going to emulate the real solution that I gave to the client in their production environment. The Reader can build upon this solution using their own ideas in the real world for similar situations. A word of caution to The Reader: this is a very minimalistic approach that I have taken to create a chatbot; however, it does not limit the user from extending its functionality by using the code given in this book. Chatbots in real life are more complicated than the code that I have given here, as it would involve sentiment analysis using nltk.corpora the nltk repository. It would also use lemmatization natural language processing techniques to give an optimum response to the user of the Python program.

This solution is and should be considered as a template code to build upon, rather than the ultimate solution, as it is not possible to write the whole source code for a production chatbot in a book because it would run into millions of lines of code. I will walk you through the code, giving you an idea as to why each part of the code has been written, including the intent and the functionality it performs and some tips as to how you could adapt it in production.

> Business Need: The business need of the solution is to emulate the work of a lab coordinator and interact with the user through a chat interface. I present to you some of the use-cases that are applicable in this case study scenario.

Pro Tip   Even before you start coding, divide your work into short use-cases and get them ratified by actual users of the system as you will be developing for them. If you skip this step, it is likely you will be developing a product that the user may reject, as you may have misunderstood some of the requirements.

> Use-Case: As a user of an automated chatbot for diabetes diagnostics, I should be able to know my past test data records in order for me to check my history.

> Use-Case: As a user of an automated chatbot for diabetes diagnostics, I should be able to know the type of tests conducted at the center and their purpose so that my doctor and I can decide on the test.

> Use-Case: As a user of an automated chatbot for diabetes diagnostics, I should be able to get the results of my tests done so that I can get a report.

> Use-Case: As a user of an automated chatbot for diabetes diagnostics, I should be able to get a recommendation on my test results so that I am able to know the future course of action.

For DIRECTPyth Diagnostic Centers, there are more use-cases that are applicable than those given here. However, to keep the process simple, we will be considering only these four use-cases for our solution.

Now we are going to look at the flowchart in Figure 4-1, which applies the process that will be followed by other chatbots while interacting with the customer. Please remember that I am using a minimalistic approach to this solution because it is not a production code; it is to give you an idea as to how to apply machine learning in the area of emulating lab coordinator in the healthcare segment.

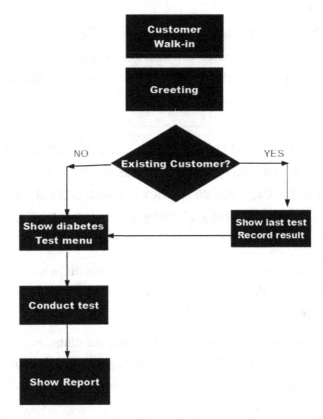

Figure 4-1. *Process of interaction between customer and lab coordinator chatbots*

In Figure 4-1 we can see that the process starts when the customer walks in and meet the chatbots in the lab coordinator, so there is no human interaction or human supervision in this process. The kiosk has sensors that detect the presence of a human being nearby and gives out a greeting to the customer. In the next part of the process, if it is an existing customer, the chatbot asks the customer for a membership ID. Now the lab coordinator chatbot has to make a decision based on the input provided if the membership id given by the customer is found in the database; then it shows the last test record result to the customer. If it is not an existing customer, then the chatbot shows diabetes tests—many that list the entire set of tests available at the lab. Once the customer has selected the test from the list, the lab coordinator conducts the test and then produces a report. In our case, in the Python program. the part where the robot asks the customer to sit near an automated testing machine for diabetes diagnosis has been marked by me, and I will indicate this in the code where the markup happens. The reason I have done this is because the Python program produces random results for the report; however, in the production environment, this data would come from the lab technician machine that undertakes the tests. In the actual world, there would be other steps that are part of the process for the report to be shared with the doctor through internal healthcare records; however I have skipped all those processes in this solution to keep it simple.

Now that we have the process flowchart for our chatbots defined, we can go into the Python code for implementing our simple chatbots.

Tip   Load the wordnet lemmatizer and punkt packages before running this example on your machine.

```
Install using the following commands:
import nltk

nltk.download('wordnet')
[nltk_data] Downloading package wordnet to
[nltk_data]     C:\Users\PMAUTHOR\AppData\Roaming\nltk_data...
[nltk_data]   Unzipping corpora\wordnet.zip.
Out[4]: True
import nltk
nltk.download('punkt')
```

Listing 4-1 shows you initialization code for our chatbots, which includes the first line declaration that our code follows UTF 8 encoding. After this we have the next set of statements, which import the GUI library tkinter and its components, such as scrawled text image and image TK, as well as time package (which is used to configure the sleep function). I have also imported the random function, as it helps our chatbots in making random choices from our answers, which we will look at later.

Listing 4-1. Loading chatbot User Interface

```
# -*- coding: utf-8 -*-
"""
Created on Sat Mar 24 10:20:18 2018

@author: PUNEETMATHUR
"""
#Loading tkinter libraries which will be used in the UI of chatbots
import tkinter
from tkinter import *
from tkinter.scrolledtext import *
from tkinter import ttk
import time
from PIL import ImageTk, Image
import tkinter

#Loading random for random choices in our chat program
import random
```

Listing 4-1 shows initial codes for our chatbots. In Listing 4-2 we see the Python code for implementing a Splash screen using tkinter package. In order to do that, we first create a new object named Splash of the tkinter window TK object, and then I give it a title that welcomes the user to the Splash screen. Then I use the Splash object to give the height and weight using the geometry function. I am creating a Splash window of 1000 by 100 pixels height and weight, so I have used 1000 x 100 in the parameter of the geometry function. Next I have given a background color to the Splash window using the configure function with parameter background equal to green. In order to display a text that asks the user to wait while the program is loading, I have used a label widget from the label object in the center library by name of w, and while initializing w, I have linked it to Splash object, which is the window in which the label is going to be created. So the first parameter is where the label gets connected with the Splash window. The next second parameter is where you enter the text that you want the label to show, and that has been entered by me as a string. The third parameter I have entered is font, where I have used Helvetica size 26 in order to show the text. The next parameter is FG, which stands for foreground color of the window, and the foreground color is the text of the label and the color in which it will be shown. In my case I have used white. In the next parameter I have used BG, which stands for background color, and I have given it a value of green. In the next statement, I hack the label so that it is ready to show on the Splash window. Once this is done, I use the update method of Splash so that the label is updated on the Windows screen. Once the screen shows up, we would like it to appear before the user for some time, and you can specify the time by making the programs sleep for X number of seconds. I have used in the next code statement time to sleep, with a parameter of 6, which denotes that the program is going to sleep for 6 seconds. You can experiment with this and see what suits your Splash screen, and you can modify the number of seconds accordingly. After the Splash screen has been shown for 6 seconds, I would like it to disappear and so I would identify the screen and then destroy it in the next two statements.

Listing 4-2. Splash Screen

```
#Splash Screen
splash = tkinter.Tk()

splash.title("Welcome to Applications of Machine Learning in Healthcare,
Retail & Finance")
splash.geometry("1000x100")
splash.configure(background='green')
w = Label(splash, text="DIRECTPyth Diabetes Diagnostics Chabot by Puneet
Mathur\nLoading...",font=("Helvetica", 26),fg="white",bg="green")
w.pack()

splash.update()
time.sleep(6)
splash.deiconify()
splash.destroy()
```

Now it is time to load the main chat window of our chatbots application, and hence in Listing 4-3 you see the code that is required to load the chat window. In the first statement in Listing 4-3, I create a window object of the TK class inside the tkinter package. And then I add a scroll bar to the window by using instantiate nS object from the scroll bar class and instantiate the scroll bar class with window so it gets associated with the window object. If you have a scroll bar and do not have a text, then it will become useless, so in the next statement I instantiate a text box with the window object. The text box is known as chat MSG, and we will be using this extensively in our program later because all the input and output from and to the user will be through this text box. In the next statement, I use focus set object in order to set the focus on the text box. In the next statement, I pack the scroll bar and use the first parameter to fix the scroll bar on the right-hand side of the window and use the y-axis for the scroll bar. In the next statement, I move the text box chat MSG to the top of the window and fill it on the y-axis. In the next statement, I configure using the config method of scroll bar to get the nd from chat MSG review. I also link the chatmsg textbox with the scroll bar to set the – s.config method and the yscrollcommand function and then linked with the value of s.config. Now the next step is to create an entry for the input user and input field by creating an object of the stringware class and then linking it with the input field by instantiating the entry class and attaching it to the window in the first parameter and the created stringware object with the text in the second parameter. If you do not do this, then your text box will not have the ability to take text and to respond back to the text. In the next statement, I hack the input field by attaching it to the bottom and filling it along the x-axis. This is where the user is going to enter all their data and going to interact with our chatbot. In the next statement I have created a variable underscore text that welcomes the user to the diagnostic center. Please remember that this is going to run as an automated program in a kiosk, so there would be sensors that would be attached to the kiosk on the arrival of a customer, and DIRECTPyth will rigger this program. However, in this code implementation, all that has been removed because it is not possible to show the entire production code in a short book like this. In the next statement, we use chat MSG, which is our text box, and insert the value of the text, which is our variable. In the next statement, we move our focus to the text box.

Listing 4-3. Creating the Chatbots Window and Welcoming the User

```
#Initializing tkinter library for UI window show up
window = tkinter.Tk()
s = tkinter.Scrollbar(window)
chatmsg = tkinter.Text(window)
chatmsg.focus_set()
s.pack(side=tkinter.RIGHT, fill=tkinter.Y)
chatmsg.pack(side=tkinter.TOP, fill=tkinter.Y)
s.config(command=chatmsg.yview)
```

```
chatmsg.config(yscrollcommand=s.set)
input_user = StringVar()
input_field = Entry(window, text=input_user)
input_field.pack(side=tkinter.BOTTOM, fill=tkinter.X)
bot_text="Welcome to DIRECTPythPyth Diagnostic Center\n"
chatmsg.insert(INSERT, 'Bot:%s\n' % bot_text)
bot_text = "Press enter to continue "
chatmsg.insert(INSERT, 'Bot:%s\n' % bot_text)
chatmsg.focus()
```

In a real-world, production-grade application in machine learning using NLP, you would need to first spend time with the businesspeople and develop a Corpus, which is nothing but a business lexicon or the jargons that are used in everyday life of the organization. Since this implementation is short, I have only given you an idea as to how a Corpus is built in Listing 4-4. You will see that I have used the Python variable type of list to create our Diagnostics Corpus. The first list is great; this is nothing but a list of the various types of greetings that our chatbots is going to give to a new user when they arrive. The next list is to add confirmation, which is yes, yay, yeah, and yo. You can add more confirmations, and this list could be quite huge as well, in order for you to comprehend what a user is trying to say. The important part of this list is that the list is learning for our chatbots, and we provide some of the ready-made answers as well as the questions that a customer can ask in this Corpus. In the next list, I use member ID, and I have used five member IDs because this is just a prototype application. However, in the real world, you would have hundreds and even thousands of member IDs, and this data would come from some flat files or databases, like mongo DB. In the next list, I use customer to capture such reactions and help our bot in order to recognize them, and this is an input where they say hello, hi, or hey. In the next list answer, I have given just two statements: the first is a positive statement and the second is a negative statement. We will look at our program later as to how this is being used in practice. In the next list, I have used some simple questions and their responses; however, they may not have been used. But it will give you an idea as to how a chatbot can react if it knows questions and responses. In the next list, I have given the test, which is nothing but the menu that pops up when a user enters their member ID. We have five tests that can be conducted; however, please remember that in the real world business of diagnostic centers, they have hundreds of tests, and on top of that they package those tests based on different

91

customer requirements, like diabetics profile test and heart condition test, just to give you an example. In the next set of test responses, I have used the options that the user can type in our previous list of tests. For example, in test responses one corresponds to the first item of the tests list, HB A1c test, and so on.

Listing 4-4. The Diagnostics Corpus

```
#Diagnostics Corpus for the chatbots
greet=['Hello welcome to DIRECTPythPyth','Hi welcome to
DIRECTPythPyth','Hey welcome to DIRECTPythPyth','Good day to you welcome to
DIRECTPythPyth']
confirm=['yes','yay','yeah','yo']
memberid=['12345','12346','12347','12348','12349']
customer = ['hello','hi','hey']
answer = ['I understand you feel happy but please stay to the point and
select one of the options',"I sympathize with you, However please do not
deviate from the topic"]
greetings = ['hola Welcome to DIRECTPythPyth again', 'hello Welcome to
DIRECTPythPyth again', 'hi Welcome to DIRECTPythPyth again', 'Hi Welcome to
DIRECTPythPyth again', 'hey! Welcome to DIRECTPythPyth again', 'hey Welcome
to DIRECTPythPyth again']
question = ['how are you?', 'how are you doing?']
responses = ['Okay', "I'm fine"]
another = "do you want another test?"
tests=['Type 1 for hbA1c test', "Type 2 for Blood Viscosity test","Type
3 for Heart rate test","Type 4 for Blood Oxygen test","Type 5 for Blood
Pressure"]
testresponse= ['1','2','3','4','5','6']
```

Now we start with the actual program of our chatbots by defining its program constructs. In Listing 4-5 we can see this code that is the heart of our chatbot. In the first part of the code, I initialize some global variables. The first one is first switch, which I have assigned a value of 1. This is used to determine if the chatbot is running for the first time. Next, I initialize a new ID. This is nothing but a new membership ID for a person who arrives for the first time at the diagnostic center. Next I have initialized the member ID (Mem ID) variable with a value of 0. In the next part of the code, I use a function known as chat, which has a parameter of event, and it gets triggered whenever a charged event occurs. Inside this function I have imported time and random package and declared the global member-id variable or condition variable as well as a first switch variable. In the next statement there is an if condition where I check if first switch is equal to 1, and if it is equal to 1 then it grids the random choice by selecting a value from the grid list, which we have seen earlier. It inserts that value from bot text variable into the chat MSG text box, and so the user is able to see a greeting when the chatbot runs for the first time. It then gives out a statement that if you are an existing member of DIRECTPyth then you can enter your membership ID; otherwise enter the value no if you are not a member based on the user input. The first switch variable now has a value of 2 and if the user enters a value it again triggers and comes into the next if statement, where first switch is not equal to 1. So this means this particular if condition will only run after the first greeting has happened for the user and this value that the user has entered is received through the input field. We use the lower function here so that we don't have to deal with uppercase and lowercase, and we take the value into input underscore get variable. This value is checked to see if the member ID entered by the user is found in the member ID list where, if you remember, we had five IDs, and if that it is found then this if condition is met and the memory function stores whatever the user has entered in input underscore get variable. Then the bot text is populated, thanking the user for being a loyal member, and a menu is shown to the user about the types of tests that are available with the last option of exiting the program. In case the user enters no, which means it is a new user and they do not have a member ID, then a new member ID is generated. Please remember that since I am creating a prototype program, I am not going into the detail of storing this new ID and creating this ID automatically. However, in the real world, you will store this value in a flat file or a mongo DB database and then increment that value to get the new user ID. In case the user enters valid values between 1 and 6 in the next if statement, I check whether the user input get statement is in test response list. The test response list, if you will recall, has numbers starting from 1 to 6 so this if statement will trigger only when the test response is met. Once a valid response is received, the bot emulator gives a message to the user to place their finger on the finger panel in the kiosk to conduct the test. It waits for 10 seconds, and I have put a delay counter here. However, in the real world there would be a sensor that would detect when the user has put their finger on the finger panel and would automatically start reading the data. In our case I have used a for loop to emulate 10 seconds and sleep the delay counter by 1 second using time date sheet the chat message. I insert those values into the chatbot, showing to the user that

I am reading their values. After the 10 steps of the for loop are done, the bot says, "Please wait, generating your report," and then it sleeps for 2 seconds. Then based on the input for the test given by the user, it generates random numbers for each test. For example, let me walk you through the if statement where the input entered by the user is a value of 1, which means that as per the menu, the user wants to conduct HB A1c test. In that case the bot generates a random number between 4 and 10, which are valid values for an A1c test and would similarly show the result to the user. After it has done that, I show you how we can add intelligence to our chatbot, which is emulating a lab coordinator, and a lab coordinator would never give an opinion on the reported results. However, we have added values for the first test HP A1c, and I have shown you how it can intelligently tell the user whether they are diabetic, prediabetic, or do not have diabetes based on the results . So in our case it looks for a value in the if condition with the variable HB A1c between 4 and 5.6. If this condition is met, then it says you do not have diabetes. Again it checks for the variable HB A1c and if the value is between 5.7 and 6.4, it says you are prediabetic. If the HB A1c variable value is greater than or equal to 6.5, then the patient is diagnosed as diabetic. This intelligence can be added for other tests as well, such as the blood viscosity test (which ranges from 30 to 44 MB), the heart rate (which has a range of 60 to 100 beats per minute), the blood oxygen (which ranges from 95 to 100), and blood pressure systolic as well as diastolic in their own ranges. You can add this intelligence in those conditions yourself, and I'll leave that up to you to modify the code and to use it more intelligently.

Listing 4-5. Chatbot Code

```
#Global variable to check first time greeting
firstswitch=1
newid="12310"
memid=0

def chat(event):
    import time
    import random
    global memid
    condition=""
    #Greet for first time
    global firstswitch
```

```python
if (firstswitch==1):
    bot_text = random.choice(greet)
    chatmsg.insert(INSERT, 'Bot:%s\n' % bot_text)
    bot_text = "If you are an existing Member of DIRECTPythPyth please
    enter your membershipid: or enter no if you are not a member"
    chatmsg.insert(INSERT, 'Bot:%s\n' % bot_text)
    firstswitch=2
if (firstswitch!=1):
    input_get = input_field.get().lower()
    if any(srchstr in input_get for srchstr  in memberid):
        memid=input_get
        bot_text = "Thank you for being a loyal member of
        DIRECTPythPyth\n Please choose a test from following menu to
        continue\nType 1 for hbA1c test\nType 2 for Blood Viscosity
        test\nType 3 for Heart rate test\nType 4 for Blood Oxygen test\
        nType 5 for Blood pressure test\nType 6 to exit\n\n"
    elif (input_get=="no"):
        memid=newid
        bot_text = "Your new Memberid is: " + newid + " Please remember
        this for future reference.\n Please choose a test from
        following menu to continue\nType 1 for hbA1c test\nType 2 for
        Blood Viscosity test\nType 3 for Heart rate test\nType 4 for
        Blood Oxygen test\nType 5 for Blood pressure test\nType 6 to
        exit\n\n"
    elif any(srchstr in input_get for srchstr  in testresponse):
            bot_text = "Please place any of your finger on the Finger
            panel above to conduct the test"
            chatmsg.insert(INSERT, 'Bot:%s\n' % bot_text)
            delaycounter=0
            for delaycounter in range(0,10):
                bot_text = str(delaycounter)
                time.sleep(1)
                chatmsg.insert(INSERT, 'Bot:%s\n' % bot_text)
            bot_text = "Please wait generating your report\n"
            chatmsg.insert(INSERT, 'Bot:%s\n' % bot_text)
```

```
time.sleep(2)
if (input_get=="1"):
    hba1c=random.randint(4,10)
    bot_text = "MemberID: " + str(memid) + " Your hbA1c
    test result is: " + str(hba1c)
    if(hba1c>=4 and hba1c<=5.6):
        condition="You don't have diabetes"
    elif(hba1c>=5.7 and hba1c<=6.4):
        condition="You are Prediabetic"
    elif(hba1c>=6.5):
        condition="You are Diabetic"
    bot_text=bot_text +  " Your condition is: " + condition
    chatmsg.insert(INSERT, 'Bot:%s\n' % bot_text)
elif (input_get=="2"):
    viscosity=random.randint(20,60)
    bot_text = "MemberID: " + str(memid) + " Your Blood
    Viscosity level test result is: " + str(viscosity)
elif (input_get=="3"):
    heartrate=random.randint(40,150)
    bot_text = "MemberID: " + str(memid) + " Your Heart
    rate test result is: " + str(heartrate)
elif (input_get=="4"):
    oxygen=random.randint(90,100)
    bot_text = "MemberID: " + str(memid) + " Your Blood
    Oxygen level test result is: " + str(oxygen)
elif (input_get=="5"):
    systolic=random.randint(80,200)
    diastolic=random.randint(80,110)
    bot_text = "MemberID: " + str(memid) + " Your Blood
    Pressure test result is: Systolic: " + str(systolic) +
    " Diastolic: " + str(diastolic)
elif (input_get=="6"):
    import sys
    window.deiconify()
    window.destroy()
    sys.exit(0)
```

```
    else:
     from nltk.stem import WordNetLemmatizer
     import nltk
     if((not input_get) or (int(input_get)<=0)):
                print("did you just press Enter?") #print some info
     else:
         lemmatizer = WordNetLemmatizer()
         input_get = input_field.get().lower()
         lemvalue=lemmatizer.lemmatize(input_get)
         whatsentiment=getSentiment(lemvalue)
         if (whatsentiment=="pos"):
             bot_text = answer[0]
             #print("Positive Sentiment")
         elif (whatsentiment=="neg"):
             bot_text = answer[1]
         #print("Negative Sentiment")
         chatmsg.insert(INSERT, '%s\n' % lemvalue)
         #bot_text = "I did not understand what you said !"
 chatmsg.insert(INSERT, 'Bot:%s\n' % bot_text)
 #label = Label(window, text=input_get)
 input_user.set(")
 #label.pack()
 return "break"
```

In this chatbot, I have used NLP to show how sentiment analysis can be done in such an application. However, please remember that the NLP that I am using is for limited use, as I cannot write millions of lines of code to emulate the real-world chat application. I have briefly used a small training set as a list but in a real scenario, you would use a file that probably would have feedback from the customers and would contain classification of positive and negative sentiments. Let us go through the code in order to briefly understand how I have done sentiment analysis in the get sentiment function. You can refer to the code in Figure 4-6 where I have imported the nltk library and then the tokenize and word tokenize from nltk in order to further analysis. In this example, I am only using three steps to perform sentiment analysis; however, please remember that there are many more steps that you need to follow for a full-fledged sentiment analysis.

In step one, I am using training data building the diabetes Corpus, and this probably is nothing but positive and negative feedback classification of responses by the customers. The positive sentiments have been classified as POS and negative sentiments have been classified as energy. After this is done I create a dictionary and tokenize each word by converting it to lowercase. After this, I create a dictionary for each word that we have to organize, and I run it through the train data set that we have been following. After this is done and we have created step 3 of locating the word in the training data, I now go to step 4 to train the classifier—in our case, naive Bayes on the sample data, so I called the naive Bayes classifier and trained it on the located world. I then get new data, which is known as test data; for example, here it is "oh my god," but you could take this and replace with the text variable of this function in order to create your test data. Once the test data is created, we need to create features out of each word that is tokenized in our dictionary, which we created in the step 3 earlier. Once this is done, we are now ready to tell how our data feature has been classified. Has it been classified as energy or POS? The function returns the value of classifier dot classify test data features. If you go back to Figure 4-1 where I defined the chat function in the condition. In the last condition of else statement, I have used a wordnet lemmatizer, and I have checked to see if input given by the data user is not an entry. Then it uses the word net lemmatizer and it gets the value input by the user in lowercase. It lemmatizes the value. Lemmatizing is the process of converting a bigger word into its root word. To give you an example, cars would have a root word of car. In the next statement, I use the get sentiment function and I give the value, which is the lemmatize input given by the user, and in return I get neg energy or POS negative or positive sentiment from the function. In the next condition, I check if the value is POS; then the bot answers a positive response answer of 0 or, if it is a negative sentiment, the bot answers a negative response. So you have seen in a very brief way how to implement a chatbots application and to use it commercially.

Listing 4-6. Sentiment Analysis

```
#Sentiment Analyzer using NLP
def getSentiment(text):
    import nltk
    from nltk.tokenize import word_tokenize

    #nltk.download('punkt')
    # Step 1 - Training data building the Diabetes corpus
    train = [("Thanks for an excellent report", "pos"),
```

```
("Your service is very quick and fast", "pos"),
("I am pleased with your service", "pos"),
("I did not know i was diabetic until you gave me this report", "neg"),
("Service - Little slow, probably because too many people.", "neg"),
("The place is not easy to locate", "neg"),
("The place is very easy to locate", "pos"),
("Not satisfied will take a second opinion", "neg"),
("No human contact everything is so robotic here", "neg"),
("can i talk to a human not convinced with your report", "neg"),
("good results", "pos"),
("good service", "pos"),
("great service", "pos"),
("excellent service", "pos"),
("amazing technology", "pos"),
("fast service and satisfying report", "pos"),
("your report sucks", "neg"),
("this report will cost me a fortune", "neg"),
("I have diabetes", "neg"),
("this report will cost me a fortune", "neg"),
("this report means i have a dreadful disease", "neg"),
("will i need to take new medication", "neg"),
("i need to take my insulin injections regularly", "neg"),
("my lipids are getting worst need to talk to the doctor", "neg"),
("oh my god very bad results", "neg"),
("bad service", "neg"),
("very bad service", "neg"),
("poor service", "neg"),
("very bad service", "neg"),
("slow service", "neg"),
("very slow service", "neg"),
("diabetes got worst is this report accurate", "neg"),
("i dont believe this report", "neg"),
("i dont like this report", "neg"),
("i am in a diabetic hell", "neg"),
]
```

```
# Step 2 Tokenize the words to dictionary
dictionary = set(word.lower() for passage in train for word in word_
tokenize(passage[0]))
# Step 3 Locate the word in training data
t = [({word: (word in word_tokenize(x[0])) for word in dictionary},
x[1]) for x in train]
# Step 4 - the classifier is trained with sample data
classifier = nltk.NaiveBayesClassifier.train(t)
test_data = "oh my god what is this"
test_data_features = {word.lower(): (word in word_tokenize(test_data.
lower())) for word in dictionary}
print (classifier.classify(test_data_features))
return classifier.classify(test_data_features)
```

```
#Start the program chat and put in loop
input_field.bind("<Return>", chat)
tkinter.mainloop()
```

CASE STUDY 2: Hospital Food Wastage Problem

In this case study, we are going to look at a very common of the hospital: food wastage. We are going to apply machine learning methods to solve this business problem.

Acadecia Hospitals is one of the leading international chains of hospitals in the US. It Was established in 1986 the a small town of Ojai, California. It was very small when it was started; however, the founder Dr. Jack Juice had a vision to make healthcare affordable and easily accessible to small-town folks. The most noticeable fact about this hospital chain is its ability to keep the operational cost of the hospital low in order to provide affordable healthcare to small-town folks. In 2017, it has more than 120 hospitals around the world, with 70 percent of them located in small towns with a population of less than a million people.

Dr. Twin Burger was sipping his morning coffee and was going through the report that he had received from the financial department about operational costs across its network of hospitals. He was the head of Acadecia Hospitals and was heading the chain by taking the vision of Dr. Juice to make healthcare affordable for people around the world. In Figure 4-2 you will see the report that Dr. Burger received that morning.

Cost Parameter per hospital	2014	2015	2016
Total Hospitals	82	103	125
Total Employees	17220	27501	42550
Average Beds	84	89	92
Absenteeism (Average total days)	19.6	22.4	20.4
Total Overtime (average total days)	6	12	15.2
Emergency room wait time (Average in minutes)	13	16	14
Total Food ordered per hospital bed per day (Kg)	178.4496	187.0602	199.6032
Average cost per kilogram of food (USD)	2.35	2.48	2.56
Food Wastage in Kilogram	74.948832	87.918294	109.78176

Figure 4-2. *Food cost report for Acadecia Hospitals*

In Figure 4-2 we can see the cost parameter per hospital report in front of Dr. Burger from the last 3 years (2014-2016). The report shows that there has been a steady increase in the number of hospitals for Acadecia; the employee strength has also increased, and the average beds have also gone up for hospital. However, for our case study, the relevant data is in the last three rows, the first row being total food order for hospital per day in kilograms. With the increasing number of hospitals, this number has also gone up. The rising food inflation is represented in the second-to-last row, which is average cost per kilogram of food in US dollars which was $2.35 to $2.56. The food wastage in kilogram has also gone from the year 2014, at 74.9 kilograms to 109.8 kilograms. The food wastage has gone up from 42 percent in 2014 to 47 percent of total food ordered in 2015 and 55 percent of food wastage of the total food order on average in all the hospitals at Acadecia. So clearly Dr. Burger was looking at rising costs in his hospitals due to the increased food wastage, as outlined in the report.

After having looked at the report, Dr. Burger understood that the problem was getting out of hand and needed some targeted solution for the problem. He remembered meeting his all-time friend during the weekend who was now working as a machine learning consultant and who had said that he could help Dr. Burger with any kind of problem that required use of technology. He shot out an e-mail to the machine learning consultant to set an appointment for discussing the problem and using technology to find a solution.

He met the machine learning consultant and showed him the data after signing an agreement with him. He asked if machine learning could help solve this problem and prescribe an appropriate solution to bring down the cost due to food wastage at his organization.

The consultant asked for more data to be produced in order for him to look at the reasons and then arrive at possible solutions for the problem. The people from the computer department at Acadecia gave him data access to look at the data store on the servers globally in the central database.

Interestingly, I am not going to cover the part of data integration and data wrangling, as we have done that in the previous case study. However, please remember that you will hardly get ready-made data that you find in this case study in a real production environment. You would need to integrate data and collect it into a single source, such as Hadoop or mongo DB or Cassandra, from sources such as flat files, Excel sheets, Word documents, PowerPoint presentations, proprietary databases such as Oracle, sQL server, and dB2—to name a few.

Now we look at the integrated data set from Acadecia on which we will build our machine learning model.

Hospital Name	Total Food ordered	Total Food Wasted	No of Inpatients	No of Meals served	No of Guests with Inpatient	Feedback	Type of Hospital
Hospital 1	659	264	67	292	30	Rural
Hospital 10	70	1	7	31	2	Urban
Hospital 100	276	12	28	122	3	Urban

Figure 4-3. *Sample Data Set*

In Figure 4-3 we look at the sample data set from Acadecia Hospitals. This is data from three hospitals, and I have removed the names deliberately to maintain confidentiality. It is also sufficiently modified from its original source in order to maintain anonymity of the clients. The data that has been collected from 125 hospitals at Acadecia includes the total food ordered by the hospital, total food wasted by the hospital, and the number of in-patient's meals served, number of guests with in-patient, and the type of hospital. All of this information is an average of all the 3 years from 2014 to 2016.

In the next steps, we will load this data set in Python and start the process of applied machine learning, which I have outlined in my earlier chapters of this book.

Listing 4-7. Loading the Data Set

```
import pandas as pd
import os
os.getcwd()

fname="Food_Raw_Data.csv"
hospitals= pd.read_csv(fname, low_memory=False, index_col=False)
df= pd.DataFrame(hospitals)
print(df.head(1))
```

Initially in Listing 4-7, I load the required Python libraries Pandas os and then I open the file food raw data .csv from the local DIRECTPyth into the hospitals Pandas data frame and then read the first record off the data frame through the head function. After having loaded the data set, we will now look at the shape of the data set, its columns, and data types to explore it further. I also look at the columns of the data frame and its data types from Listing 4-8 and the shape of this data frame constitutes 125 rows and 8 columns. By giving df.com, we can see all the 8 columns starting from total food ordered, total food wasted, number of in-patients, number of meals served, number of guests with in-patient, feedback, type of hospital, and total number of beds. After this, we look at the data types of each column; the numeric columns are total food ordered by a particular hospital, total food wasted by a particular hospital, number of in-patients admitted in the hospital, number of meals served in a day in the hospital, number of guests with in-patient in a hospital, and the total number of beds in a hospital. The non-numeric columns are hospital name and feedback, which is the rating given by the patients and the guests on the hospital's food quality, but we are not going to use this in our model.

Listing 4-8. Looking at the Shape and Size of the Data Set and Its Structure

```
print(df.shape)
(125, 8)

print(df.columns)
Index(['Total Food ordered', 'Total Food Wasted', 'No of Inpatients',
       'No of Meals served', 'No of Guests with Inpatient', 'Feedback',
       'Type of Hospital', 'Total No of beds'],
     dtype='object')
```

```
df.dtypes
Out[72]:
Total Food ordered              int64
Total Food Wasted               int64
No of Inpatients                int64
No of Meals served              int64
No of Guests with Inpatient     int64
Feedback                        object
Type of Hospital                object
Total No of beds                int64
dtype: object
```

In Listing 4-9 we can see through the df.org null that there are no null values, and we verify this with bf.in for all the values that are non-null for each data type. This way we are sure that each column and each row is populated in our data set so there are no missing values.

Listing 4-9. Checking for Missing Values

```
#Check if there are any columns with empty/null dataset
df.isnull().any()
#Checking how many columns have null values
df.info()
df.isnull().any()
#Checking how many columns have null values
df.info()
<class 'pandas.core.frame.DataFrame'>
Index: 125 entries, Hospital 1 to Hospital 99
Data columns (total 8 columns):
Total Food ordered              125 non-null int64
Total Food Wasted               125 non-null int64
No of Inpatients                125 non-null int64
No of Meals served              125 non-null int64
No of Guests with Inpatient     125 non-null int64
Feedback                        125 non-null object
Type of Hospital                125 non-null object
```

```
Total No of beds            125 non-null int64
dtypes: int64(6), object(2)
memory usage: 13.8+ KB
```

Now that we have checked the missing values, let us move on to exploratory data analysis by looking at the mean, median, and mode of the numeric columns of our data set and see in Listing 4-10 through the df.com mode undefined. To briefly understand our results from the mean function, the total food ordered average is 319.18 and the average food wasted by hospital is 54.68 kilograms. The number of people is 33 and on average the number of meals served by a hospital is 140. The average number of guests with in-patient is 8. On average, the hospital has a total of 64 beds. If we look at the median values for the same columns, we see a huge difference between total food ordered with the median value of 255 and total wasted stands at 23. The number of in-patients stands at 26 and number of meals served stands at 113. The number of guests with in-patient is 7, and the total number of beds close to the mean value at 66. If median and mean are close enough, then it means our data set is normal or near to normal, and the characteristic is that the values of each of these columns for mean, median, and mode will be near to equal if the data set has a normal distribution. However, we can clearly see that our data set is not normally distributed. Another thing that the difference between the mean and median tells us is that we are dealing with outliers, and there are more outliers in total food wasted, number of meals served, and total food ordered columns. The rest of the columns are close to each other, and hence there may not be many outliers in them.

Listing 4-10. Detecting Outliers

```
df.mean()
Out[75]:
Total Food ordered            319.184
Total Food Wasted              54.680
No of Inpatients               32.952
No of Meals served            141.224
No of Guests with Inpatient     8.800
Total No of beds               64.776
dtype: float64

df.median()
Out[76]:
```

```
Total Food ordered              255.0
Total Food Wasted                23.0
No of Inpatients                 26.0
No of Meals served              113.0
No of Guests with Inpatient       7.0
Total No of beds                 66.0
dtype: float64
```

```
df.mode()
Out[77]:
   Total Food ordered  Total Food Wasted  No of Inpatients  \
0              110.0               0.0               23
1                NaN               NaN               25

   No of Meals served  No of Guests with Inpatient Feedback Type of
   Hospital  \
0               97.0                              2.0        B
Urban
1                NaN                              NaN      NaN
NaN

   Total No of beds
0              44.0
1               NaN
```

Listing 4-11. Exploratory Data Analysis

```
#How is the data distributed and detecting Outliers
df.std()
df.max()
df.min()
df.quantile(0.25)*1.5
df.quantile(0.75)*1.5
df.std()
Out[79]:
Total Food ordered        220.918186
Total Food Wasted          81.394658
No of Inpatients           22.565266
```

```
No of Meals served                97.742244
No of Guests with Inpatient        8.358886
Total No of beds                  20.279047
dtype: float64

df.max()
Out[80]:
Total Food ordered                     921
Total Food Wasted                      454
No of Inpatients                        91
No of Meals served                     407
No of Guests with Inpatient             38
Feedback                                 C
Type of Hospital                     Urban
Total No of beds                       100
dtype: object

df.min()
Out[81]:
Total Food ordered                       2
Total Food Wasted                        0
No of Inpatients                         0
No of Meals served                       1
No of Guests with Inpatient              0
Feedback                                 A
Type of Hospital                     Rural
Total No of beds                        30
dtype: object

df.quantile(0.25)*1.5
Out[82]:
Total Food ordered                   238.5
Total Food Wasted                      7.5
No of Inpatients                      25.5
No of Meals served                   105.0
No of Guests with Inpatient            3.0
Total No of beds                      66.0
Name: 0.25, dtype: float64
```

```
df.quantile(0.75)*1.5
Out[83]:
Total Food ordered              679.5
Total Food Wasted                87.0
No of Inpatients                 70.5
No of Meals served              300.0
No of Guests with Inpatient      18.0
Total No of beds                123.0
Name: 0.75, dtype: float64
```

In Listing 4-11, we move to detecting outliers to detect that we first look at the standard deviation, which tells us about the dispersion of our data in each column, and then we look at the max and min values to find out the range of each column in our data set. Then we use the quantile function, and we use the 25th percentile and the 75th percentile and multiply that by 1 to get the lower-bound outliers and the upper-bound outliers. From the quantile 0.2, for example, we can see that total food ordered has an outlier lower limit at 238.5 whereas the 75th percentile X 1.5 for the column total food order gives us a value of 679. In practical terms, for the column total food ordered, any value below 38.5 and any value above 679 will be treated as an outlier. You can similarly look at the other columns like total food wasted, number of in-patients, number of meals served, etc.

Listing 4-12. How Many Outliers in Any Particular Columns

```
#How many Outliers in the BPSystolic column
df.columns
df.dtypes
df.set_index(['Hospital Name'])
df['Total Food ordered'].loc[df['Total Food ordered'] <=238.5].count()
Out[84]: 55

df['Total Food ordered'].loc[df['Total Food ordered'] >=679.5].count()
Out[85]: 11
```

Now we look Figure 4-3 in which I am giving you an example of how to count how many values in a particular column, like total food ordered, are not meeting the lower-bound and upper-bound limit of the outliers. We can see that for total food ordered, with the lower outlier limit of 38.5, there are 55 values that are less than this number. Similarly for the upper-bound outlier limit of £679, the total food ordered column has 11 values that lie beyond this threshold limit.

Why do we need to know this? For one thing, any machine learning consultant will look at this value because they need to take the decision of whether to discard, keep, or modify the outliers. In this case, I make the decision to keep the outliers because if I remove them I will be losing out on a significant percentage of data set (66 rows out of 125 rows will be lost) and the learning that these rows can bring will also be lost with them. However, this is not a rule that you must follow in every model building exercise. You should independently think as to what is relevant and good for your data set and the model that you are building.

```
#Visualizing the dataset
df.boxplot(figsize=(10, 6))
df.plot.box(vert=False)
df.kurtosis()
df.skew()
import scipy.stats as sp
sp.skew(df['Total Food ordered'])
```

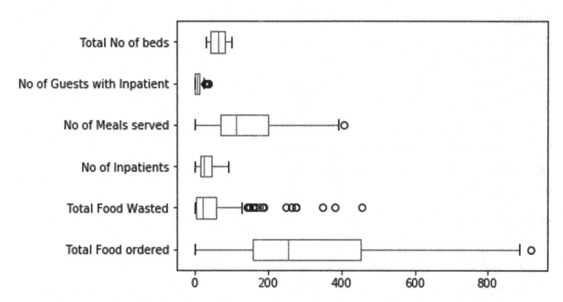

Figure 4-4. *Visualizing the structure of data set*

In Figure 4-4 we try to visualize our data set by doing both horizontal and vertical orientation of the box plot, and graphically it is very clear that the total food ordered is more spread and has outliers at the end of the tail. Total food wasted in comparison is much less dispersed; however, it has a lot more outliers at the end of the tail.

Similarly readers will recall from Chapter 3 that kurtosis shows the thickness in the distribution of our data set. This means the thickness, and if the peak is toward the left then it is known as leptokurtic. If the distribution is fatter tails, then such a distribution is compared to a normal distribution and the value of kurtosis is equal to 3. Excess kurtosis means that the value of kurtosis will be greater than 3, and less kurtosis would mean value of kurtosis would be below 3. If the value of kurtosis is less than 0, then it is called a platykurtic distribution. Keeping this in mind, let us now study four variables given in Listing 4-13. The kurtosis values for total food order is negative (–0.1) so it is platykurtic. The total food wasted is above 3, at a value of 7. This means there is more peaked in the data and excess of kurtosis and the distribution is mesokurtic. The columns number of in-patients and number of meals served are platykurtic, as they are less than 0; similarly, total number of beds is also less than 0. The column number of guests with in-patient is 2, which means it is not less kurtosis, as the value is less than 3.

Listing 4-13. Looking at Skew and Kurtosis

```
df.kurtosis()
Out[91]:
Total Food ordered              -0.150535
Total Food Wasted                7.432315
No of Inpatients                -0.299269
No of Meals served              -0.155185
No of Guests with Inpatient      2.008910
Total No of beds                -1.224649
dtype: float64

df.skew()
Out[92]:
Total Food ordered               0.756837
Total Food Wasted                2.570979
No of Inpatients                 0.712854
```

```
No of Meals served            0.754662
No of Guests with Inpatient   1.476908
Total No of beds             -0.028728
dtype: float64
```

In Listing 4-13 we look at the skew and kurtosis for each of the columns, and you will recall from Chapter 3 that if the skew number is less than 0, then we say the distribution is negatively skewed; if the skew is equal to 0, then the distribution is said to be symmetric; and if the skew value is greater than 0, then we say the distribution is positively skewed. Skew tells us in which direction the tail is skewed. Negatively skewed results have a long left tail, and positively skewed results have a long right tail. From Listing 4-13, we can see that total food order has positive value of 0.7, total food wasted is also positively skewed at 2. Number of in-patients is positively skewed at 0.71, number of meals served is also positively skewed at 0.7, number of guests with an in-patient is highly skewed at 1.4, and total number of beds is slightly negatively skewed but closer to 0 at −0.02.

```
df.hist(figsize=(10, 6))
Out[95]:
array([[<matplotlib.axes._subplots.AxesSubplot object at
0x0000019D18C1F940>,
<matplotlib.axes._subplots.AxesSubplot object at 0x0000019D18F2CB70>],
       [<matplotlib.axes._subplots.AxesSubplot object at
        0x0000019D18F64B70>,
<matplotlib.axes._subplots.AxesSubplot object at 0x0000019D18F9FC50>],
       [<matplotlib.axes._subplots.AxesSubplot object at
        0x0000019D18FDAC50>,
<matplotlib.axes._subplots.AxesSubplot object at 0x0000019D18FDAC88>]],
dtype=object)
```

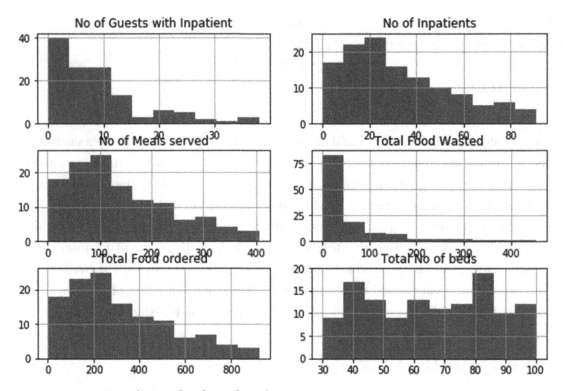

Figure 4-5. *Visualizing the data distribution*

In Figure 4-5 we can clearly see visually how the columns in the data set are distributed. This shows that none of the data in the columns follows the normal curve.

Now we move to the next step of recognizing any relationship between the data, as we are talking about numeric data in our model building exercise. In Figure 4-6 we can see the result of the correlation values of various columns, and our main focus of the case study is to create a model based on the total food wasted values, which need to be predicted based on the other data. The other data is available, so looking at the correlation values, the most significant that I choose are that the total food wasted in relation to number of patients has a correlation value of 0.7; total food wasted has a relationship to number of meals served of a positive correlation of 0.7; total food wasted has a positive correlation which is very high to the number of guests with in-patients, at 0.9; and the total food wasted in correlation to total food order is 0.7. I propose to build a prediction model for total food wasted based on these four inputs. We can see that probably the number of guests with in-patients in a correlation with total food wasted stands at 0.9, so Acadecia Hospitals probably needs to look at the reasons as to why an increase in in-patients is leading to food wastage in their hospital facilities. This single-most determining factor can save them a lot of money in food waste.

```
df.corr()
Out[96]:
```

	Total Food ordered	Total Food Wasted \
Total Food ordered	1.000000	0.770522
Total Food Wasted	0.770522	1.000000
No of Inpatients	0.998059	0.765459
No of Meals served	0.999994	0.770236
No of Guests with Inpatient	0.696581	0.934847
Total No of beds	0.410256	0.357904

	No of Inpatients	No of Meals served \
Total Food ordered	0.998059	0.999994
Total Food Wasted	0.765459	0.770236
No of Inpatients	1.000000	0.998056
No of Meals served	0.998056	1.000000
No of Guests with Inpatient	0.697330	0.696443
Total No of beds	0.411096	0.409509

	No of Guests with Inpatient	Total No of beds
Total Food ordered	0.696581	0.410256
Total Food Wasted	0.934847	0.357904
No of Inpatients	0.697330	0.411096
No of Meals served	0.696443	0.409509
No of Guests with Inpatient	1.000000	0.296937
Total No of beds	0.296937	1.000000

Figure 4.22 Correlation for all the numeric column variables

```
df.plot.scatter(x='Total Food Wasted', y='No of Guests with
Inpatient',s=df['Total Food Wasted']*2)
Out[98]: <matplotlib.axes._subplots.AxesSubplot at 0x19d190eec50>
```

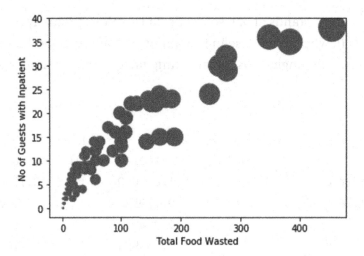

Figure 4-6. *Visualizing the correlation with a scatter plot*

Now Figure 4-6 shows you a way to look at this correlation and create a scatter plot that clearly shows a link between total food wastage and number of guests with in-patients. We can clearly see a pattern in the graph. Although we have two categorical columns, feedback and type of hospital, because our case study does not require any calculation or understanding for them, we are going to ignore them for our model building exercise. Next I move to the step of data preparation where I split the data into feature and target set. The first data frame is wastage, which is our target data set for which we need to predict the total food wasted based on the other columns. In order to create a features data frame, I drop off total food wasted, which is our target column, the feedback column, the type of hospital column, and the total number of beds column from the data frame. This is depicted in Listing 4-14.

Listing 4-14. Preparing Features and Target Data Sets

```
wastage = pd.DataFrame(df['Total Food Wasted'])

dropp=df[['Total Food Wasted','Feedback','Type of Hospital','Total No of
beds']]
features= df.drop(dropp, axis=1)
wastage.columns
features.columns
```

```
Out[102]:
Index(['Total Food ordered', 'No of Inpatients', 'No of Meals served',
       'No of Guests with Inpatient'],
      dtype='object')
```

Next we move on to the step of shuffling our data and splitting it into a training and testing set in the ratio of 80 percent to 20 percent. This can be seen in Listing 4-15.

Listing 4-15. Shuffling and Splitting the Data

```
from sklearn.cross_validation import train_test_split
from sklearn.utils import shuffle

# Shuffle and split the data into training and testing subsets
features=shuffle(features,  random_state=0)
wastage=shuffle(wastage,  random_state=0)
# Split the 'features' and 'income' data into training and testing sets
X_train, X_test, y_train, y_test = train_test_split(features, wastage,
test_size = 0.2, random_state = 0)

# Show the results of the split
print("Training set has {} samples.".format(X_train.shape[0]))
print("Testing set has {} samples.".format(X_test.shape[0]))
Training set has 100 samples.
Testing set has 25 samples.
```

Next I move on to building and evaluating the model. I will be using two regressors: one is the linear regression model and the other is linear SVC (support vector machines). You can see the library imports and their initialization in Listing 4-16.

Listing 4-16. Results of Regressors

```
import matplotlib.pyplot as plt
import numpy as np
from sklearn import linear_model
from sklearn.metrics import mean_squared_error, r2_score
from sklearn.svm import LinearSVC
```

```
#Creating Linear Regression object
regr = linear_model.LinearRegression()
linear_svm = LinearSVC().fit(X_train,y_train)
Figure 4.26  Model Evaluation and Initializing

regr.fit(X_train,y_train)
y_pred= regr.predict(X_test)
yy_pred= linear_svm.predict(X_test)
#Printing Codfficients
print('Coefficients: \n',regr.coef_)
print(LinearSVC().fit(X_train,y_train).coef_)
Coefficients:
 [[ 3.84820846 -4.81910798 -7.39895629  7.71902335]]
[[ -3.53041635e-02   5.09097801e-02   3.14979916e-02  -3.88312025e-01]
 [ -2.32668818e-02  -1.42174073e-01   7.43984582e-02  -1.16573785e-02]
 [  4.72789182e-02   1.47150837e-01  -1.36891194e-01  -5.32241337e-02]
 [  2.93890989e-02  -1.19191185e-01  -2.58725709e-02  -3.82878378e-02]
 [  4.11308074e-02   2.64727641e-02  -9.78443211e-02  -5.51862063e-02]
 [  7.00718282e-02  -8.10166533e-02  -1.22951514e-01   1.71447192e-01]
 [  3.42043753e-02  -2.05910747e-02  -6.20141160e-02  -9.89629458e-02]
 [  2.77961883e-02  -4.46751024e-02  -4.37038593e-02   2.66465015e-01]
 [  1.13547353e-02  -2.71632958e-02  -2.08526490e-03   1.70754244e-01]
 [  3.32914578e-02  -1.67505293e-02  -5.77349454e-02   2.09845962e-03]
 [  4.77186007e-02  -8.23837686e-02  -9.30268666e-02   3.78425737e-02]
 [  3.41540305e-02  -7.34444501e-02  -6.46481812e-02   3.54015691e-02]
 [  3.84521437e-02  -6.41689817e-02  -7.31629621e-02   2.70787385e-01]
 [  4.87625884e-02  -6.84474198e-02  -8.67811679e-02  -5.64164062e-02]
 [  1.49537087e-02  -3.77585007e-02  -1.36249294e-02   7.99620681e-02]
 [  4.89155675e-02  -9.21493872e-02  -8.01503822e-02   1.77140915e-01]
 [  4.24949470e-02  -4.87499272e-02  -7.78022864e-02   1.34518802e-01]
 [  3.50542029e-02  -3.54090045e-02  -6.63975873e-02   1.09584692e-03]
 [  9.38169848e-03  -3.67554573e-02  -1.71349625e-02   2.41221242e-01]
 [  1.00033106e-02  -4.53600521e-02  -6.24499229e-03   1.58324477e-01]
 [  1.41868325e-02  -3.95136457e-02  -1.76177176e-02   2.42552491e-02]
```

```
[  2.67055967e-02  -3.86757704e-02  -5.58150253e-02   2.54908921e-01]
[  4.79369084e-02  -6.20604669e-02  -8.98633410e-02  -7.57650121e-03]
[  3.08510176e-02  -8.53705374e-02  -5.20465381e-02   2.20385612e-01]
[  1.73454354e-02   1.98721103e-02  -4.24878889e-02   9.81570693e-02]
[  1.24536489e-02  -4.20971569e-02  -1.23960336e-02   3.52634992e-02]
[  2.57398024e-02  -9.16159713e-02  -4.47215477e-02   2.19305087e-01]
[  4.23505923e-03   6.72353051e-04  -6.50834658e-03   1.49214594e-01]
[  2.53837094e-02  -6.98875557e-02  -4.85734903e-02   2.22530149e-01]
[  1.43908959e-02  -4.75516908e-02  -1.95433533e-02   1.51543940e-01]
[  2.74067987e-02  -7.52560330e-02  -4.01603079e-02   1.10143783e-01]
[  4.64045608e-02  -4.05773937e-02  -8.79857548e-02   1.03748880e-02]
[  1.90491415e-02  -4.10809528e-02  -3.62574033e-02  -1.81196597e-02]
[  2.22912356e-02  -2.72874169e-02  -4.39681811e-02   1.09394978e-01]
[  4.20384279e-02  -3.25727010e-02  -8.51492094e-02  -6.37752010e-03]
[  2.61534393e-02  -2.94261743e-02  -5.41846630e-02  -2.75644483e-02]
[  2.45319444e-02  -5.09991059e-02  -5.06126410e-02   2.02505939e-01]
[  2.61919602e-03  -1.25839053e-02  -6.30409084e-03   1.80773339e-01]
[  2.74789306e-03  -2.73580886e-02  -6.50473121e-03   2.01205405e-01]
[  2.44669007e-02  -7.03696516e-03  -4.64750958e-02   2.60881871e-02]
[  1.51200603e-02  -6.89484027e-02  -8.71324723e-03  -8.82744952e-02]
[  2.65609136e-02  -4.97286727e-02  -5.75957648e-02   3.38979678e-02]
[  7.11056619e-03  -3.27401201e-02  -1.46946498e-02   1.84639962e-01]
[ -3.19488770e-03  -1.29730299e-02  -6.65748840e-03   2.30931190e-01]
[  2.39725322e-02  -4.20831865e-02  -5.23242642e-02   6.14469586e-02]
[  6.08374964e-03  -3.24197530e-02  -1.01534653e-02   1.56827822e-01]
[  6.69569094e-03   4.31666176e-03  -3.94068509e-02   1.51761293e-01]
[  4.25886521e-04  -2.49710716e-02  -1.34306904e-02   2.29936692e-01]
[ -1.00182507e-03  -2.39362307e-02  -8.88224128e-03   2.23843885e-01]
[  1.51225156e-02  -4.74318832e-02  -3.73751734e-02   1.50716919e-01]
[  2.45229013e-02  -5.96876827e-02  -5.15767695e-02   1.86736550e-02]
[  1.13573008e-02  -2.92617710e-02  -3.19670746e-02   1.29940982e-01]
[  1.33635906e-02  -3.62729876e-02  -2.39250008e-02   1.03188376e-01]
[  1.22517696e-02  -4.33917684e-02  -1.70961907e-02   8.42211744e-02]
```

```
[   7.24558495e-03   -3.29668719e-02   -1.44697007e-02    1.50876782e-01]
[   9.93726094e-04   -3.39403174e-02   -9.35154827e-03    2.01139275e-01]
[   4.76853411e-03   -1.52811320e-02   -2.65559075e-02    1.66170095e-01]
[   3.07916719e-03    3.05077312e-05   -2.62159469e-02    1.62382755e-01]
[   1.07347039e-02   -4.44424820e-02   -3.08244532e-02    1.32283650e-01]
[   1.24123818e-02   -4.00221036e-02   -3.10893289e-02    1.28289289e-01]]
print('Coefficients: \n',regr.coef_)
Coefficients:
 [[ 3.84820846 -4.81910798 -7.39895629  7.71902335]]

plt.plot(X_test, y_pred, linewidth=3)
plt.show()
```

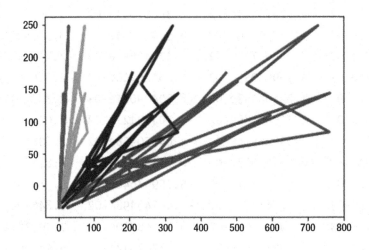

```
line = np.linspace(-15, 15)
for coef, intercept in zip(linear_svm.coef_, linear_svm.intercept_):
    plt.plot(line, -(line * coef[0] + intercept) / coef[1])   #HOW DO WE KNOW

plt.ylim(-10, 15)
plt.xlim(-10, 8)
plt.show()
```

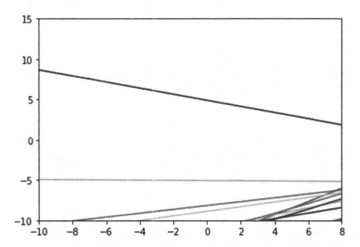

Figure 4-7. *Linear regression versus linear SVM visualization*

In Figure 4-7, we see the results of linear regression as well as the coefficients from linear SVC while we see that the coefficient from linear regression has four parameters, as expected. However, linear SVC is a bad method to use in this particular case, because it gives us many more divisions in order to predict the solution. In order to make you understand this concept, I will plot in Listing 4-17 the results of linear regression with the prediction and the graphical representation used in the case of linear SVM. When we compare the graphs of linear regression and linear SVM, we see that there are more boundaries in linear SVM as compared to only four in the case of linear regression. So we should use linear regression for building our model.

Listing 4-17. Predict Using Linear Regression Using Our Model on the Amount of Wasted Food Based on Four Parameters

```
predicted= regr.predict([[820,81,363,35]])
print(predicted)
[[ 312.23258101]]
```

I use the last step in Listing 4-17 to predict at random by giving four values for our dependent and independent variables to get the total food wastage in a particular hospital.

That is all I have for this chapter on case studies. I hope you enjoyed going through the case studies as much as I had the pleasure in presenting them to you.

## CHAPTER 5

Pitfalls to Avoid with Machine Learning in Healthcare

In this chapter I am going to share my experience and knowledge that I have gathered over the years in building both machine learning and non-machine learning applications. The main objective of this chapter is to make you aware of the common miss that people make when implementing machine learning in their business environment. I will be highlighting some of the pitfalls that the machine learning teams and organizations who are implementing machine learning need to avoid. You may have come across these in your work environment, or some of them may be new to you; however, this scenario that I give from my experience is something that you will cherish and we'll know an expert opinion on how to avoid these issues. From that perspective I would like you to read all of the six pitfalls that I talked about in this chapter. I will be using and giving various examples from my experience without naming the clients to maintain anonymity as to how, when the teams did not focus on these principles, it led to the project either being delayed or terminated. In my capacity of having worked as a program and project manager for more than 17 years, I cannot stress enough on the fact that if you do not follow these principles, your machine learning project is also bound to fail.

© Puneet Mathur 2019
P. Mathur, *Machine Learning Applications Using Python*, https://doi.org/10.1007/978-1-4842-3787-8_5

Meeting the Business Objectives

Meeting the business objectives is something that I have already discussed from Chapter 1 onward. However, here I am not only going to highlight the importance of building a machine learning application for the sole objective of meeting business needs but also give you real-world examples where when the machine learning development team did not follow this principal, the project ended in disaster.

In an assignment for one of my clients I was introduced to a very talented and young team that was developing an AI application. The team was comprised of machine learning engineer testers, documentation experts, and other cross-functional experts. The team was working under pressure due to strict schedule timelines for the launch of the application. The team was using scrum Agile methodology for their development, and in order to gain status of their project I started attending their daily standup. I understood that the team was in the middle of the development and had been given several warnings by the product owner on the application being developed. There were several experienced engineers working on the team, and it was supervised by an experienced manager as well. The following week there was a meeting between the team and the product owner, and I got an insight into what the product owner thought about the application that was being developed.

In the product demonstration, the product owner had agreed to the application that was shown to him in parts during the various sprints that the team had; however, when the team integrated the application, the product owner gave the feedback that this application did not meet the business objective. Anybody who has worked on a 1.0 application has experienced this kind of a scenario. Suddenly when the application was shown in parts to the product owner, the product owner agreed that the parts were good and meeting the business objective; however, when the application was integrated it did not meet the business objective.

This generally happens and did happen in this case where one of the business objectives of the application was that it would automate the manual process and apply machine learning algorithms to speed it up in the domain of healthcare; however, when the application got integrated where the GUI, the setup and configuration modules, the machine learning engine, and the web reporting modules were brought together, it took much more time for the application to create an automated process that it defeated the original business objective of building the application. Each of the models, such as setup and configuration, engine, web reporting, and the GUI were developed by different teams in iterative cycles known as sprints. They did not think about building an efficient fast application by using search algorithms and technologies, which would lessen the time it takes for a human to do the same task that was being automated by this application. When you develop applications that have specific business objectives to be met, nobody should ignore those business objectives while developing the applications. Otherwise, it would lead to a failure and the project getting terminated as a result of losing sight of the business objective.

This is advice that I will give to all my readers: pay attention to the business objectives and ask each team if the module that they are building would meet the business objective. Will the application be better than the human that is performing the job? Will this application be faster than the human that is performing this job? IF you as a team think that this application is going to be better than the manual task then how much time or how much reduction in process is this automation going to provide?

These are some of the questions that everybody from a team member to the product owner to the manager needs to ask every day about the application meeting its business objective. Most of the time the teams spend grappling with issues in technology, such as which algorithm to use, which language to use for the Goa, which technology to use for the web reporting app, and how to make each module communicate with each other, rather than looking at the primary business objective—in this case, providing fast and efficient replacement of human efforts. If the team loses sight of the business objective, the parts of the application will be successful; however, when they are summed up they will be termed as a failure and the project may get scrapped as a result. In all of the meetings, whether they are business meetings, team meetings, product owner meetings, or any other kind of review meetings, the topic of discussion has to be whether the application that we are building as of now will meet the primary business objectives or not. If the application is going to meet the business objective, then by what percentage, and this should be measured based on some realistic tests conducted by the team. Only when we bring this kind of rigor to putting the business objective first can we then hope that the application is going to meet its business objectives.

This is Not a Competition, It is Applied Business!

Another important mindset that every applied machine learning engineer needs to have is that they are developing for the business and that this is no longer a hackathon or a competition. I say this based on my experience of having talked to many machine learning teams as well as interacting with machine learning engineers on social platforms like LinkedIn, and I saw that the common belief is that machine learning is all about knowing statistics, common machine learning algorithms, and programming language like Python or R. But when the same machine learning engineer who was selected based on winning the hackathon or competition, they step into the business world, and they fail to meet the business objectives of the machine learning application. I will now highlight the differences between applied machine learning and machine learning used in competitions; this will help you understand how applied machine learning is different from popular machine learning. Table 5-1 shows this difference.

Table 5-1. *Differences Between Applied Machine Learning and Popular Machine Learning*

Parameters	Applied Machine Learning	Popular Machine Learning
Objective	To solve a business problem	To get the highest rank in competition
Code ownership	Proprietary and patentable by the organization	Public not patentable
Focus	Apply for business success	Hack to score
Means to achieve	End-to-end working application	Code that meets the competition criteria
Technical achievement	Application meets business needs	Code meets top rank criteria

In the table you can see there are five types of parameters on which I have differentiated between applied machine learning and popular machine learning. The first is objective. In the case of applied machine learning, the objective is to solve a business problem. The business problem could be related to automating human effort or creating an innovative application that would use artificial intelligence and machine learning to do new tasks for the end customer of the business. The objective is clearly to meet the issues and the problems that a business is facing and to apply machine learning to solve them. In the case of popular machine learning used in competitions, the objective is to get the highest rank in the competition. One could argue and say that you can't get the highest rank in the competition without meeting or solving the business problem given in the competition. Because there are at least hundreds of participants in the competition who are able to solve the business problem given for the competition in their own way, they may not get selected as the winner because they do not rank as the highest. In hackathons or competitions, criteria are never applied to see which participant's solution is optimally solving the business problem; however, it is to see if the solution given is able to meet a certain accuracy level. Meeting or exceeding and accuracy level may not mean that this solution optimally solves the business problem identified. You may have a very accurate machine learning algorithm, but it may not solve the business problem because it does not take into account the issues that the business is trying to address. In such cases the popular machine learning approach will create disastrous machine learning solutions.

The next parameter is code ownership. In the case of applied machine learning, usually the code credit Python machine learning team is owned by the organization and is patentable and proprietary to it. In contrast to this, with the popular machine learning in competitions, the code is not patentable as it can be accessed by the public. There is no copyright attached to the solution, as it can be seen by anybody who is participating in the competition or the hackathon. This is true for competitions that are run on websites like kaggle.com.

The next parameter is focus. Here, the applied machine learning focuses on business success and creating a solution that not only meets but exceeds the business objectives. With machine learning applications, like we have seen in our case study of lab coordinator, the chatbots in the kiosk are able to replace the lab coordinator with certain limited functions and are able to give the business a success. In the case of popular machine learning, the focus is on using hacks in the code to score higher in accuracy or whatever benchmark the competition is targeting. An example of such a focus is that there are some algorithms like gradient boost or Ada that have become popular with competition participants because they are able to give a higher accuracy level. Accuracy level does not mean a guarantee that your solution is going to solve the business problem. There are various reasons why although you may have a high accuracy machine learning solution, it may not meet the business objectives. Some of these could be related to efficiency of the solution. It could also be that we are trying to do a trade off with bias and variance in our machine learning algorithm.

The next parameter is the means to achieve the application or the business objectives. In the case of applied machine learning, the means are to create an end-to-end working application that emulates to solve its business needs. However, in the case of popular machine learning, the purpose is to write code that meets the competition criteria.

The next parameter is technical achievement. In the case of applied machine learning, it succeeds only when the application meets business needs. In popular machine learning, the code succeeds only when it meets or is the top rank criteria. In my opinion, this is a significant difference in the way a machine learning engineer has to unlearn and relearn these parameters and the differences in the approach and change their mindset toward becoming applied machine learning engineer.

Don't Get Caught in the Planning and Design Flaws

The purpose of planning is to provide a structure to application development and to identify risks that could potentially derail the project. Some common planning flaws are:

> *Failure in identifying key business objectives for the machine learning applications.*

> *Failure in identifying all the modules needed for the applications.*

> *Failure in identifying benchmarks for application performance.*

Some of the design flaws are:

> *Failure in creating feedback architecture for the machine learning application.*

> *Failure in identifying integration challenges due to technology.*

> *Failure of the prototype.*

At the top of my list for the planning flaws is the failure in identifying key business objectives for the machine learning application that is being developed by the organization. To give you an example, a particular client asks for a machine learning application that replaces the front desk at a healthcare facility. This particular business objective is in itself not of much use in understanding how to convert it to interactive machine learning application. Different themes can be interpreted in different ways. For example, one team could say since we need to replace the entire front desk system, we need to build a robot. Some other team may say that we need to build a kiosk computer that could give the arriving customer options to interact with the hospital. Another team could interpret that as building an application that would assist the front desk staff. So it is not just helpful in defining the business objective but also in identifying what part of the process needs to be replaced or emulated. If this is not done correctly then different teams and different people will come up with their own ideas of arriving at solutions for the business problem identified, hence it is very important to identify those key business objectives that are important for the machine learning application.

The next failure is in identifying all the models that are needed for the application during application planning. I have seen various themes discovering that, for example, they need a configuration module that they had not thought about earlier in order for the application to work properly. Discovery of such models is a costly affair when done during the middle of development activity. Hence, it is prudent that the team does efficient planning and identifies all the models that the machine learning applications would require in order to run successfully. In our example, if the configuration module is to be developed in the middle of the development cycle, then it requires replanning and rescheduling and then reworking the cost of the machine learning application. If it turns out that the module is small and does not require many days of work, then there may not be a need to go back to the business owners in order to identify if the replanning is ratified by them. However, if this turns out to be a major development activity requiring weeks of development and testing activities and is something that will affect integration of the software, then this is an example of missed planning or bad planning. It is important that the team doing the machine learning application does a lot of planning activity in identifying all the various kinds of models they will need for this application before they start to design and code.

With the next failure in planning I put forward a very common problem that leads to a machine learning application failure—that of identifying performance benchmarks once the application moves into production. The reason I say this is very common is because many algorithms related to machine learning are computer-intensive, and if the machine learning application uses things like deep learning neural networks, then performance benchmarks are extremely important during such application building. I can tell you from my experience that when a machine learning application was built for a prominent customer and was moved into production, the algorithm ran for more than 12 hours in order to compute a prediction value as to whether a customer would buy the product from the website or not. When the team started planning, they never thought about putting in any application performance benchmarks, as all of the machine learning engineers were from the popular machine learning field, and they had no experience in applying machine learning to business. So although the application had a high accuracy level after using deep learning models, it failed to meet the business objective of predicting the values of whether a customer would buy a product or not and who has visited a website within the real-time status. During the application development life cycle of a machine learning application, these performance benchmarks have to be put in the form of test cases when the application is integrated and brought together to work. This will ensure that the machine learning application is able to perform as per the expectations of the business objectives.

Now we move to the design flaws, the first being failure in creating a feedback architecture for the machine learning application. This is another very common issue, wherein the machine learning architect fails to create a feedback loop in the design of the software, and the machine learning application does not take feedback from the real-time production system and is later junked by the business as giving inaccurate results. Let me clarify as to what I mean by feedback architecture for the machine learning application. Any machine learning team can plan, design, and develop a machine learning application that predicts certain business parameters of a process. In the real world, one can hardly find an application that does not does have 100 percent accuracy levels. Every algorithm has a certain accuracy level, and this means that the algorithm will make some predictions that are erroneous, classified as Type 1 and Type 2 errors. If the machine learning application does not learn from predicting erroneous values, then it is said to have a design flaw in feedback architecture. Feedback architecture demands that the machine learning application learns from the errors that it makes and improves itself in its performance the next time. This is known as true learning and emulating the learning process that human beings perform every day.

In the next design flow failure, I talked about identifying integration challenges due to technology. In machine learning application, you can create chatbots—for example, the one that I created in Chapter 4 for our case study for emulating lab coordinator. I created the GUI using Python; however in the real world when you go to implement such an application, you will hardly build artificial intelligence using Python. You would use a machine friendly language like C# or Java in order to create the front-end application. The next integration challenge in such an application would be that the intelligence of the chatbots is being run in Python, however the goal is showing up in dotnet and how do these two integrate together? This could be achieved by using various plug-in technologies that integrate C# into Python or Python into C# and then making them talk to each other through these plug-in libraries. This is just an example of the kind of technological integration challenges that one could face while designing a machine learning application. Another example would be that if the chatbots need to interact with a human being through website, then they will need a way to connect to the Python code from the web front-end GUI. This can be achieved through services and technologies like flask, which allow the integration process.

The next failure I talked about was that of the failure of the prototype. In this failure, the team builds a proof of concept and has a prototype shown to the business owner; however, when we try to implement the prototype in the real world, we face multiple problems. These problems commonly relate to scaling of the technology used such as the prototype for 10 users. However, when we are scaling this up to thousands of users, it hangs. In such cases, although we had a prototype, it failed when it was scaled up. We could also, in some cases, have a prototype that uses a certain type of technology, but when the technology is used to create a certain feature that was not built when the prototype was being developed, it fails and we realize that this technology is not appropriate for the kind of prototype application that we are trying to build. So prototype failure is also one of the design failures that machine learning applications can face, and this can lead to termination of the machine learning application project as well.

Choosing the Best Algorithm for Your Prediction Model

This is another big reason why machine learning applications fail. I recommend using the scikit-learn cheat sheet for algorithm selection. It is the best way to navigate the complex process of selecting the best algorithm for your machine learning algorithm [1].

Let me run you through an example using the case study from Chapter 4 of this book as a reference. I come to the orange start button, and the next question it asks is, "Do you have a sample that is greater than 50?" In our case, if you will recall, we had a sample of 125 hospitals, which is greater than 50. So in our case, there was no need to get more data. We move to the next circle, which asks, "Are you predicting a category?" In our case, we were predicting food waste in kilogram, which is quantity and it is not category, so we say no and we move to predicting a quantity. Then it asks to predict a quantity using yes or no. We say yes. It asks, "Is it less than 100,000 samples?" We say yes, because we have only 125 samples. The next question is, "Are there few features that should be important?" We say no, because most of the numerical features are important in our case. We pick up SVR kernel linear regression, and we see that it does not work, so the next part of the arrow takes us to ensemble regressors, and we choose linear regression regressor to solve our identified problem. So in this book you have seen how I have used the cheat sheet to arrive at the best machine learning algorithm.

Are You Using Agile Machine Learning?

Agile scrum-based software development methodology is very popular these days and is being used in organizations throughout the world. Agile methodology has proven its ability to speed up software development and to empower the teams in making decisions by themselves. I talk about agile machine learning because there are various machine learning applications that are being developed not by software organizations but by business organizations, such as retail stores or hospitals or financial companies. In such a scenario, when they develop in-house applications, they should also use the most modern software development methodologies in order to be successful. Agile gives the ability and flexibility to a machine learning application development team to change course in the middle if the application does not meet the business needs. Machine learning is a trial-and-error effort, and one cannot say that there is definitely going to be a solution for a particular problem. The trial and error could be based on selection of the algorithm, the selection of the data set, or the selection of the technology. If the team works in a waterfall approach, then they lose the benefit of agile that allows the team to correct its course in the middle. Agile gives you the framework of integrating product owner into the development cycle and take early feedback so that surprises don't crop up at the end of the application development. Agile also gives democracy to the team, as there are the team members who make major decisions while implementing the work, and it is they who take up required work voluntarily in order to complete the application on time. Agile scrum type of development with machine learning applications also brings transparency, allowing everyone to see what the machine learning engineer and other cross-functional team members are doing on the project. Since some of the development cycles could end in failures due to the trial-and-error approach of machine learning, it is better to let the stakeholders know immediately that an approach is not working than to keep them waiting until the end of the cycle, as happens in waterfall model. Looking at all these benefits, I highly recommend that whenever you bring together a machine learning applications team, you start using agile form of development.

Ascertaining Technical Risks in the Project

The biggest risk in developing machine learning applications is that it is a trial-and-error-based process. Sometimes the algorithms work on certain types of datasets and sometimes they underperform on other types of datasets. There is no single answer in the best algorithm selection despite having a cheat sheet (which we discussed earlier). In spite of this limitation in the business world, a machine learning consultant is under pressure to deliver the best solutions for the client. Even if the right algorithm is found, the hyper-parameter optimization takes a long time to determine the right parameters for the algorithms. Deep learning algorithms such as ANN and RNN require very high computational power and processing time in order to arrive at the optimum set of parameters.

There are other technical risks as well, such as requirement of high computational power through use of GPUs, and RAM for deep learning applications is something that, if not planned out properly for the production environment, can lead to derailment of the entire project. I have received many SOWs from my industrial clients who want industrial vision applications implemented on 4 GB RAM with 1,1 GHZ CPU with an ordinary GPU, and I have to inform them of the minimum computational requirements for neural network-based systems.

Another risk that I have found with most of my clients is that they have hired a team of machine learning engineers from the market; however none of them has the competence to produce a production-ready machine learning application, as they have never done this. Such technical resources are a liability, rather than an asset, for the organization. They have to then hire a consultant like me to guide them in building a machine learning algorithm end-to-end. Experienced machine learning engineers with knowledge of implementing machine learning applications are hard to find.

Aligned to the risk of getting machine learning engineers from hackathons who do not know applied machine learning is that they may know programming languages that are not used in the company where the application is being built. With one of my clients, they had hired machine learning engineers who knew Java and R and did not know Python. The application was being developed in Python, and they were all having difficulties learning and implementing code. They somehow managed to write code, but when it came to testing and removing defects, they struggled because, due to their inexperience with Python programming language, they had written an inherently buggy performance-lagging application. In the end, to speed up the process, they had to hire a consultant like me to help them out. This happens when hiring managers are under pressure to put together a team of machine learning engineers, and everybody is in a hurry to get the project started. Skills are definitely a big risk if people are not selected for the project carefully and can lead to delays. Machine learning does not just require programming skills; it needs a person who knows math and statistics in-depth and who knows how the algorithms work. It also needs knowledge of an SQL database, such as MongoDB or Cassandra, as well as a web server-based integration engine such as Flask. Machine learning also requires excellent analytical skills; the ability of the machine learning engineer to analyze the outcome of algorithms is also very important. Another often overlooked skill for a machine learning engineer is the ability to understand and cater to the business objectives. This ability is gained when you apply the process of applied machine learning, which I have outlined in this book. By using some of the techniques I have outlined, you can develop quick and robust applications for your clients.

Another very important pitfall is creating machine learning applications without having data. If you see, in the case study in Chapter 4, I had data for only 125 hospitals. Creating an application for such a small size of data is not advised because it is an underuse of technology. The machine learning algorithms and the underlying technology is capable of using petabytes of data. I have come across several clients who do want to build machine learning applications, however when I asked the simple question, "Where is your data?" they were not able to pinpoint any clear sources of data for the machine learning application that they wanted me to build. What they showed me was data that could not exceed even 1 gigabyte. If you end up using machine learning applications for such small data sizes, then you may not get the required returns by investing in applied machine learning. So even before you start to conceive a machine learning application, you must ask within your organization whether you have the data to build a machine learning application for this task. For example, if you want to create a bot that is going to replace the doctor, then do you have data of all the symptoms, diseases, their causes, and medications with their compositions compiled in some textual format that the machine can read? This is a very small example of what you need; however, machine learning application requires much more data than what I have talked about.

In my opinion the most important ability of any machine learning team is the ability to translate the technical machine learning jargon into business language. This single-most ability differentiates between a popular machine learning engineer and an applied machine learning engineer. Telling the business head that the SVM algorithm is best for predicting customer churn does not have any meaning to them unless you tell them that I have developed this algorithm that can predict when the customer is going to turn away from the business. A lot of times, cutting away the jargon can make it easier for the people from the business world to understand machine learning. I often ask machine learning engineers to think if they had to explain their most preferred algorithm in machine learning to a layperson, how would they do it in three sentences? The key here is to not just cut the jargon but also to maintain brevity. In the business world, it is extremely important to communicate the right thing with the right words at the right time with the right tense. Only then can we hope that the business is going to understand the value that the machine learning application is bringing to the organization (or not).

Another extremely important pitfall to avoid in any machine learning application is data privacy. We have seen in the recent data leaks at Facebook and other organizations that public data and the way it is dealt, transmitted, stored, and secured is very important for the business to continue in the long run. Any machine learning application requires petabytes of data, and ignoring the data privacy aspect of the application would mean that we are putting the organization at a risk. Careful planning needs to be done not just at the design stage of the application but also at the implementation stage. Security of data, when it is transmitted, and where it is stored need to be properly thought through. If flat files are being used to store the data, then are they secure enough? Who is going to access them? Are they stored on secure servers? Who is this data going to be shared with? How do we ensure that in the long-term, the date remains secure and nobody steals even from inside the organization? Failure in securing data privacy for the machine learning applications can lead to legal battles and extremely bad results for the organization. If the organization has a data privacy policy, then we need to check and ask if this machine learning application is meeting the organization's data privacy policy. The user story of the machine learning application need to include data breach test cases in order to crash and certify that the machine learning application is able to securely transmit data and store it without any type of hackers or parties who are not supposed to access the data able to access it.

End Note

[1]   Buitinck et al., 2013. API design for machine learning software: experiences from the scikit-learn project, `http://scikit-learn. org/stable/tutorial/machine_learning_map/index.html`

## CHAPTER 6

Monetizing Healthcare Machine Learning

This chapter is about ideas in healthcare wherein using machine learning technology would help organizations in monetizing these ideas. I present to you just three ideas that, as per my research in the healthcare sector and after having consulted experts from the healthcare field, brought me to the conclusion that these three ideas not only need more attention but are going to be the focus for the healthcare industry in the future. Some of the things that I tell you in this chapter may sound far-fetched and far from reality, but you will realize as there's progress that these ideas are definitely going to take shape and are going to be implemented in the healthcare industry. Of course these ideas are good for any startup to pick up and start working on. It is not that there are no startups working on these ideas, but I am presenting you a fresh view of the ideas in how to monetize them as far as machine learning is concerned. The first idea is about a communications application. The second idea involves connected patient data networks. And the third idea is about IoT in healthcare. While I tell you about these ideas, I will also tell you about some of the pitfalls and the dangers that exist in the current state where these ideas stand.

Intro-Hospital Communication Apps

In order to introduce you to the idea of intro-hospital communications applications, I would first like to take you through a personal hospital encounter that ratifies and tells about the need for intro-hospital communication.

In 1998, my mother was hospitalized and she had fallen ill. However, based on the scan reports, none of the doctors were able to diagnose any form of cancer. It was when her stomach that was opened that the doctor was surprised to find a tumor

135

© Puneet Mathur 2019
P. Mathur, *Machine Learning Applications Using Python*, https://doi.org/10.1007/978-1-4842-3787-8_6

ball in her intestine and made an emergency decision to remove it. While I am not talking here about the diagnostic error that the doctor made, I am going to talk about the communication error that happened and that could have killed my mother even before she died at a later date. After her operation was performed, she was given regular injections, and since she had anemia, she was also administered blood infusions. There were nurses on the staff who would change their shifts in a 24-hour pattern, and each nurse was supposed to communicate any change in medication or a change in the vital signs that were being monitored by the doctor. In the case of my mother, one of the staff failed to communicate about the change in medicine to be administered through intravenous means. This was a nurse on night shift (when the people are least alert), but since the doctor had talked about the change in the medicine and rotated on the prescription, I had the name of the medicine and I checked what the nurse was administering intravenously in the saline that was being administered. I found out that she was again going to administer the old drug, which was causing inflammation in my mother, and the last nurse had failed to communicate about the change in medicine to the new nurse. This is an example of communication errors that happen inside hospitals day in and day out. If the people who are attending to the patient are not alert, then these kinds of errors do not get noticed and the patient suffers.

I now take your attention to an article in the Times of India, an Indian newspaper. The article is titled, "Medical Negligence— 70% of Deaths Are a Result of Miscommunication." This article was published in the newspaper in 2016. The article highlights the fact that in the US, there are 44,000 to 98,000 deaths that happen due to these kinds of errors. In India, it is more alarming due to high population—5 million people die due to such human errors [1; https://timesofindia.indiatimes.com/life-style/health-fitness/health-news/Medical-negligence-70-of-deaths-are-a-result-of-miscommunication/articleshow/51235466.cms].

When we talk about miscommunication, there are some areas where this miscommunication is more prone than others. The highest risk is when a patient is transferred or handed off between the medical providers. I gave you my personal example of miscommunication where the nurse failed to communicate on the change in medication for my mother because it can be very critical to share the information that needs to pass regarding the patient medication, and it has to pass between doctors, nurses, and pharmacists. In this idea for creating an app for intro-hospital communication, the app should have a good GUI that is available on any android or iPhone for the hospital staff to download. The goal should have certain characteristic features that are not available in an ordinary app. For example:

a) The graphical user interface should have large fonts and large controls, like buttons text boxes, and labels. The reason for keeping the GUI elements large is that the healthcare professionals, be it nurses, doctors, or pharmacists, all are under pressure to take care of multiple patients at the same time. And even then a medical emergency can come at any time. So if the graphical user interface elements are plotted on the phone screen and are not large enough to read, then it may lead to erroneous selection and entry of data.

b) The graphical user interface needs to have very minimal data entry requirement from either the nurses, doctors, or pharmacists. The idea here is that the more open you keep data entry in the form of text boxes, the more you are opening the gates for human error. Almost all the options for entering data have to be free-field in the form of drop-down box options, etc. This will ensure that the open-ended data entry will not happen, and there will be reduction in errors.

c) The app should be common for nurses, doctors, pharmacists, and any other healthcare professional working in the hospital. This is important because we want a single source of communication to happen between the staff of any hospital. I will give you an example of how this app can reduce the communication gap that happens among staff. The app would have detailed information of nurses when they change shifts. The entry screen for a nurse for handover to the next nurse would require her to select all the patient IDS that are pre-populated from the hospital patient database. For each patient ID selected, there would be details of the current medication that is being administered and the required intervals of monitoring the patient. Since this is a single app that is common to the doctors, the moment a nurse selects a patient ID who is in the risky zone of being handed off either from an operation or during a regular shift, the app would start blinking and alert the nurse that a doctor has prescribed a new medication and the information that needs to be handed over to the next shift person. In fact the new medication changed by the doctor would come through the app because the doctor would have a screen for the patient ID selection and would select that changed medication from the drop-down menu of the app. This alerting system would apply and send out SMS communication as well to all the nurses connected in their shift to a particular patient ID. In practical terms, this may look like overcommunication, but please remember we are dealing with human lives and any communication is extremely important and cannot be treated as overcommunication. The alert of change in medication goes to the doctors themselves, to the nurses connected with taking care of patient, and also to the pharmacists who are administering the medicine. You may say that even after having received an alert about a change in a patient's medication, the nurse, pharmacist, or any other healthcare staff can ignore the communication, and the error may happen. However, when the nurse opens her shift schedule in the app, the app would show an alert about change in medication, change in the word of the patient, change in the dietary requirement, or any other kind of a change. It is hard to ignore an alert when it shows up on the personal screen of the healthcare professional. I am not saying that this will remove the miscommunication by 100 percent; however, introducing such an app inside the hospital will definitely reduce the communication errors. There are certain characteristics that the app should have. One thing that nobody wants to do after a grueling session of surgery or patient care is data entry for electronic patient health records. I am not going into the legal aspect of electronic patient health records; however, I am going into the ease of maintaining electronic health records from the perspective of healthcare professionals. They are going to be the users of this app, and hence they need to be consulted before the app is finalized regarding what makes them more comfortable while making selections from the mobile screens. In order to make an app that does not require the healthcare professional to enter open-ended text, such as text boxes, there needs to be research done on each aspect of the hospital process that a healthcare professional undergoes so that nothing is missed that requires the healthcare professional to enter data in open-text format. This requires extensive study of any hospital's processes and then converting it into suitable GUI options. This application will fail if it requires the healthcare professional to enter a lot of data or select a lot of options from multiple screens. The options should be minimal, and the screens should also be kept minimal so that the busy healthcare professionals don't get entangled in the web of data entry in the app.

I will give you an example of extensive research that has to happen in order to build this app. In Chapter 4, I tried to emulate in Case Study 1 the work done by a lab coordinator. We can hardly call that Python application to replace a lab coordinator; however, that app does give a structure to a narrow approach to machine learning application building that we need to take. To know all the work that a lab coordinator does, one needs to carefully study and note all the tasks or activities that a lab coordinator performs during the day. Once these tasks are known, then we need to see what kind of workflows take place between these tasks. The next thing we need to see is what kinds of actors are involved for each of those tasks. By actors, I mean the people who are interacting with the lab coordinator, such as lab technicians, doctors, nurses, or patients. The next, most important part that needs to be understood is for each of those tasks and the workflows, what kind of data is needed and flows between them. The team that is building this app needs to carefully divide the data into structured, semi-structured, and unstructured data. To give you an example, a lab coordinator may make some handwritten notes on a lab report and that will constitute unstructured data. Structured data is stored in proprietary traditional databases, such as Oracle DB, SQL server, etc. Semi-structured data is stored in flat files or XML files and files like csv or JSON. If the lab coordinator uses any of these forms of data, it needs to be documented and then a decision needs to be made on how to deal with unstructured data. In my opinion any unstructured data, such as handwritten notes, are a serious threat to the medical fraternity. The reason is that handwriting can be misinterpreted and can lead to confusion. Open text is very much open to misinterpretation. So the app should aim at asking the healthcare professionals in converting all such open-ended text to structured data. It may seem difficult, but it is possible to look at all the things done by a lab coordinator over time and then come up with the common things that are put in the handwritings. This does require extensive work, and that is why I mentioned in the beginning that there is extensive research required for such an app to eradicate the miscommunication from the hospital system.

Connected Patient Data Networks

We come to our next idea on monetization that is connected patient data networks. The moment we talked about anything that has to do with data we have to talk about data privacy. Data privacy in the healthcare industry is of more importance than in any other sector because it deals with personal data of every human being. This data, if led to the wrong sources, can lead to disastrous circumstances. In the current healthcare system, there are multiple hospitals at multiple levels, and there are independent doctors and healthcare consultants who are not able to see a unified view of a patient health record. There is no unified system of maintaining patient case history. To give you an example, when a new patient arrives at any hospital around the world, the doctor starts prescribing medicine and treatment after checking some of the vital signs, such as heart rate, blood pressure, oxygen rate, and 17 common lab tests that need to be performed on the patient. If the patient shifts from one hospital to another, the same process is repeated by the doctors at the new hospital. From the patient's perspective, this is a huge cost for them and something that could be avoided if we had a centralized connected patient data network.

Imagine that you have undergone a treatment for a certain disease at Hospital A. However, you are not satisfied with the treatment that they are giving you, and you want to shift to another hospital. The biggest hurdle apart from logistics is that of data. The data that the hospital has collected for you is not communicated to Hospital B, and that is where the problem lies. If we have a connected patient data network, then the data that Hospital A collects about a particular patient will be available to Hospital B once the patient authorizes Hospital B to access its data.

The hospitals and their data systems are currently working in silos, and they do not maintain any central record for the patients that can be accessed outside of their systems. The biggest roadblock in creating this connected patient data network is that of data security and data privacy. If there can be a secure way of storing such centralized information or it can be decentralized using the block chain technology that does not require a centralized means of storing information, then we can reduce the cost of healthcare for the patients significantly. Another problem that the connected patient data network is facing is that of proving the identity of the patient. This roadblock can be overcome by introducing biometric authentication. However, we need to say that no biometric authentication system around the world has been 100 percent successful. The last roadblock that I see for the connected patient data networks is that if we have some kind of an organization that stores such large amounts of data, it may eventually turn to data terrorism, like we have seen with bigger US corporations in recent times. Illegal data mining without the patient's knowledge is a bigger threat to this kind of a network. The advantage of data mining could be that it could lead to unearthing of finds in patient diseases based on the medication that they have been provided. So when we are building such an application, we need to weigh the pros and cons of building such an application.

Another problem with connected patient healthcare records is that the cost of maintaining such a record system would need to be borne by someone. Either the hospital or the patient needs to bear the cost of maintaining data on the system. There could be both the models that could work as well. The patient could be charged X amount of a subscription for storing data on the electronic record system (this could be a monthly or yearly fees). On the other hand, the patient could be asked to pay to access a particular patient's record for a certain period of time. Of course, if you ask the hospital to pay, it would ultimately be factored in the hospital bills that it charges the patients. So it would be indirectly charging the patient for maintaining their electronic health records. The third model is where both the patient and the hospital pay. The patient pays for the duration that the electronic health record is maintained, and the hospital pays for the duration that it accesses a particular patient's health record. The first model, where the patient pays, and the third model, where both the patient and the hospital pay, are hard to maintain in poor economies. The wealthy patients will be able to pay for maintaining their electronic health records. In the much poorer economies, there has to be a public system of maintaining such electronic health records in the future. This needs to be done for each citizen of the world.

IoT in Healthcare

The IoT, or Internet of Things, is the network of physical devices, vehicles, home appliances, and other items embedded with electronics, software, sensors, actuators, and connectivity that enables these objects to connect and exchange data [1; `https://en.wikipedia.org/wiki/Internet_of_things`].

In simple layman's terms, IoT is small devices that are embedded with common things, such as paintings. etcetera to give them the ability to connect and exchange data. You may say, "What is the use of having data collected from a simple thing like a painting?" However, think about this: a painting can collect a lot of data, such as the visitor's face, visitor's profile, their expressions on seeing the painting, the distance of the audience from the painting, the average number of visits to the painting, the number of people who did not stop or look at the painting, etc. This is just an example of how enabling a simple wall painting with the IoT platform can get more data about the reactions from people.

In healthcare, especially the IoT is coming up in a big way. The main reason is that healthcare is an industry that is always under pressure to save lives and heal people from dreadful diseases. In the nature of this industry, the hospitals and healthcare professionals have an attitude of early adoption of technology for the good welfare of patients. There are many areas where IoT is making its entry in the healthcare field, some of them being activity trackers that are embedded into the patient skin to track cancer treatment. The most prominent use of IoT, in my opinion, will be in the space of having sensors to help doctors crack treatment of sick patients. We have seen that communication is a big problem in the current healthcare industry. IoT-enabled devices sending out messages to doctors, nurses, and pharmacists based on their senses are going to prove to be a boon for them. So I am going to concentrate on application for monetizing using IoT sensors in this section.

In order to monetize technology from the IoT for remote health monitoring, we can look to build a remote health monitor catering to specific diseases. The Cape COD v belt uses sensors at the patients' homes and could collect data on patients' heart rates, oxygen levels, and sugar levels. This kit would have not only embedded sensors, which a patient could strap on to their chest, but would have additional transmitters that would connect to the internet and relay the patient's information to the doctor on a real-time basis. The key thing for developing such a kit is that it would require a regular subscription from the patient in order to be monitored and the data to be transmitted to the hospital at regular intervals. The central monitoring system that connects this data from the sensors through the internet would alert the doctor in case they find that there is some abnormality in the vital readings of the patient. It is important that the medications are also monitored through these sensors. We can develop sensors that would recognize the presence of a certain chemical in the blood that would give an indication that a particular medicine has been consumed by the patient. This type of remote health monitoring can not only be used at patients' homes but can be used inside hospitals on patients' beds in order to monitor them. There are some key advantages for both patients and the hospitals for having IoT-based sensors monitor their health. The patient being monitored can be assured that there is not going to be any human error and the machine is going to send out alerts whenever there is a change in vital signs of the patient. From the hospital's side, it will free their staff from the monitoring activities that they do, and they can deploy that monitoring staff to other work that is important and requires attention in the hospital. I can clearly see the future hospital, with emergency beds for more urgent issues, and for diseases that are non-critical, the patients will be monitored at their homes. When this type of healthcare environment evolves, we would definitely have focused healthcare facilities. Of course, these types of systems will have less human touch and more machine presence. In order to build the remote monitoring IoT devices, you would also need a central electronic patient database system, which I have already discussed in this chapter. We are talking about developing this patient health monitoring remote system for the future; hence, we should also look at having physicians replaced by robots who connect to these remote health monitoring systems and send out alerts to the required people, like emergency staff, when a critical monitoring alert is generated. So in that scenario we would have staff attending to emergencies and not use staff for doing mundane patient health monitoring jobs. There are apprehensions that robots will take over all the work in the healthcare industry. However, I would like to show you that this may be true for some jobs, but there will always be a requirement for expert and emergency staff who would help the automated system to deliver better healthcare services to the patient.

Figure 6-1 presents the complete idea by taking three actors in this use-case:

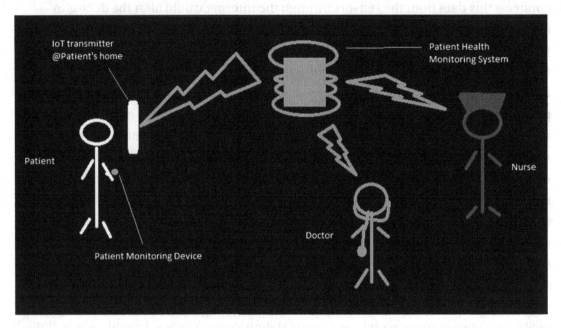

Figure 6-1. *IoT-based patient health monitoring system*

The first is the patient, the second is the doctor, and the third is the nurse. All these three actors are critical to patients during critical illness. We can see from the figure that the patient has a kind of strapable monitoring device, and at their home they have an IoT transmitter device that transmits specific vital statistics information about the patient after receiving it from the patient monitoring device. The IoT transmitter sends the statistics about the patient to the centralized patient health monitoring system at the hospital. The patient health monitoring system is automated, and it uses machine learning to predict criticality of a patient's health in advance and sends alerts to the doctor and nurse. To give you a scenario of how this can work, let's take an example where a patient is critically ill from a heart attack and is being monitored post-surgery at their home through the IoT monitoring kit. The patient's heart rate, oxygen level, and other key vital statistics are being transmitted from the patient monitoring device to the IoT transmitter at the patient's home, and this information is relayed at 1-hour intervals to the hospital patient health monitoring system through the internet. The patient health monitoring system has the intelligence to increase or decrease the level of frequency of monitoring data that is to be transmitted back to it from the patient monitoring device. Since the patient health monitoring system uses machine learning, it is automatically able to predict a critical heart condition in advance based on the learning that it has gained from a huge amount of patient data that is available to it. It turns out prediction alerts to the doctor, nurses, and the emergency teams about a potential heart condition for a patient already being monitored. This ability to predict is completely missing from the current human setup of having doctors and nurses monitoring the patient. So just by introducing IoT and a centralized patient health monitoring system, we are able to bring a level of predictability of the onset of a disease in the patient. Such a system would rid the lower staff of mundane repetitive activities of monitoring a patient and the process that is currently so error-prone that it leads to 70 percent of the deaths that happen due to medical errors. The entire staff at the future healthcare facility that would be using IoT-based patient health monitoring system would be ready for any eventuality that takes place for the patient in advance. They would also be prepared to take up emergency procedures with precision. It will drastically improve the level of healthcare that we provide to our patients in the current environment. This is the system that I want you to visualize and build for the betterment of the healthcare industry.

Monetization of this IoT service will be of three types. First the hospital that is implementing this IoT would need to bear the cost of keeping IoT service alive 24/7. Second the patient would have to bear the cost of initially installing the sensor kit at their homes. The next cost is that of the subscription where the patient pays for the service for whatever length they use. For example, hiring this service for 10 days of monitoring could cost X dollars to the patient. The subscription will also cover the cost of accessing and billing information through the internet at periodic intervals.

End Note

[1]   Buitinck et al., 2013. API design for machine learning software: experiences from the scikit-learn project, `http://scikit-learn.org/stable/tutorial/machine_learning_map/index.html`

## CHAPTER 7

Overview of Machine Learning in Retail

At a data science conference in Bangalore a few years back, I was approached by a prospective client from the retail industry. He had a clear goal for data science to help their company increase their retail business. The current team was not able to get a breakthrough and was looking for someone experienced to guide them. The client informed me that the retail industry was undergoing a change, with e-commerce portals disrupting the way sales used to happen. He explained that his company had lost nearly 25 percent of the market in the last 3 years to online retailers like Flipkart, Amazon, and Bigbasket. The trend did not look healthy and he wanted to know if it was possible to use targeted marketing through machine learning to boost sales.

Retail is an industry that has both functional segmentation and also has a value segmentation that we will see in this chapter. Retail spans across various industries where business-to-consumer transactions happen very frequently. In business-to-consumer transactions, the goods or services move from producer of goods and services to the consumer. The consumer then directly consumes these goods or services. Let us understand this through an example. There are retail departments in most of the major banks around the world, such as the retail division of Citibank or Bank of America and other such banks. In major fashion houses around the world, there are retail divisions that cater to directly selling fashionable clothes and accessories to the consumer. Similarly, there are retail divisions in all major companies, like producers of soaps and toiletries. These dedicated retail divisions have the responsibility of ensuring that the consumer gets the products to send services produced by the organization. When we talk about retail in an organizational context, we are talking about their retail divisions. Now let us look at how this term is used overall in an organization or sectors. There are dedicated companies that have their main business as retail. Such companies do not do any other activity, like producing the goods and services. A good example of this type of

© Puneet Mathur 2019
P. Mathur, *Machine Learning Applications Using Python*, https://doi.org/10.1007/978-1-4842-3787-8_7

organization is Walmart, which is from the category that is also called brick and mortar organizations. Amazon.com is an example where retail is done online through the internet.

We have direct selling organizations in the US as well that also act as retailers where the producer organizations have their own retail stores. Companies like Dell, which sells computers for both end consumers and to organizations as well. It has direct selling stores that it uses to reach the end consumer. In both scenarios the goal of the organization is to reach the end consumer and make them make a buying decision.

The retail industry globally is undergoing a change due to the widespread use of the internet among households, leading to companies like Amazon offering customers fast home delivery options. The key thing to note is that these e-commerce retailers are able to use technologies such as robotics, artificial intelligence, and machine learning. The clear differentiation in the business approach can be seen from Table 7-1.

Table 7-1. *Different Retailer Types and Their Offerings*

Retail Type	Focus	Differentiation	Break-even	Logistics	Cost
Brick & Mortar	In-shop experience	DiscountsBranding	Short cycle	Retail storesWarehouses	High
Online Retailer	Ease of accessSave customer time	Home deliveryDeep discounts	Long cycle	Warehouses	Low
Hybrid	Extension of in-shop experience	Known brand value	Medium cycle	Retail storesWarehouses	Medium

We can see from Table 7-1 that currently there are three types of retailers. The first is brick and mortar retailers, the second is online-only retailers, and the third is hybrid retailers. The brick and mortar retailers focus on providing customers with an in-shop experience where the customer walks into the shop and has a look at the range of products on display and then makes a buying decision. They differentiate themselves by giving discounts and branding their retail stores. In comparison to other retailers, the brick and mortar retailers have a shorter break-even cycle. A brick and mortar retailer has to manage the logistics of retail stores and warehouses as well. The brick and mortar stores have a higher cost because they have to maintain retail stores and warehouses. For the online retailers, the focus is on ease of access to their online shop and saving the customer time by not traveling to the retail stores. The customer is able to order from the comfort of their home. An online retailer differentiates themselves by giving the option of home delivery of the chosen products by the customer and giving deep discounts for the products that they offer. Online retailers have a very long cycle to break even. A case in point is Amazon, which took more than 10 years to attain profitability. Online retailers do not have retail stores, and hence they have to manage only the warehouses to store their products. The cost of operation of an online retailer is significantly lower than a brick and mortar retailer because they do not have to manage the real estate of retail stores. There is a third category of retailers now popping up due to the popularity of online retailers, and they are hybrid retail stores. They have both brick and mortar retail stores and online websites to sell their products. They focus on the expansion of in-shop experience to customers who have already purchased from the brick and mortar stores. They differentiate based on the fact that a loyal customer knows about the brand value of the brick and mortar store so from the comfort of their home they can hope to get the same brand value. Since the hybrid model adds the cost of online retailer, the break-even cycle for a hybrid store is medium. The logistics advantage of a hybrid store is that it already owns retail stores and warehouses; however, it needs to open more warehouses for distribution of its products in various cities. That is why we come to the next summer tour of cost where they have the highest cost of all the three types of retailers.

Retail Segments

Figure 7-1 explains the various segments that exist within the retail industry. This segmentation is at a high level to give the reader an understanding of how the overall business of retail is segmented. The first segment is specialty retail, and these are stores that cater to the focused needs of the buyer, such as clothing, office supply, handicraft, etc. In the US there are stores like Staples and Office Depot that cater to office supplies; similarly, there are chains like Barnes & Noble for books, and Mattel for children's needs. These are stores that cater to the specific needs of the buyers such as children, books, office supplies.

Figure 7-1. *Retail segments*

The next segment is food and beverages. There are various world-reknowned global companies like McDonald's, Pizza Hut, and Dominos that cater to this segment. Other food companies like Citarella Gourmet foods to just name a few.

Another popular retail segment is work, home, and lifestyle. Stores like The Story in New York, Spell and the Gypsy collective, Song from Vienna, and Macy's (which now has more than 600 stores with global presence) are all examples of home and lifestyle retail stores.

The next segment is general retailing, and in the top of that list is Walmart, which sells products in all categories. Similar to Walmart is Amazon; however, Walmart used to be more of brick and mortar operation and Amazon is largely retail. Home Depot also sells general retailing products like garden products, home improvement products, building materials, and other services related to general retailing.

The last segment of retail concerns retail logistics, and this is more of a back-end operation for the retailers where they partner by outsourcing their transportation practices. The reason why I have categorized logistics as a separate retail segment is that it is the most important decision in the retail business, wherein a business has to decide based on its logistics on where to locate stores, warehouses, and distribution facilities. Sometimes a big retail store giant has to build warehouses and distribution centers near major ports and major inland hubs in their respective countries because a lot of goods that are sold by these stores are imported and then repackaged and sold in their stores. There is a surge in large million square foot distribution centers around the world because of these import and export transactions in the retail Industry. There are also mega-sized distribution facilities around the urban areas that have popped up in the suburban areas of major urban markets around the world where land is cheap. These mega-sized distribution facilities are used as a regional or central hub by the retail store chain in order to manage its retail operations. Deciding on where to open a brick or mortar retail outlet to serve the customer demand is a very important decision for the retail company. The location of a retail outlet that fails and underperforms costs the company in terms of lost revenue, lost opportunity, and lost time. It is logistics that makes the retail sector more costly in terms of operations because of the movement of goods involved in it. In the healthcare industry, the real estate is used by a hospital similar to a retail store. However, this is different in the finance world, which we will see in the third section.

Retail Value Proposition

Value proposition as defined by Google dictionary is marketing and innovation, service, and features intended to make a company or product attractive to customers. The words "innovation," "service," and "feature" are important here in order to determine the value proposition of retail industry. In Figure 7-2, I present to you the value proposition that each retailer type gives to its customers.

Figure 7-2. *Retail customer value proposition*

Here I have divided the retail sector into three value segments. The first is direct product service offerings. The three characteristic features of this type of retail business are that it is business-to-consumer-oriented, there are direct selling stores for the consumer to buy products, and there is an option of directly buying online. A good example of this kind of company is Dell Incorporated. It sells to customers all over the world through direct company stores and it also has a direct online website that allows the people to place orders for various computer types.

In the next categorization, I place experience-based offerings by retail companies. Three characteristic features of this type of offering are that they are generally situated in large malls, they are luxury stores, or they are exclusive stores. Examples of such stores are Jeffrey Gallery d, Crush Boutique, The Velvet Fly, and Blake, to name just a few.

The third type of offerings are those that provide price and revenue advantage to the customer through online offerings. The three characteristic features of this type of offering are that these types of retailers provide deep discounts on their websites, they also provide home delivery stores, and they provide unique product launches that are exclusively launched through the e-commerce channel, such as mobile or other electronic devices. Examples of this are Amazon and alibaba.com.

You can say that the value a customer gets is of three types. However, you need the first two segments' direct offerings and experience-based offerings with the traditional way of selling goods and services to the customer. Wine price revenue offerings are a recent advancement in the retail industry that is threatening to disrupt the direct and experience-based offerings. There are various shortcomings in the direct product service offerings; for example, when a person walks into the store of a direct retailer, the customer does not have a choice of checking competitive prices of its rivals. Even in the experience-based offerings, where there are luxury stores and exclusive stores, they do not offer the comfort of choosing a product from home. A customer needs to walk into the companies exclusive or specialty store in order to choose its products. This limitation is being exploited by the online e-commerce retailers who are sharing the customers by giving them experience through videos and customer review videos of other buyers in order to let the customer choose between different competitive products.

In a typical retail store set up, there are some common departments like store management, marketing management, merchandising management, human resources management, finance and accounting management, and customer support. We will now look at how machine learning is being applied in some of these departments. An important thing to note is that the customer generally faces only the marketing department or the customer support department, and the rest of the departments work in the back end. From that perspective, I will first take up customer support and marketing management in retail organizations to discuss machine learning applications.

The Process of Technology Adoption in the Retail Sector

Figure 7-3 depicts the process of technology adoption taken from this book's healthcare section.

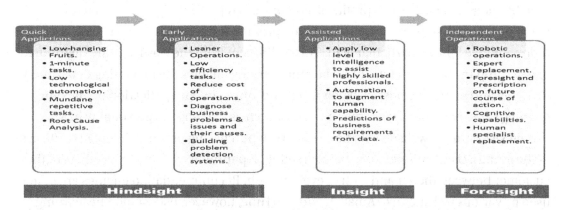

Figure 7-3. *Process of technology adoption*

In customer care and customer support, machine learning and artificial intelligence are being used by automating some of the customer service tasks, automating internal customer service processes, automating product deliveries, and automating the front office. Automation in customer service can happen through simple things like automated e-mail or SMS responses to the customer to automate the use of chatbots or robots for giving service to customers outside of normal operating hours. The intelligent use of machine learning in customer service will be the ability to predict the next customer complaint as soon as a customer buys the product as well as machine learning to find out the profile of a satisfied customer. Another application for customer service is where a customer logs a complaint and it is routed to skilled agents who are bots, and they provide recommended solutions just like any technician would do. If the resolution does not work for the customer, then the complaint is transferred to a human being. Customer service becomes more predictive when it is able to estimate when customer service calls will be at a peak, enabling the organization to gear up in taking those calls during those predicted times. In customer service, I will categorize the process of technology adoption at an early applications stage because it is currently replacing low-efficiency tasks, such as taking customer complaints and diagnosing the problems and issues faced by the customer and giving out simple solutions. It needs to move to the next level of assisted application, where it is able to apply intelligence and assist the highly skilled professionals who solve the next level of customer problems. It also needs to predict the business needs from the customer service data that it creates and has access to.

In marketing, machine learning is being applied by companies to profile the leads that they acquire and create a profile of similar sales representatives, and then the machine learning software matches both the profiles and recommends the best sales representative for that particular lead. This is different from the way leads are distributed in any company based on territory. Machine learning enables the marketing department to profile and match the best salespeople for the job. A similar application of machine learning is the creation of customer personas, such as creating the personality of a certain visitor to the website who has a history of purchasing products in the first 10 days of the month. Using this persona, the marketing department can customize offers to that customer between the 1st and 10th of every month. Recommendation engines are being used by various websites like Amazon and YouTube; however, using machine learning by creating customer personas and then recommending based on a match between the products and their persona adds more intelligence to a recommendation engine. A very common usage of robots is in customer care, where they are being adopted in retail stores or marketing offices that interact with the customers directly. This trend is going to increase because creating a bot and maintaining it is cost-effective and provides a unique experience to the customer as well. The bots will be able to answer anything, and they will be at a level where they will be able to convert just as any other human being. From the technology adoption perspective, this is still in the assisted applications stage, where low-level intelligence is being used by these parts and they have automated the human capability. They are able to predict business requirements based on data by giving the customers the related products that the company or organization offers.

In the current state of things, I do not see the technology at the level of independent operations as far as customer service and marketing is concerned. However, in another 5 to 6 years, we will be able to see the increasing trend of bot-based marketing, where the bots are used to interact intelligently with humans after reading, analyzing, interpreting, and intelligently understanding customers' data. The bots will be able to have an edge over the human marketers because they will have the ability to analyze process and take out meaningful information from the vast amount of data, which humans are not capable of handling.

The next department is the merchandising department. The key activities of the merchandising department in a retail store are purchasing the right product at the right price and at the right time. It is also responsible for inventory control or warehousing of products. Machine learning is being used to determine purchase cycles of a department store and find out the peak times when the customer demand for a particular product undergoes a spike. Stores can then be ready before the start of that peak demand activity. This is just one of the ways machine learning is helping purchase the right product at the right time. Another application on purchases is the use of robots in warehouses to intelligently store products that are faster moving near the exit doors, rather than those that have a higher storage life. The robots use algorithms like Markov chains in order to determine the fastest path to reach, move, and transport a particular product inside a huge warehouse. Instead of having people catalog and find a particular product in a huge warehouse facility spanning thousands of square meters, the robots intelligently move goods once they receive an order.

The Current State of Analytics in the Retail Sector

Descriptive Analytics: This field of analytics is invoked to know the answers to questions for projects that have already happened, such as what is the status of X Sales in the past?

Traditionally the retail sector has been using descriptive analytics to produce reports about its sales for any given product category, and this has had a big impact with the top management while making various decisions. Product-wise, sales reports product wise discount reports, store wise and product wise sales reports are some of the examples where descriptive analytics has been used traditionally. This trend is not going to go away. We will see the use of descriptive analytics in the retail sector; however, we will also see the emergence of other analytics, which I discuss in the next section.

Diagnostic Analytics: This type of analytics is used to know the root cause of a phenomenon, such as a project success or a failure. Why did the X Project fail? What are the positive lessons we can learn from this product launch success? All such questions can be answered using diagnostic analytics. In the retail sector, diagnostic analytics has also been used to analyze certain outcomes, such as failed product launches or successful product launches, and to find out the root cause of such successes and failures and then emulating them in the coming product launches. Diagnostic analytics also looks at the past and then tries to bring out the reasons for success or failure with the basic concept of the future follows the past. This may not always be true as the customer preferences and the environment to which the customer has been exposed keeps on changing. So we need to go to the next level of analytics, which is predictive in nature.

Predictive Analytics: This type of analytics is used for determining the outcome of an event in the future, such as project success or failure, project budget overrun, or a schedule slippage for an ongoing product launch. This analytics is something that brings about the actual ability to avoid situations in the future. For example, by using predictive analytics we can predict if a product launch is going to succeed or fail. There could be various parameters that the machine learning model code takes into account for analysis before coming to such a conclusion. However, the whole purpose is to give a sense to the top management on the direction that the business is going to take. Even this does not solve the problem, but it nearly tells or acts as a warning signal of a failure or a deviation from the plan in the future. In order to be able to do something about the deviation, we need the next level of analytics.

Prescriptive Analytics: In this field of analytics, the maximum value of analytics is achieved, as it builds upon the prediction made based on predictive analytics, and it prescribes actions that should be taken for the future. In prescriptive analytics, it uses machine learning to build a future plan of action that is based on past failures in similar situations, such as failed product launches, and gives out specific activities that need to be carried out in order for the product launch to be a success. With the retail sector getting prescriptive analytics, it is now truly able to do course corrections even before the failures happen. You may say that if a company does not fail in its retail operations, then it would see multiple growths happening. Yes, this is the aim of machine learning for moving from hindsight to foresight in retail operations.

## CHAPTER 8

Key Technological Advancements in Retail

Scenario 2025

In the not so distant future year of 2025, there lives a robotic engineer named Jenny. Her house is completely run by a house monitoring robot called GENIE. Jenny's house is equipped with a lot of smart common items, such as a smart refrigerator and smart cupboards. Jenny woke up and was made ready for the day by her house robot, which gave her a bath and prepared her breakfast. Like everyone else in the year 2025, Jenny works from her home office, which is upstairs. She moves upstairs to take an early morning conference call with her robot boss from her home office. She does not have to worry about ordering common household items and food since her entire house is smart and connected to her house monitoring robot. Her smart refrigerator creates a list of items that are getting exhausted, like butter, cheese, jam, etc. The machine learning application inside the smart refrigerator uses sensors and images to check on the number of items which need reordering. In this age, the smart refrigerator talks to Jenny and finds out her preferences for a new product, which she orders for herself. Based on this feedback, the refrigerator remembers and removes the things from the reordering list that Jenny does not like. Her house has smart cupboards that have smart containers for each common product, a separate smart jar for coffee beans, salt, sugar, etc. Smart containers weigh the quantity that is stored in them and flash an alert to the smart cupboard when they reach a perfect reorder threshold weight inside them. These tools aggregate all the orders at the end of the week and send them to the house GENIE. The house GENIE collect the orders from the smart refrigerator the smart cupboard and other such devices and then shows the complete order to Jenny. The house GENIE also finds out from the internet the current offers and discounts that are available for each of the products to be ordered and shows Jenny the cost savings that she can have by selecting them. After the house GENIE reports

© Puneet Mathur 2019

P. Mathur, *Machine Learning Applications Using Python*, https://doi.org/10.1007/978-1-4842-3787-8_8

the order list, it takes voice feedback from Jenny and makes modifications to the order and then places it. In this new modern world, all the retail stores have their own marketing robots that connect to the house monitoring robots and take orders. Drones are used by the retail stores to make home delivery of products. The items arrive at Jenny's home, and the house robot takes delivery after checking all the items through visual inspection—another use of visual machine learning. The biggest advantage for Jenny is that she does not have to be involved in mundane tasks, and the robots carry them out with efficiency. This is how the retail industry is going to change our society in the future.

Does this sound far-fetched or too distant?

Today it may sound like science fiction to you; however, in the near future this is going to turn into reality. Look at some of the technological advancements that have been made, and this will assure you that the future is going to help us do things more efficiently with the use of technology like artificial intelligence, machine learning, and robotics. Smart refrigerators that are shown in the 2025 scenario can use visual analytics by creating a simple machine learning-based deep neural network to identify whether an item in the refrigerator is nearing replenishment requirement. It can also have sensors to determine the distance of objects kept in the refrigerator from the walls. A robotic arm inside the refrigerator could help hold the product while it takes pictures of it to determine its level. Another thing that the smart refrigerator in our scenario needs is the ability to talk. The chatbot technology already exists where we have bots talking in a somewhat intelligent manner with the customers. However, machine learning will need to advance further in order to move from text-based conversion technologies to audio-based technologies. What I mean by this is the chatbots would need to understand the audio that is being transmitted to them by the user and would need to process the answers in real-time. The smart chatbot in the smart retail store will need to understand a narrow application of finding out the feedback from the user on a particular product inside it. This conversation with the user has to happen in order for the robot to determine if it needs to order this product again. It needs a programmed approach where it wakes up at a certain frequency, which the user of the smart refrigerator can set up using the home GENIE system, to let the smart refrigerator wake up and start collecting data for the next order. For example, a user can set a biweekly cycle to replenish the products inside the refrigerator. Once this is set, the smart refrigerator then reads the labels and scans the barcode to determine its contents. It determines and records the frequency at which a particular product is being used and gives a list of used products that have been in the refrigerator for a long time. This, of course, helps reduce the expenses that a person puts into buying products that they do not use. Such a report will definitely help the user in making better decisions.

Another application we saw was that of the IoT-enabled smart cupboard. This smart cupboard has a smart charge that stores certain products used by the household. There are sensors and machine learning applications inside the smart cupboard chips that wake up at a certain frequency and determine if any particular product needs to be re-ordered. The user sets the threshold for re-ordering a product; for example, rice stored in a smart jar can be re-ordered if its quantity reaches the threshold of 20 percent of the stored value. This alert is sent by the smart charge through the smart cupboard sensors, which record the alert and send it to the home GENIE system. The home GENIE collects all these awards and shows them to the customer once a day to get feedback from them. We have the technology now to implement search a scenario; however, some company needs to do actual research and then create such a system.

Narrow vs Broad Machine Learning in Retail

As we saw in the healthcare sector, there is a similar trend in the retail sector where there is suddenly a massive growth of narrow machine learning technologies rather than broad applications.

There is trend of falling footfall in the malls and people increasingly moving away from the best buy culture to selective-based buying culture. There is also a shift in peoples' buying patterns wherein they are no longer spending on clothes but they are spending more on travel gaming and other such entertainment activities [1; https://risnews.com/top-8-retail-trends-watch-2018].

In my opinion, this is not a surprising trend but something that the retail sector should have thought about and prepared itself for much more in advance. One of the reasons for moving away from experience-based buying to selective-based buying is the rise in traffic all over the world. The traffic conditions become horrible on weekends, with everyone trying to buy at the same time and clogging the roads. So people are opting for online home-based delivery models where the deliveries are made to their home without them having to venture into traffic.

In order to cater to such urban shoppers, the big malls will have to reinvent themselves by creating community self-driving stores. What I mean by this is that there are going to be mobile self-driving stores that would drive through a particular community based on their social media activity and give the option to that community to come out of their houses and buy the products instead of driving to the retail stores. The community-based self-driving retail store could be a big truck converted into a small shopping mall that is smart enough to track users' facial reactions to a particular product displayed inside it. Such a smart store would also record the customer's current color preferences and could talk to the customer by directing them to the colors similar to the one they are wearing. It could also gently ask the customer if they have any color preference. This is one example of how the retail sector is going to use technology to cater to the changing patterns and needs of the buyers. The smart store would also cater to returning customers of a particular community by knowing their preferences in advance. It could return with certain items ordered by the customer the last time they visited the smart community self-driving store when perhaps that product was not available. This type of store could be similar to Amazon Go, where a customer profile is used with a card to track what items they purchase during their visit to the smart community self-driving store. The store would declare its next visit through channels like social media promotion campaigns targeted to people living only in that community area based on their geo-location-mapping. This will bring the promotional costs down for the retail companies, as targeted promotions will help them reach only those who are likely to buy from the location near them.

The Current State of Retail Institutions Around the World

In Figure 7-1 you can see that we have three types of retail institutions. The first type is a typical brick and mortar organization. This is the traditional way of selling products by making the customer come to the store and then buy it products. Some brick and mortar organizations do have websites; however, those websites are only for giving information about their store's company and its products as well as to advertise promotional offers. Their main concentration is to bring the customer to the store.

The next type of retail institution is an online retailer. This type of retail organization has its primary concentration and focus on bringing the customer to its online store website. The online retailer uses social media blogs and other internet services to bring the customer to its website. Being an online retailer does not mean that they do not have a brick and mortar presence. This really means that brick and mortar is used for warehousing purposes and merchandising purposes only.

The third type of retailer is the retailer that has both brick and mortar stores and an online e-commerce site to serve its online customers. The advantage that a brick and mortar store gains by creating an online e-commerce site is that of credibility. The shoppers who have been to the stores of that company know the company very well, and since they have been loyal returning customers they know the products that they buy from these stores. So it is convenient for such a customer to order frequently used or purchased items from a brick and mortar store through its online website. Increasingly most of the brick and mortar stores are moving to this business model due to falling footsteps of the customers.

To explain to you the current state of retail institutions around the world, let us take the example of a big retail store chain in the US. TJX is a big US retailer with a revenue of more than 33 million US dollars annually and 35,000 employees overall. It has eight divisions. Its operations of retail stores span across the world in countries like Canada, the UK, and Europe. It primarily deals in products like clothing, footwear, wedding items, food, furniture, jewelry, beauty products, and housewares. This retail giant has various brands, such as TJMaxx, HomeGoods, HomeSense, Marshalls, Sierra Post, and Winners. Marshalls is a brand that concentrates on fashion, home goods, and other accessories and is a brick and mortar retail store chain of the TJX group. TJMaxx is another of the brands that does not offer online sales. Similarly HomeGoods retail store brand of the TJX group does not offer an online shopping facility. The TJX group has another set of retail stores that follow the hybrid model by having stores as well as an online facility to buy goods, including Sierra Trading Post, which has clothing and footwear for men, women, and kids as well as furnishings, jewelry, home, and fashion items on sale. A customer can look at its offerings online and order them for delivery to their homes. TJX has another brand of retail stores related to style and fashion clothing known as Winners, which also does not give any online option to buy its products. You have to go to a Winners store to check out its new arrivals and then make a buying decision. Similarly, TJX has another brand of retail stores called HomeSense, which also does not offer any online shopping facility.

Another example of a brick and mortar retail chain that has now provided the facility for the customer to buy through e-commerce internet sites is Home Depot, which offers home furnishings, upholstery, and other home services both through its retail stores and online website. Walmart is also an example of a similar store that has a huge brick and mortar presence; however, it is now allowing customers the option of ordering online. Made in America is also an example of a store that has both a brick and mortar presence and online facility to shop its goods.

Importance of Machine Learning in Retail

The retail sector is different from most of the other sectors because it depends on activity, on logistics, or on supply chain management. This is also a factor where large organizations like TJX, Walmart, and Macy's—to name just a few—have a lot of in-house data from customers being generated every minute. Billing happens as long as the store remains open, and every customer will have a huge amount of data. Target was one of the first stores to build an accurate model to predict what a customer would buy next. In a story that was published in the media, Target was in the middle of a controversy where its machine learning systems were able to predict the pregnancy of a teenage girl even before her father became aware of her pregnancy. The store collects data about every customer that is linked to their credit card, name, or e-mail address, and they create a bucket of the items a person is buying at their store. Using the buying patterns of pregnant ladies, it was able to detect a pattern where pregnant ladies were buying scented lotions around the beginning of their second trimester. So the machine learning system was able to profile a pregnant woman as a shopper because of a sudden spike in buying lots of scent-free soap, extra big cotton balls, hand sanitizers, and washcloths. Target used this data to send the pregnant ladies specific coupons around the times when specific stages of their pregnancies were predicted by its system. In this case, the system was so accurately able to predict the pregnancy of a teenage girl in Minneapolis that its systems sent out offers to the teenage girl about baby clothes and cramps. When the father saw this in the mail, he became furious and went and spoke to the Target store manager angrily, and the manager apologized. However, when the father talked to his daughter after going home, she revealed that she was pregnant. The father later apologized and said you know what is going on in my house better than I do [2; https://www.forbes.com/sites/kashmirhill/2012/02/16/how-target-figured-out-a-teen-girl-was-pregnant-before-her-father-did/#4a9c59c86668]. This is a classic example where technology is being used through machine learning and is predicting peoples' events based on their buying behavior. It also raises issues of data privacy and the fact that by mining data, large corporations are trying to control people's lives. All these concerns need to be sorted out before machine learning in retail actually starts predicting every aspect of human life.

Personally, on social media, I see no people complaining about a complete erosion of privacy the moment they step out of their houses. There are reported cases where a family goes to a restaurant, is about to order, is discussing what they would like to have, and the man utters the word "pizza" many times while in conversation with his daughter. Suddenly he receives an SMS on his mobile device saying that the restaurant in which he is sitting is giving him a 25% discount on pizza if he orders it today. He is stunned that he has just said pizza several times to his daughter and now he has received an offer for the pizza. This overuse of technology looks good from a retailer perspective; however, from the customer perspective this means that their conversation inside a restaurant is not just being heard and recorded but is also being analyzed and acted upon. Machine learning and audio analytics make this possible. Before this machine learning technology goes mainstream and is applied to every retail counter, the privacy issues need to be addressed.

The important thing to note is that this kind of application of technology is simply not capable of being applied through a human being. Human beings cannot discover patterns from such a huge amount of data. In order to discover an event like pregnancy among ladies, a company like Target or Walmart would need petabytes of data in order to discover frequent patterns among them. The training data also would need to be fairly accurate in order to make an accurate prediction. Because, as the saying goes, garbage in, garbage out. This would require the customers to be able to give permission to the store to analyze and reach conclusions.

Now I take you through a survey done online with experts from the retail industry on finding out through the Delphi Method which segments of the industry would fall under the level of technology adoption. This survey is very similar to the survey done in the healthcare section of this book. The key segments identified in a preliminary survey by the retail experts are store management systems, digital commerce, supply chain management, merchandising, and customer management. The purpose of carrying out this survey is to bring to the reader a clear understanding of where the technology adoption maturity lies in each area of retail. The experts are dispersed across organizations with brick and mortar stores, online retailers, and hybrid organizations.

Some of the key areas where retail has machine learning applications are:

1. **STORE MANAGEMENT SYSTEMS**

2. **DIGITAL COMMERCE**

3. **SUPPLY CHAIN**

4. **MERCHANDISING**

5. **CUSTOMER MANAGEMENT**

The store management systems involve managing the internal arrangement of various products on the store shop floor. It also involves the use of skills to display the most attractive offers near the areas customers frequent more. This has largely been an area where a store manager uses their own experience to position the most lucrative offers in front of the customers. Not only that, store management involves classifying goods into similar categories and putting them together so that it is easier for the customer to compare among different brands of the same product. Although this sounds like a simple activity, if you consider the fact that any large store anywhere around the world has thousands of products in different categories to display, it almost turns out to be a nightmare for the store management. Filling up the product on the shelves from warehouse inventory is also something that needs careful handling. All over the world, store managers have been experimenting with store shop floor designs and displays that attract the customers the most. Determining products that have a seasonal promotional value such as Christmas displays and gift items during December or any other local or regional festival is also the job of store management. This activity has largely been a human-driven activity that requires some skills and experience to know what works and what does not work in increasing sales for the stores.

Digital commerce is a fast-growing area and something that most customers would migrate to in the near future. Most of the brick and mortar stores have now got their own websites, like Walmart has walmart.com, TJX has TJx.com, Macy's has macys. com, and Target has target.com. When a company extends its services from a brick and mortar setup, it is easier for it to ship products to people's homes. The company has saved on warehousing of goods, which an exclusive online retailer would need to do. The added advantage that a brick and mortar store offers is that it has a loyal customer base that keeps on coming back for more orders. So when a customer orders products from such stores, they know that they can go to a physical store and lodge a complaint with their customer service desk if the product sent to them is not up to the mark. The online retailers such as amazon.com and alibaba.com do not have any major physical store presence; however, they have the use of machine learning to give better recommendations to a user based on their past buying patterns.

Supply chain management deals with the logistics that are essential for retail store to function. It has the back-end activity that a customer does not see directly and involves keeping the suppliers of thousands and millions of products connected and updated with upcoming requirements. Orders with the suppliers are placed in advance by the major retail chains so that the inventory does not dry up in any of the stores. The critical thing to note here is that a poor supply chain system can cost a retail store chain millions of lost dollars. If more products are ordered than what the market demands, it would lead to stocking up of more materials, and this would increase the warehousing cost to the retail store company. If fewer products are ordered than what the market demands, then it will lead to customer dissatisfaction. That is why supply chain management is said to be the heart of the retail industry. Some stores follow the practice of having warehouses closer to their store locations; however, some store chains follow the practice of having stores near their suppliers. Both the approaches have worked for different companies, and there is no right or wrong formula for working out this critical activity.

Merchandising is another very important activity that determines if the store will be profitable or not. I say this because merchandising involves ensuring that the store is properly stocked in inventory and that the products are priced competitively. A merchandiser who works behind the scenes in retail store chains ensures that they are up to date with consumer sales trends, allowing them to buy the type of products at a price that is right for the retail chain to make a profit. To give you an example, planning for a Christmas sale starts at least 6 months in advance by the merchandising managers who plan by buying a particular type of products looking at past Christmas sales reports and new product launches that align with Christmas sales. They also determine what kind of products get prioritized in store displays so that the customer is attracted toward them in order to make a favorable buying decision. The key skill that a merchandising manager has is that of negotiating the lowest price of inventory items that are bought by the retail chain. Scheduling the buy is an important skill that merchandising managers use in order to ensure that the stores are stocked with the right goods at the right time. The merchandising experts in major retail store chains ensure that they know which merchandising strategies will appeal most to the customers as they keep abreast of the consumer changes or buying patterns that are happening throughout the year. Merchandising also includes evaluation and monitoring of merchandise cost and negotiating contracts for a win-win situation.

Customer management involves getting new customers and increasing the loyalty of existing customers. This segment of a retail store chain monitors the new flow of customers to the store to ensure that there is revenue growth for the store chain. Old customers who come back to buy more products are equally important because they make repeated purchases and spread good word about the brand. If a store has only new customers coming in with a decline in old customers, then this shows that the promotional schemes run by the store are effective, but when a customer buys goods from the store chain they are not happy with the experiences. In such a situation, after some time even the new customer flow will stop as a bad word-of-mouth will spread about the store chain. Having a scenario where only old customers are coming in and very few new customers visit the store is also not a very healthy situation. This shows that the promotional schemes of the store chain are not being accepted by new customers, and it is possible that they are going to compete because of better offers. In such a scenario the old customers, when they see the better offers in the market, might also move toward the new competitors and slowly abandon the store chain. So in both the cases, the store chain loses business. Customer management practices in any store chain should really take care of both the old customers and ensure that new customers also come in with competitive offers in the market. Now let us look at the survey and its research methodology.

> **Research objective:** The primary objective of this research is to use expert opinion in finding out and mapping two parameters of artificial intelligence and machine learning: (1) the current technology maturity level of artificial intelligence and machine learning in the key areas of retail industry and (2) the technology adoption process inside the retail industry.

> There were 16 initial key areas identified by the expert groups in the first iteration. These areas were then reiterated with the expert group to find out among them important demo areas that would evolve in the future. The expert group was able to identify five areas in retail that would be important for the retail industry to

advance further. The research study does not provide the results of this iterative selection of the key areas, but it starts from the point where the experts have selected these five key areas. I have already discussed in this chapter those five areas, from store management to customer management.

Research sample: The group of experts that was selected were from a total population of 125 experts. The experts were comprised of retail professionals who had worked in the industry for more than 20 years at positions from customer care, to a management expert in a retail institution, a director of a retail facility, chief executive officer of a retail organization, or academic professors who had worked on research in the retail industry with accepted and published papers. I have covered all the experts from each of the areas in retail such as supply chain management, customer care, merchandising, CEOs, and AI experts—to name just a few. A total of 20 such professionals shortlisted for this study. There were no absentees nor attrition in this study.

Information needed: In order to make decisions and to support them, various secondary data (e.g., published papers on the state of machine learning and AI in retail) were provided; some examples are those of Target or Walmart. The required information in order to create a map between the two parameters mentioned earlier was based on the experts' understanding of the current state of technology implementation in the five areas starting from store management through customer management. To make the decision-making of the expert explanations on the levels of technological maturity the phase-wise identification of technology was provided to them. Beyond this there was no other information provided, so care was taken not to create a bias in the minds of the experts. The information needed for this study was contextual, theoretical, and expert knowledge. There was also a requirement for the experts to use their tacit or inherent knowledge, which they possess from being associated with the retail industry for so long.

Research Design Overview:

The primary steps involved in this research are the following:

1. Define objectives of the research.

2. Find experts who are willing to help in this research study.

3. Design questionnaires that will gather information and involve less writing effort by the experts.

4. Administer the questionnaires to the experts.

5. Gather responses to the questionnaires and analyze them to see if consensus has been achieved.

6. Iterate and administer more questionnaires until the experts reach a consensus on a particular key area.

7. Once a consensus is reached, move on to the next key area and reiterate the questionnaire until a consensus is reached. Until the time consensus is reached, more information is provided based on the previous responses provided by the experts.

8. Analyze and create a map of the technical maturity levels and phases of adoption of AI and machine learning.

Data Collection Methods

Literature regarding retail was not a data to be collected for this study. The test study that was conducted (which I mentioned earlier) was that of taking expert help in narrowing down from 16 to 5 key areas that are going to be important for the future of the retail industry. This is an important thing because in our study expert we are using judgment on what is going to be the focus of the retail industry based on their past experience. We have used the Delphi Method of study from a paper entitled "The Delphi Method" by Chittu Okoli and Suzanne De Poweski as a research tool, example, design, consideration, and applications [1; https://www.academia.edu/399894/The_Delphi_Method_As_a_ Research_Tool_An_Example_Design_Considerations_and_Applications] as it is the best research tool for collecting expert opinions for our study.

The questionnaire method was used for data collection from the experts through e-mail and online administration of surveys.

Data Analysis

During a particular iteration when the data was collected, Microsoft Excel software was used to record the expert's response in a tabular format. For any given key area, a graph was made to check whether there was a consensus reached, and if the graph showed sufficiently well that there was consensus, then the iteration was stopped. So the data analysis was done manually with the help of computer software. The mapping of technology maturity and phases of technology adoption was undertaken using Excel software to create a technology map graph. This was also done with the help of Microsoft Excel.

Ethical Considerations

It is possible that bias could have slipped into the study had we not made sure that the results and the responses of the experts were kept anonymous and did not affect the outcome of this study. So due care was taken to ensure that the experts were not known among themselves. As I have already mentioned, there are in the retail industry two groups of people: one whose members like technology and the other whose members do not like technology. We did not do an expert selection based on these specific criteria, so this study could very well be biased on such grounds and we have not tested for this.

Limitations of the Study

Qualitative research has as its biggest limitation that of not being able to exactly quantify the outcome of the future, and this is very much applicable to our study as well. However, by using categorical variables in our questionnaires, we have tried to take the quantitative analysis of our outcome as well. Mapping of the technological adoption and understanding of the technological maturity is not something that a normal human being can do unless they have been associated with the industry; that is why we chose experts to carry out the study. However, it is possible that some of the experts may not have sufficient knowledge or exposure to the advances in artificial intelligence and machine learning. We acknowledge that this could be a limitation to the study.

Examining the Study

We already know from Figure 1-1 from this book that there are four phases of technology adoption. In Figure 8-1 we look at this mapping.

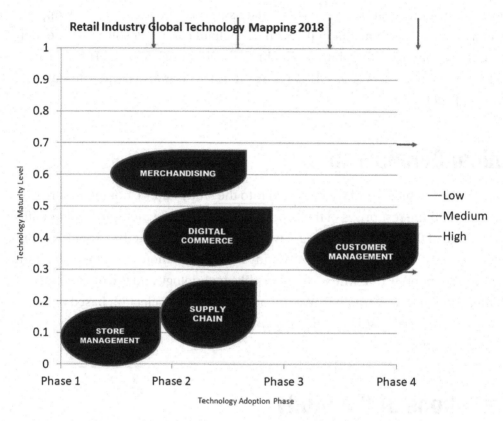

Figure 8-1. *Retail industry technology adoption phases*

From Figure 8-1, there are two axes: the x-axis represents the technology adoption phase as outlined in Figure 8-1 and the y-axis represents the technology maturity level. The technology maturity application level. **The maturity application level is divided into Low, Medium, and High. Low means the technology is at a research stage and is not in production yet. Medium means the technology has been implemented in production with some hits and misses and needs more research to move into mainstream production. High means the technology is well-researched and is ready to move into production or is being used in a production environment,** such as retail stores, etc.

Presented here is data in tables and figures with its analysis of the Delphi Method of research.

Table 8-1. *Data on Delphi Method of Research Used in the Study*

Topic	No of retail Experts		No of Iterations
Delphi Method	Invited	Shortlisted	
Current Application of AI & ML in retail	125	20	4
Future Application of AI & ML in retail	125	20	5

We have already discussed this data in the methodology section of this chapter. Now we look at the data and its graphical representation regarding the parameter of technology maturity level of AI and machine learning in retail.

Now we look at State of AI & ML in Store Management in Retail sector in Figure 8-2.

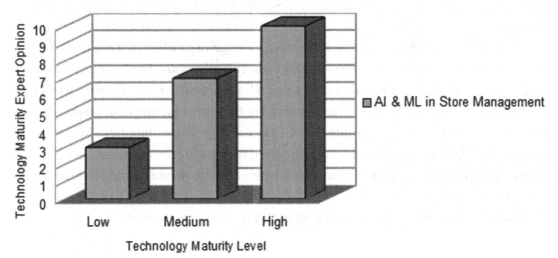

Figure 8-2. *State of AI and ML in store management*

In the area of store management, with regards to the first parameter of technology maturity levels of AI and machine learning in the retail industry, 50 percent of the experts felt that it has a high level of maturity. The identification of store management at the high level of maturity means that the technology has been implemented in this area of production and it is being used in mainstream production. A good example of this area would be The Robot Merchandiser employed by Best Buy stores, known as "chloe" (`https://www.businessinsider.in/I-went-to-Best-Buy-and-encountered-a-robot-named-Chloe-and-now-I'm-convinced-shes-the-future-of-retail/30-seconds-later-she-brought-me-my-purchase-and-passed-the-DVD-to-me-through-a-chute-/slideshow/49507844.cms`).

The robot communicates with the store customers using a touchscreen and is able to get them their selected products for purchase within 30 seconds. The Chloe test was started in 2015 in the Chelsea neighborhood of New York. The test robot looks more like an automated industrial arm but is able to communicate through a screen it displays behind a glass screen for its posting. In this robotics store, the floor robot has completely replaced employees and retrieves merchandise for its customers every day. It is able to travel the entire floor space inside the store. There is intelligence in the Chloe robot where it is able to track customer buying patterns and is able to predict buying of fresh inventory for products that have a high demand.

Even Walmart is deploying robots for store management where it has successfully tested shelf scanning robots in a few of its stores. The robots are 2 feet tall and they use a camera to check if any items are out of stock. The robots also check for wrong prices or missing labels on items. They are connected to the store management system so that a human can look at any problem, such as missing prices or incorrect prices for stocks. The robots are programmed to stop when they see a customer approaching. This is an application of assisted operations where the robots are helping humans do a better job.

Now let us look at another area: digital health records in Figure 8-3.

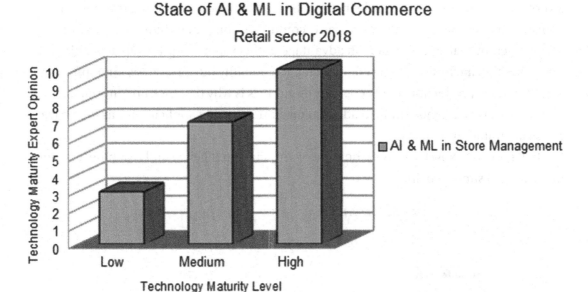

Figure 8-3. *State of AI and ML in digital commerce*

Our experts conclude that this is at a high state of technological maturity, with 80 percent of our experts concluding this opinion. We can see in Figure 8-3 that some of them (about 15 percent) also feel that the level of maturity is at a medium level. Medium means that the technology is not yet moved into mainstream production and has had a few hits and misses here and there. However, high state means that the research has moved into production.

North Face, which is an outdoor clothing retailer, is using machine learning-based IBM Watson engine on its website to personalize the shopping experience of its online customers. Download the app on their phone and speak right into the app just like you would speak to a human salesperson. The virtual salesperson asks a series of questions of the customer that helps them in learning the customer's preferences and offers products matching the customer's needs. Another good application of machine learning is the great recommendations engine at amazon.com. Another good example of the use of machine learning by an e-commerce retailer is shown in how Netflix uses big data and machine learning to study how a film is consumed by the viewer, including studying the release of full seasons of episodes of shows and when to auto-play the next episode and optimize recommendations related to a particular film. Machine learning at Netflix is saving them 1 million US dollars per year. This is over and above the revenue increase they get out of recommending products and auto-playing the next show or film. This is a very intelligent use of machine learning, where it is not only increasing revenue for the company but also reducing its costs. The e-commerce companies have been quick to adopt machine learning and gain an advantage as their operations are already digital. It only takes the machine learning engineer team to identify business areas for application and then write production-ready code for them. This is why the brick and mortar companies take a lot more time to adapt to machine learning applications, as they have physical limitations to tackle.

In Figure 8-4, Now we look at the state of artificial intelligence and machine learning in the area of supply chain.

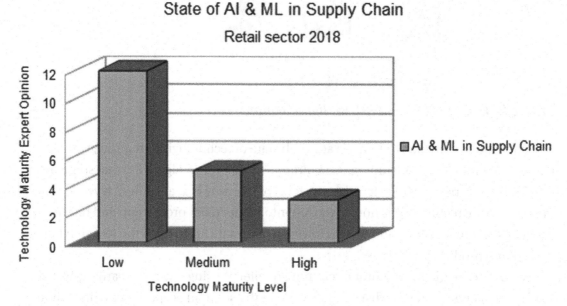

Figure 8-4. *State of AI and ML in supply chain*

After the five iterations our experts told us that the technology adoption maturity is at a very low level; 60 percent of our experts tell us with certainty that this is the case. The area of supply is also known as logistics. Machine learning is being supplied by Amazon where it is used in forecasting, planning, and optimizing in real time the millions of goods needed at fulfillment network. Amazon applied machine learning to large volumes of data for different problems: Recommendations, sales operations, planning, automating, and machine learning, wherein it identifies search products that to be ordered through its suppliers based on forecast.

Walmart is using AI and machine learning in the way it delivers its products to the customers. It is using machine learning for its Walmart associate deliveries program in which machine learning selects the best route to deliver orders more efficiently to its customers. This is helping shoppers to avoid checkout lines at Walmart stores. Walmart uses machine learning to learn what the customers want and then making it available at the right price at the right time and at the right place [4; https://scsolutionsinc.com/news/Walmart-turns-to-ai-to-serve-you-better].

Now we look at another key area—that of merchandising in Figure 8-5.

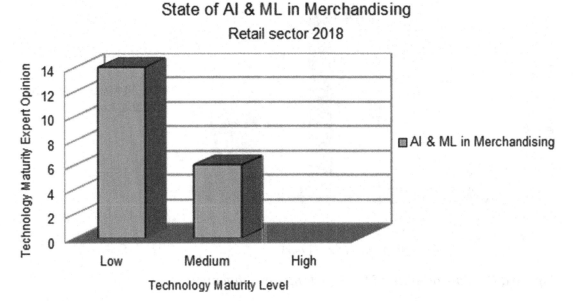

Figure 8-5. *State of AI and ML in merchandising*

We can clearly see that our experts tell us that the technology maturity is at a low level. Sixty-seven percent of our experts felt this was so after four rounds of iteration, when a consensus was reached. One good example of this is the Manthan Systems case study [5] on merchandise analytics used by a retail corporation in Peru that successfully utilized merchandizing data by implementing machine learning on it. The solution by Manthan was able to utilize 350 Gigabytes of unused data in its data warehouse, and the data discovered patterns by generating reports based on season and comparing various trend analysis. Through this system, using merchandise analytics on current data communication with the suppliers also became very easy as the stock in hand, sales forecast, and the current purchases for all were put together in the same system in order to predict the demand in the future [5; https://www.manthan.com/downloads/case-studies/Ripley-peru.pdf].

We now look at an interesting application of artificial intelligence and machine learning in the area of customer management in Figure 8-6.

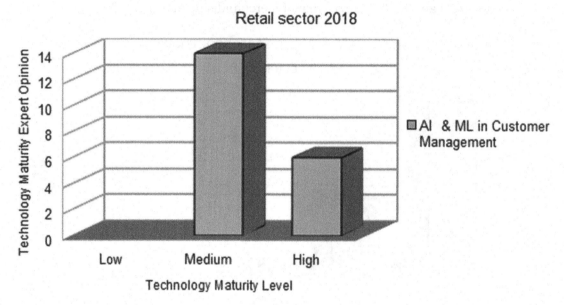

Figure 8-6. *State of AI and ML in customer management*

Our experts told us after four iterations that the technological maturity in this area is at the medium stage, and 70 percent of our experts concluded this. We all know about the customer product recommendation engine from amazon.com that has helped it generate 55 percent of repeat orders. The recommendation engine is a nice online replacement for a physical salesperson. Here, however, there is hardly anybody to talk to and a person just gets a notification on the screen about a recommended product. It is not easy to show recommendations just like that, but there has to be machine learning applied to it so that a customer gets to see a recommendation that they will actually buy. Merely showing what the customer has last purchased from the store is not a good recommendation. We see this goof up happening on many websites that claim to use machine learning for recommending products to existing customers. The real crux of a good recommendation engine is to create a business model after studying data from millions of users and then studying their behavior patterns with products that are generally bought together. After unearthing such patterns we can hope that the machine learning algorithm will recommend something that a person will buy. The current searches that a person is trying to do for the product should not be the only influence for what is being recommended to the customer. We will look at creating a recommendation engine, although at a very small scale, so that you get an idea of what an actual recommendation engine would entail. Another customer management use of machine learning is the creation of chatbots. Good examples of chatbots are eBay and Sephora. At eBay it is known as a shopbot, a virtual personal shopping assistant that helps people find items they want by giving certain details like price and description [6; `https://ww.ebay.com`].

Phases of Technology Adoption in Retail, 2018

Now we move on to the second parameter of our research study, which is that of phases of technology adoption in retail (which I have already discussed in Chapter 1), where we have four phases from the quick applications phase to the independent operations phase. After analyzing we can see from Figure 8-7 that for the use of artificial intelligence and machine learning in store management, 40 percent of our experts say that it is in the Phase 2 level.

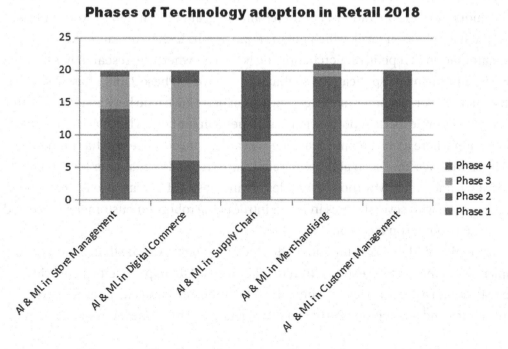

Figure 8-7. *Phases of technology adoption in the retail industry, 2018*

You will recall that I have classified Phase 2 as early applications, where the machine learning is being used for problem detection systems and automating low-efficiency tests. The focus is to diagnose the root cause of business problems. Our experts have classified digital commerce as the Phase 3 stage, which means it has reached assisted applications. You will recall when a technology is in the assisted applications, as it has a good level of automation, it uses a low level of intelligence, and it is just skilled professionals. In our case, they could be merchandising professionals, store managers, customer care people, or marketing staff. We have seen through this retail section where I have shown you that customer care is trying to implement robotic operations by putting robots in front of the customer for service. However, for digital commerce that is more or less automated, we are yet to see robots independently managing the operations of websites without use of human specialists in the background. This is the reason why our experts have classified its technology as assisted applications. Next we look at supply chain management, and it is classified as a high Phase 4 level of implementation, according to 55 percent of our experts. Supply chain management involves use of property operations, and we have seen that there is a very high use of robots at the warehouses of Amazon, Walmart, and other retail giants that are using machine learning algorithms like Markov chains to optimize their inventory storage. This is the reason why our experts have classified this technology as reaching independent robotic operations. For merchandising, after five iterations our experts have put it as a Phase 1 level, which means applications technology automation and automation of repetitive merchandising is an area where the research has to be done for improving its applications so that it can move to Phase 2 and Phase 3 stages subsequently. For customer management, our experts have a tie between Phase 3 and Phase 4, with our experts reporting back at 40 percent for both. The phase is assisted application where a the machine learning is at an advanced stage and has predictive ability as well. We have seen abilities of retail stores to predict customer buying behavior in advance and that is why those examples are in Phase 4. They are also in customer management, with several stores in Japan introducing robots for customer service and greeting customers on the floor.

With this, I end the presentation of the study that took me more than 3 months to implement along with the experts from retail industry. I do hope that it will provide the reader with a concise view of where the retail industry stands with respect to its applications and adaptation of artificial intelligence and machine learning.

End Notes

[1] https://www.academia.edu/399894/The_Delphi_Method_As_a_
     Research_Tool_An_Example_Design_Considerations_and_
     Applications

[2] https://www.businessinsider.in/I-went-to-Best-Buy-and-
     encountered-a-robot-named-Chloe-and-now-

[3] Chloe Robot at Best Buy Stores: https://www.businessinsider.
     in/I-went-to-Best-Buy-and-encountered-a-robot-
     named-Chloe-and-now-I'm-convinced-shes-the-future-
     of-retail/30-seconds-later-she-brought-me-my-
     purchase-and-passed-the-DVD-to-me-through-a-chute-/
     slideshow/49507844.cms

[4] https://scsolutionsinc.com/news/Walmart-turns-to-ai-to-
     serve-you-better

[5] https://www.manthan.com/downloads/case-studies/Ripley-
     peru.pdf

[6] https://ww.ebay.com

CHAPTER 9

How to Implement Machine Learning in Retail

The three most promising areas in retail are:

- **Retail consumer buying patterns**

- **Customer management**

- **Supply chain management**

In the retail industry, the top-most item that has huge potential is applying machine learning to understand retail consumer buying patterns. Although there have been some advancements in this area, such as the creation of recommendation engines, this is just the tip of the iceberg. Consumer buying patterns are a human behavior that needs better understanding by a machine in order for it to derive any benefit out of data. A buyer purchased a product due to an inherent need, does some kind of a research on the type of product, evaluates the various purchasing alternatives, and then makes a buying decision. Although this looks simple, think about a time when you had to buy something recently and how you went about buying that product. The fact that you recognized the need to buy the product was just the starting point. You could have Googled about the product or asked your friends and family who might have used that product for their opinions. If you were searching for a movie, then you would have looked at the various movie reviews online or in many mobile apps. Once you have done your research and are convinced that you should buy this product, you could then look at the various alternatives from where you could purchase this product, including online sales or brick and mortar stores. That time available to you for buying the product is also

© Puneet Mathur 2019

P. Mathur, *Machine Learning Applications Using Python*, https://doi.org/10.1007/978-1-4842-3787-8_9

an important decision-making criteria. For example, if you do not have time to go to a brick and mortar store, you would prefer buying the product online. After evaluation of alternatives, you then make the buying decision. In order to understand this consumer buying pattern, a machine needs to learn how human beings make a buying decision. Machine learning can be used for implementing marketing personalization. This involves understanding the buying needs of the customer and then creating a customized promotional offer to that target customer. Another way in which machine learning is being applied is by learning the past buying behavior of consumers and then giving recommendations to them. E-commerce stores like amazon.com have been successfully doing this. Matching products to a consumer preference with the machine learning algorithms can play a crucial role in determining the right positioning of brands to the right consumers. This is an area where a lot more research needs to be done and commerce applications need to be built. Two sales strategies that can be used to provide offers to customers by recognizing their behavior patterns are upsell and cross-sell. Upsell is when a customer is given choices for more premium, better-quality products than the one that is initially chosen by the customer. Cross-selling is giving the customer an alternative of existing brands from the one chosen by the customer. Both these strategies can be included in the recommendation engine in order to test and create a good promotional offer recommendation system.

In customer management the organization is looking to implement a strategy right from the stage of acquiring a new customer to creating or promoting brand loyalty at the first purchase and then to implementing a strategy for repeat purchases. Using machine learning to understanding new and changing buying needs of the customers, looking at the competitive products and their offerings, and then giving promotional offers that are better than that of the competition can be done by implementing online sentiment analysis toward competitive products and data mining for those sentiments that lead to a buying behavior. For example, in sentiment analysis done for a competitive product, we may find out that a promotional campaign run by the rival organization using a particular celebrity has given a boost to the sales of that company. Now in order to be successful, our company will also have to do something similar in order to acquire new customers. Such an intelligent use of machine learning can help greatly in marketing intelligence strategies. A deep analysis of data from first-time buyers can yield a lot of benefits on how and why first-time customers make their buying decisions with a particular company. Using machine learning on such data sets can give you hidden buying patterns that have not been explored so far. Loyal customer data sets are from those customers who buy repeatedly from a particular organization. We can do data mining to understand and unearth critical buying patterns. In this chapter, we are going to see one such example of the implementation of data mining in which we will be unearthing the hidden dimensions of consumer buying patterns using clustering in unsupervised learning.

Using machine learning to give effective promotional offers is another aspect where machine learning can be used for boosting sales. If an organization creates a database of past promotional offers and the consumer's actions based on their background, it can help a machine learning application to unearth those patterns that constitute a successful promotional offer. For example, office-goers like offers that involve using the company's app to buy their products.

Machine learning in supply chain management is hard because the physical movement of goods and services is involved in this process. While implementing machine learning for improving the supplied parameters, we need a lot of data, such as the lead times from suppliers to calculate the optimum inventory, etc. The data source may come from different systems, which is the primary challenge for implementing machine learning in supply chain management, and adding to this complexity is the fact that data on supplies is used in database systems with very different formats and processes. For example, vendor data may come from the procurement management system, while data on transportation may come from transport management system. In some cases, the data may result in external systems that do not talk to the company's supply chain systems directly. Another challenge for such diverse data is that of data provenance, where the quality of data and its accuracy is in question. The biggest challenge for implementing machine learning for supply chain management is creating a single repository that has up-to-date data and that has been cleansed properly. If you fail to create a supply chain management application in machine learning you will have to architect a machine learning solution that has middleware database management capabilities as well as the ability to integrate various sources of data within minutes.

Implementing Machine Learning Life Cycle in Retail

Now I am going to take you through an implementation of machine learning in the retail industry. Here, I am going to use the unsupervised learning technique to show you how to do data mining with a retail data set. The data set used in this example is fictitious and suitable for you to understand how to use it. We are aware of the unsupervised learning technique and we have a solution architecture in mind; however, it has not been found because we do not know what model we are going to build into the steps of data preparation, which is given in Chapter 3. Machine learning life cycle. At this stage after data preparation, such as cleaning up and pre-processing the data, we are stuck at the step on exploratory data analysis in order to find any patterns in the retail data set. I want you to understand that at this stage we are not looking at building a solution or a model, but we are asking if there are any patterns in the available data set. We are mining the data to make any meaning out of it. Here the focus is on the machine finding out any patterns or dimensions in the data set versus re-defining any predefined learning to the machine as we do in a supervised learning technique. I will only be showing you how to build an unsupervised model with the retail data set; however, at the end of this exercise, you will get the dimensions, if any, that can be further used to develop a supervised learning model. Generally, we use unsupervised learning techniques to unearth buying patterns and then create prediction models based on the dimensions that have been discovered using unsupervised learning. I will help you to use supervised learning and create a model similar to what I did in Chapter 3 using the data that is being developed by applying unsupervised learning technique. This will help you implement in the real-time production environment once you start working on a live retail data set. This data set is in the form of a flat file, which is available at the following URL: `http://www.PuneetMathur.me/Book009/`. Let us now jump into implementing unsupervised learning on this data set.

Information   All the code used in this exercise is tested for compatibility with Python 2.7 in Anaconda environment. It should work on 3.x as well; however, it has not been tested.

Unsupervised Learning

In Listing 9-1, I have first suppressed some basic warnings about import of libraries from matplotlib otherwise a lot of warnings makes it impossible to interpret results. Before we proceed further, let me explain the structure of the code. I have divided this code into two parts: the first part is all the functions that we need for data visualization and processing, such as PCA output, the output the Y plotter, and channel output; and the second part of the code is where the actual implementation of unsupervised learning technique occurs. In the second part, I use step-by-step summation of the previously defined functions and use force and features to figure out hidden dimensional patterns in this retail data set.

Listing 9-1. Importing Necessary Libraries

```
import warnings
warnings.filterwarnings("ignore", category = UserWarning, module =
"matplotlib")
warnings.filterwarnings("ignore", category = UserWarning, module = "cross_
validation")
# Importing libraries
import matplotlib.pyplot as plt
import matplotlib.cm as cm
import pandas as pd
import numpy as np
import pandas.plotting
```

Let me now try to explain the four functions that I have defined in the first part of the code given in Listing 9-2.

Listing 9-2. Function to Output PCA Results

```
def pcaOutput(good_data, pca):
    '''
    Visualizing the PCA results and calculating explained variance
    '''

    # I am doing Dimension indexing through pca components
    dims = dims = ['Dimension {}'.format(i) for i in range(1,len
    (pca.comps_)+1)]

    # Creating the PCA components pandas dataframe from the dimensions
    comps = pd.DataFrame(np.round(pca.comps_, 4), columns =
    good_data.keys())
    comps.index = dims

    # Calculating PCA explained variance for each component
    ratios = pca.explained_variance_ratio_.reshape(len(pca.comps_), 1)
    variance_ratios = pd.DataFrame(np.round(ratios, 4), columns =
    ['Explained Variance'])
    variance_ratios.index = dims
```

```
# Creating a bar plot visualization for better understanding
fig, ax = plt.subplots(figsize = (14,8))

# Plotting the feature weights as a function of the components
comps.plot(ax = ax, kind = 'bar');
ax.set_ylabel("Feature Weights")
ax.set_xticklabels(dims, rotation=0)

# Displaying the explained variance ratios
for i, ev in enumerate(pca.explained_variance_ratio_):
    ax.text(i-0.40, ax.get_ylim()[1] + 0.05, "Explained Variance\n
    %.4f"%(ev))

# Returning back a concatenated DataFrame
return pd.concat([variance_ratios, comps], axis = 1)
```

The PCA output function gives results of the principal component analysis run
on the retail status in this function. I first create dimensions and then copy into it all
the PCA components by running a for loop. Then I create components in the Pandas
dataframe from the dimensions, after which I calculate the PCA explained variance
for each component. The explained variance will be used as a measure to select those
features that are independent of each other. After this is done, I create a bar plot
visualization by plotting the feature weights as a function of the components. This
function returns the concatenated Pandas data frame, which contains the explained
variance ratios and components.

Now let us look at the next function, clusterOutput, in Listing 9-3.

Listing 9-3. Cluster Output Results

```
def clusterOutput(redData, preds, centers, pca_samples):
    '''
    Visualizes the PCA-reduced cluster data in two dimensions
    Adds points for cluster centers for-selected sample data
    '''

    preds = pd.DataFrame(preds, columns = ['Cluster'])
    plot_data = pd.concat([preds, redData], axis = 1)
```

```
# I am Generating the cluster plot
fig, ax = plt.subplots(figsize = (14,8))

# Creating the Color map to distinguish between clusters
cmap = cm.get_cmap('gist_rainbow')

# Coloring the points based on assigned cluster
for i, cluster in plot_data.groupby('Cluster'):
    cluster.plot(ax = ax, kind = 'scatter', x = 'Dimension 1',
    y = 'Dimension 2', \
                    color = cmap((i)*1.0/(len(centers)-1)),
                    label = 'Cluster %i'%(i), s=30);

# Plotting the centers with indicators
for i, c in enumerate(centers):
    ax.scatter(x = c[0], y = c[1], color = 'white',
    edgecolors = 'black', \
                    alpha = 1, linewidth = 2, marker = 'o', s=200);
    ax.scatter(x = c[0], y = c[1], marker='$%d$'%(i), alpha = 1,
    s=100);

# Plotting transformed sample points
ax.scatter(x = pca_samples[:,0], y = pca_samples[:,1], \
            s = 150, linewidth = 4, color = 'black', marker = 'x');

# Plot title
ax.set_title("Cluster Learning on PCA-Reduced Data - Centroids with
Numerical markingr\nTick marks denote Transformed Sample Data");
```

In the clusterOutput function, I am using the input of reduced data, the predictions the centroid centers, and PCA samples to visualize and add points to the clusters center for given samples. In the first set of statements, I first create a Pandas dataframe with the predictions column called plaster, and then I create concatenated Pandas data frame which has predictions and reduced data. I now generate a cluster plot with subplots of size 14 by 18 and use a rainbow colormap. Then I plot all of the points groupings by cluster and iterate the data. I also use the for loop for plotting centers with indicator cross-marks in the color black for the sampled data.With this you will be able to visualize the cluster plot to which the sample belongs.

Visualization and Plotting

Next, in the code, I used the plotter function, which takes clean data to reduce data and PCA as input in code Listing 9-4.

Listing 9-4. Biplots for Sample Data

```
def biPlotter(cleanData, redData, pca):
    '''

    Building a biplot for PCA of the reduced data and the projections of
    the original features.
    Variable cleanData: original data, before transformation.
    Creating a pandas dataframe with valid column names
    redData: the reduced data (the first two dimensions are plotted)
    pca: pca object that contains the components_ attribute

    This function returns: a matplotlib AxesSubplot object (for any
    additional customization)
    This function is inspired by the script by Teddy Roland on Biplot in
    Python:
    https://github.com/teddyroland/python-biplot
    '''

    fig, ax = plt.subplots(figsize = (14,8))
    # scatterplot of the reduced data
    ax.scatter(x=redData.loc[:, 'Dimension 1'], y=redData.loc[:,
    'Dimension 2'],
        facecolors='b', edgecolors='b', s=70, alpha=0.5)

    feature_vectors = pca.components_.T

    # we use scaling factors to make the arrows easier to see
    arrow_size, text_pos = 7.0, 8.0,

    # projections of the original features
    for i, v in enumerate(feature_vectors):
        ax.arrow(0, 0, arrow_size*v[0], arrow_size*v[1],
                head_width=0.2, head_length=0.2, linewidth=2, color='red')
```

```
    ax.text(v[0]*text_pos, v[1]*text_pos, cleanData.columns[i],
    color='black',
              ha='center', va='center', fontsize=18)

  ax.set_xlabel("Dimension 1", fontsize=14)
  ax.set_ylabel("Dimension 2", fontsize=14)
  ax.set_title("Principal Component plane with original feature
  projections.", fontsize=16);
  return ax
```

In Listing 9-4, I am building a biplot for the reduced PCA data, and I am projecting
on the original features. Data to the Y-plotter function is sent through three parameters:
clean data, read data, and the last wearable PCA. The purpose of defining this biplot
function is to create the biplot and then return it back to the color. You will notice I have
created a figure of size 14 by 8 as subplots and used scatter diagram to print dimension
1 and dimension 2 because we are using a two-dimensional plan. I have used arrow
size and text positions to allow projecting arrows from the centroid. In the next for loop,
I have used projections of the original features by going through feature vector and
populating the arrows with their respective size, length, and line width with the color of
red. The next text appears in the text position with the color of black. I have used a font
size of 18 in this biplot. For the x-coordinate and y-coordinate for dimensions 1 and 2,
I have used a font size of 14; however, you can adjust this according to your requirement.
The title uses font size of 16 and then the function returns the plot back to the caller.

In Listing 9-5 we see a function that gives channel output results by visualizing the
PCA reduced cluster data in two dimensions. Here channel is nothing but the data
points, which show the selected sample data.

Listing 9-5. Channel Output Results or Sample Data Projection on the Graph

```
def channelOutput(redData, outliers, pca_samples):
    '''

    Here we are Visualizing the PCA-reduced cluster data in two
    dimensions using the full dataset
    Data is labeled by "Channel" points added for selected sample data
    '''

    # Check that the dataset is loadable
    try:
```

```
        full_data = pd.read_csv("retail.csv")
    except:
        print "Dataset could not be loaded. Is the file missing?"
        return False

# Create the Channel DataFrame
chl = pd.DataFrame(full_data['Channel'], columns = ['Channel'])
chl = chl.drop(chl.index[outliers]).reset_index(drop = True)
labeled = pd.concat([redData, chl], axis = 1)

# Generate the cluster plot
fig, ax = plt.subplots(figsize = (14,8))

# Color map
cmap = cm.get_cmap('gist_rainbow')

# Color the points based on assigned Channel
labels = ['Segment 1/Segment 2/Segment3', 'Retail Customer']
grouped = labeled.groupby('Channel')
for i, chl in grouped:
    chl.plot(ax = ax, kind = 'scatter', x = 'Dimension 1',
    y = 'Dimension 2', \
                color = cmap((i-1)*1.0/2), label = labels[i-1], s=30);

# Plot transformed sample points
for i, sample in enumerate(pca_samples):
        ax.scatter(x = sample[0], y = sample[1], \
            s = 200, linewidth = 3, color = 'black', marker = 'o',
            facecolors = 'none');
        ax.scatter(x = sample[0]+0.25, y = sample[1]+0.3,
        marker='$%d$'%(i), alpha = 1, s=125);

# Set plot title
ax.set_title("PCA-Reduced Data Labeled by 'Channel'\nTransformed
Sample Data Circled");
```

In the first part of channel output function, we try to load the data set again and then we build a channel dataframe that contains the complete data. We then drop the outliers column because it is no longer needed, and then I concatenate the reduced data with the channel data frame. After this, a subplot with 14 by 8 size is created with a rainbow color map like we did previously, and then I assign these labels to the three segments for the retail customer. In the for loop, I have used each channel data to move through the grouped channel data in order to plot them on dimension 1 and dimension 2, respectively. In the next set of for loops, I enumerate it through the PCI samples in order to create a scatter plot that is black in color, and the caterer function takes the inputs of each sample and then creates the output. In the last line, I define the plot title. Now that we have finished understanding the functions, let me explain to you how I am going to execute or implement the unsupervised learning technique using them.

Loading the Data Set

First, we will be importing libraries and then importing the data set. After that we will have a look at data by describing it. Now because we are doing exploratory data analysis I will select three samples from the data set.

The selection of the sample is done so that we can explore the data and see if there are any patterns emerging out of it. After selecting three indices I now move to create a dataframe of those samples by name of samples. I drop the rest of the columns, as they are not required, so the samples data set is comprised of only the sample data that I will be using in the sample data sets to calculate deviations from mean and median. This is required in order to understand if there are any huge outliers in the particular features. After this, I move on to creating a decision tree regressive for scoring using the R2 score for each of the features. This step allows us to filter out those features that are not independent. I then use a natural algorithm to scale the sample data and then produce a scatter matrix. After this we look at the outliers, and for that, there is a function that enumerates all the outliers for the given features. After removing the outliers we are left with good data that is then used for principal component analysis (PCA). After doing a fit of the good data, I then use the PCA output function that we saw earlier to get the PCA results, and then I call the biplotter function to create a biplot. Then I subsequently call the cluster output function to display the implementation of clustering.

From Listing 9-6, after implementing the code we can see that the retail.csv file has been loaded and has 440 samples with 30 features each.

Listing 9-6. Loading the Data Set

```
# This is Necessary for a newer version of matplotlib
import warnings
warnings.filterwarnings("ignore", category = UserWarning, module =
"matplotlib")
warnings.filterwarnings("ignore", category = UserWarning, module = "cross_
validationb")
warnings.filterwarnings("ignore", category=DeprecationWarning)
import matplotlib.pyplot as plt
import matplotlib.cm as cm
import pandas as pd
import numpy as np

# Load the retail customers data set
try:
    data = pd.read_csv("retail.csv")
    data.drop(['Region', 'Channel'], axis = 1, inplace = True)
    print "Retail customers data set has {} samples with {} features
    each.".format(*data.shape)
except:
    print "Data set could not be loaded. Is the dataset missing?"

Retail customers data set has 440 samples with 30 features each.
```

In simple terms, there are 440 rows and 30 columns. Let us now have a look at the data set in detail in Table 9-1.

Table 9-1. *Describing the Data Set*

	Bread	Milk	BathSoaps	FrozenFood	Detergents	
count	440.000000	440.000000	440.000000	440.000000	440.000000	...
mean	12000.297727	5796.265909	7951.277273	3071.931818	2881.493182	...
std	12647.328865	7380.377175	9503.162829	4854.673333	4767.854448	...
min	3.000000	55.000000	3.000000	25.000000	3.000000	...
25%	3127.750000	1533.000000	2153.000000	742.250000	256.750000	...
50%	8504.000000	3627.000000	4755.500000	1526.000000	816.500000	...
75%	16933.750000	7190.250000	10655.750000	3554.250000	3922.000000	...
max	112151.000000	73498.000000	92780.000000	60869.000000	40827.000000	...

	Chocolates	Shampoo	ReadytoEat	LEDBulbs	PackagedWater	
count	440.000000	440.000000	440.000000	440.000000	440.000000	...
mean	1524.870455	1172.447727	639.102273	1838.736364	26792.865909	...
std	2820.105937	527.238879	369.311261	396.316449	9186.632655	...
min	3.000000	192.000000	17.000000	1164.000000	10811.000000	...
25%	408.250000	751.750000	329.750000	1495.500000	19412.500000	...
50%	965.500000	1202.500000	647.500000	1808.000000	26530.000000	...
75%	1820.250000	1625.500000	951.250000	2169.500000	34425.750000	...
max	47943.000000	2020.000000	1240.000000	2562.000000	43085.000000	...

(continued)

Table 9-1. (*continued*)

	FitnessEquipments	NasalSpray	Detergents.1	Juices	Butter
count	440.000000	440.000000	440.000000	440.000000	440.000000
mean	9.875000	4457.306818	223.106818	1288.706818	18678.575000
std	5.547501	979.522344	99.645453	754.998453	10419.614651
min	1.000000	2851.000000	52.000000	38.000000	202.000000
25%	5.000000	3522.250000	138.000000	651.000000	9690.250000
50%	10.000000	4486.000000	222.000000	1252.000000	19584.000000
75%	15.000000	5326.500000	304.250000	1931.500000	27397.750000
max	19.000000	6125.000000	539.000000	2589.000000	35969.000000

	Jelly	Diapers	Toasters	Movies	Popcorns
count	440.000000	440.000000	440.000000	440.000000	440.000000
mean	219.047727	31805.109091	120.011364	22.984091	2300.545455
std	93.574304	38012.651316	126.492916	12.707583	1273.548161
min	59.000000	12.000000	0.000000	1.000000	58.000000
25%	137.750000	8612.000000	31.000000	12.000000	1207.500000
50%	219.000000	19022.000000	85.000000	23.000000	2316.500000
75%	299.000000	42623.000000	169.000000	34.000000	3419.000000
max	381.000000	371120.000000	1122.000000	45.000000	4512.000000

This retail customer's data set has 440 samples with 30 features each.

```
8 rows × 30 columns
```

We can see that the code output gives us the mean standard deviation, minimum, and maximum of each feature or column. The first column (bread) has a mean of 12,000.29, standard deviations of 12,647, minimum of 3, and maximum of 112,151. What this means is that for bread the customers of this retail chain have been ordering an average of 12,000 pieces of bread per year, and they have been ordering a minimum of 3 breads and a maximum of 112,151 breads. The rows denoted by 25%, 50%, and 75% stand for the 25th percentile, 50th percentile, and 75th percentile of the bread data. You can look at the rest of the columns from milk to popcorn to get an idea of what those 30 items mean for this retail chain. This data pertains to a particular retail chain for a year of data, and it shows entries of sales that happen in dollar terms for each of these items. This is a global data set and does not constitute individual buying transactions. It is divided between channels. A value of 2 means a brick and mortar store and a value of 1 means the channel is an online retailer. Similarly, the data has a column region that is used to denote the regions in which the sales have taken place.

Now I move to the next step in Listing 9-7, which shows a selection of three indices by me and the creation of the samples Pandas dataframe and the output of the samples dataframe.

Listing 9-7. Selecting Samples

```
#   Selecting three indices of my choice from the data set
indices = [225,182,400]

# Creating a DataFrame of the chosen samples
samples = pd.DataFrame(data.loc[indices], columns = data.keys()).reset_
index(drop = True)
print "Chosen samples of Retail customers dataset:"
display(samples)
display(samples)
Chosen samples of Retail customers dataset:
```

	Bread	Milk	BathSoaps	FrozenFood	Detergents	Chocolates	Shampoo	\
0	12680	3243	4157	660	761	786	2008	
1	694	8533	10518	443	6907	156	842	
2	4446	906	1238	3576	153	1014	1933	

```
     ReadytoEat  LEDBulbs  PackagedWater    ...       FitnessEquipments  \
0           600      1694          36590    ...                       3
1           230      2298          18582    ...                      17
2          1232      1603          26071    ...                       8

     NasalSpray  Detergents.1  Juices  Butter  Jelly  Diapers  Toasters
Movies  \
0          2948           294    1613   33305    349    16628       127
23
1          4236           138    1406   32028    322    42072         7
35
2          5868           270    1134    9964     90     4952        44
23

     Popcorns
0        2291
1        3490
2        2256

[3 rows x 30 columns]
```

The reason for selecting three samples is to get an idea of how the data looks. You can select even more samples than this if you have a larger data set. However, the plot will become complex and difficult to understand if you add more than five samples.

Visualizing the Sample Data Set

In Figure 9-1, we see the code to visualize the samples data set.

```
pd.DataFrame(samples).transpose().plot(kind='bar', stacked=False,
figsize=(8,8), title='Retail customers dataset')
Out[46]: <matplotlib.axes._subplots.AxesSubplot at 0xa1a59860>
```

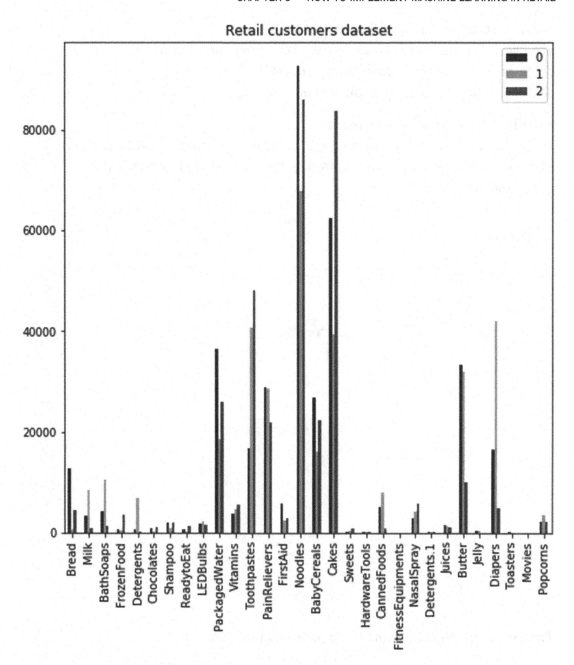

Figure 9-1. *Visualizing the retail customer samples data set*

We can see that the third sample has a high order of cakes and noodles and the third
highest for toothpaste. Sample one is highest in noodles, butter, LED bulbs, and baby
cereals. After noting the various revenue for each of the three samples we can then move
on to check the three samples against mean and median. This can be seen in Figure 9-2.

```
# Calculating deviations from Mean and Median
#to check how much the 3 samples deviate from the Center.
delta_mean = samples - data.mean().round()
delta_median = samples - data.median().round()

#display(delta_mean, delta_median)
delta_mean.plot.bar(figsize=(10,4), title='Compared to MEAN', grid=True)
delta_median.plot.bar(figsize=(10,4), title='Compared to MEDIAN',
grid=True);
```

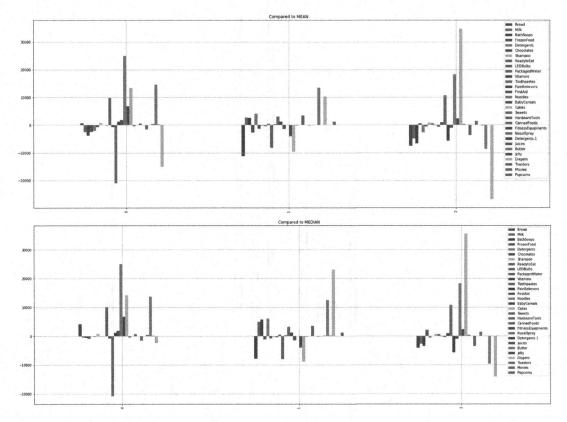

Figure 9-2. *Sample comparison to mean and median*

In the code, we see that in the first sample compared to mean, the highest amounts
of items ordered relate to detergents, which are higher amounts than those ordered by
an average retail store. Similarly, butter is also ordered most in this sample as well. From
the mean, nasal spray is an item that is at the lowest in orders from this sample retail
store. Similarly, diapers are also something that is away from the mean and ordered far

less than at an average retail store. In the second sample, the highest orders from the mean were for butter and diapers. And the lowest orders from the mean were for bread, cakes, and packaged water. In the third sample data, we see the highest orders for cakes, noodles, and toothpaste, which are away from the mean. Similarly in the negative were diapers and butter, which were ordered far less than those ordered by an average retail store. Now that we have looked at comparisons to mean let's also look at a comparison to median. The trend in mean and median is not significantly different. However, we do find some differences in the median chart where, in sample one, the bread is ordered more than the median store. In the case of the second data set, most of the other items remain the same; however, the significant difference is for shampoo, which is ordered higher than a median store. In the case of the third sample data set, both the mean and median are almost identical.

Feature Engineering and Selection

Now we move to the next step of looking at the R2 score of each feature in order to determine its importance. For this we will need a small function known as SCORER() function, which will use decision tree regressor to determine an R2 score for a particular feature. Our features are stored in the data frame, and using a for loop and the scorer function we will loop through each column of a data frame in order to calculate its R2 score value.

In Listing 9-8 you can see the output of running this scorer function on dataframe.

Listing 9-8. Scoring the Features

```
#Importing Libraries
from sklearn.cross_validation import train_test_split
from sklearn.tree import DecisionTreeRegressor

#Broke down the logic into a scoring function and a For loop
def scorer(feature):
    #   Make a copy of the DataFrame, using the 'drop' function to drop the
        given feature relevant_data = data.drop([feature], axis=1)
```

```
    # Split the data into training and testing sets using the given
    feature as the target X_train, X_test, y_train, y_test =
    train_test_split(relevant_data, data[feature], test_size=0.25,
    random_state=45)

    # Create a decision tree regressor and fit it to the training set
    regressor = DecisionTreeRegressor(random_state=45).fit(X_train, y_train)

    # Report the score of the prediction using the testing set
    score = regressor.score(X_test, y_test)

    print("The R2 score for feature {:16} is {:+.5f}".format(feature, score))


for feature in data.columns.values:
    scorer(feature)
The R2 score for feature Bread            is +0.95214
The R2 score for feature Milk             is -0.65329
The R2 score for feature BathSoaps        is +0.93408
The R2 score for feature FrozenFood       is -1.44912
The R2 score for feature Detergents       is +0.73558
The R2 score for feature Chocolates       is -12.74963
The R2 score for feature Shampoo          is -1.06275
The R2 score for feature ReadytoEat       is -0.57883
The R2 score for feature LEDBulbs         is -0.75093
The R2 score for feature PackagedWater    is -1.34695
The R2 score for feature Vitamins         is -0.98001
The R2 score for feature Toothpastes      is -1.26507
The R2 score for feature PainRelievers    is -0.74436
The R2 score for feature FirstAid         is -1.02262
The R2 score for feature Noodles          is -0.73669
The R2 score for feature BabyCereals      is -1.49739
The R2 score for feature Cakes            is -1.12935
The R2 score for feature Sweets           is -1.23246
The R2 score for feature HardwareTools    is -1.44181
The R2 score for feature CannedFoods      is -1.44300
The R2 score for feature FitnessEquipments is -1.51559
The R2 score for feature NasalSpray       is -0.53323
```

```
The R2 score for feature Detergents.1      is -1.34752
The R2 score for feature Juices            is -1.14858
The R2 score for feature Butter            is -1.16000
The R2 score for feature Jelly             is -1.04652
The R2 score for feature Diapers           is +0.98407
The R2 score for feature Toasters          is +0.95279
The R2 score for feature Movies            is +0.99948
The R2 score for feature Popcorns          is +0.99792
In [52]:
```

In the listing are two scores. In Listing 9-8 we can see the R2 scores of bread, bath soaps, detergents, and vitamins are positive. Other features that are positive include diapers, toasters, movies, and popcorn. The negative scores are for milk, frozen food, chocolate (which is at a highest of -12), shampoos, packaged water, toothpaste, first aid, noodles, baby cereals, cakes, sweets, hardware tools, canned foods, fitness equipment, detergents, juices, butter , and Jelly—to name a few. I do not recommend that we use the features that have a positive score for the purpose of unsupervised learning because these features show some kind of relationship between one feature with the other positive feature. Also, the information these features deliver seem to be contained to a large extent in other features so it would be appropriate to drop them as they would be redundant for our unsupervised model. For the negative scoring features, I recommend keeping these features since they are not showing a relationship with other features and hence are independent to identify the customer-specific behavior from them alone.

In Listing 9-9 you can see the code that is required to remove the redundant features.

Listing 9-9. Code for Removing the Redundant Features

```
#Now selecting Only relevant features from the R2 score of each feature
#print(feature)
selected_features=[]
cntftr=0
for feature in data.columns.values:
    scorer(feature)
    if scorer(feature)<=0:
        print("This Feature is fit for selection ", feature)
        print("Counter Feature is: ",cntftr)
```

```
        #selected_features[cntftr]=feature
        selected_features.insert(cntftr,feature)
        cntftr=cntftr+1
# Create a data set with only the features with a negative R2 score from
above for loop
display(selected_features)
data=data[selected_features]
```

I am not implementing a code here to remove these redundant features; however, I will most certainly show you the code on how to drop the redundant features. It is a for loop that goes through the column values of the dataframe, and it creates a list of all the selected features based on the if condition. The if condition is important here because we are using the square function, which I have outlined in Listing 9-1, and we are checking whether for that particular feature the value is less than or equal to 0. If the value is negative, then we treat that feature to be fit for the selection we selected. Otherwise the if condition ignores if the feature has a score that is greater than 0. By the way, you can implement feature selection based on the R2 score.

Visualizing the Feature Relationships

Next, I am plotting a scatter matrix for each pair of features in the data using the Pandas plotting package. This can be seen in Figure 9-3 in detail.

```
pd.plotting.scatter_matrix(data, alpha = 0.3, figsize = (24,12),
diagonal = 'kde');
```

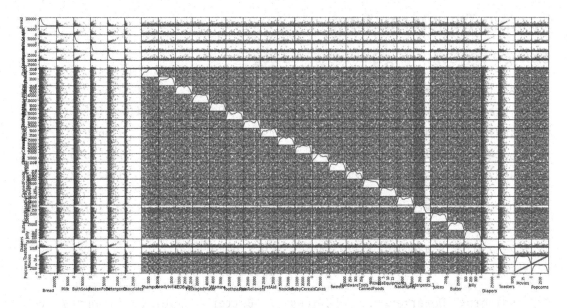

Figure 9-3. *Scatter plot of all the features*

In Figure 9-3, although the scatter matrix of the features are crowded, at the left-most graphs and uppermost graph, we do see some patterns with some of the features such as bread, milk, bath soap, frozen foods, detergent, chocolates, and shampoos.

```
data.corr()
```

In order to further look at whether the relationships exist between various features among themselves, I have used correlation on the entire data set (the output is too long for the book, so run the command yourself if you want to examine it in detail). The correlation table shows that there are some items or features that have a high level of correlation between them, such as bread and toasters, diapers and bath soap, detergents and diapers, bath soap and diapers, and movies and popcorn. All these features are positively correlated with values above 0.9 for correlation coefficient. This means that people at these retail stores frequently buy these items together.

Sample Transformation

Listing 9-10. Converting Data to Natural Log

```
display(log_samples)
        Bread      Milk  BathSoaps  FrozenFood  Detergents  Chocolates  \
0   9.447781  8.084254   8.332549     6.49224    6.634633    6.666957
1   6.542472  9.051696   9.260843     6.09357    8.840291    5.049856
2   8.399760  6.809039   7.121252     8.18200    5.030438    6.921658

     Shampoo  ReadytoEat  LEDBulbs  PackagedWater  ...  FitnessEquipments  \
0   7.604894    6.396930  7.434848      10.507530  ...           1.098612
1   6.735780    5.438079  7.739794       9.829949  ...           2.833213
2   7.566828    7.116394  7.379632      10.168579  ...           2.079442

    NasalSpray  Detergents.1     Juices      Butter     Jelly    Diapers  \
0     7.988882      5.683580   7.385851   10.413463  5.855072   9.718843
1     8.351375      4.927254   7.248504   10.374366  5.774552  10.647138
2     8.677269      5.598422   7.033506    9.206734  4.499810   8.507547

     Toasters    Movies  Popcorns
0   4.844187  3.135494  7.736744
1   1.945910  3.555348  8.157657
2   3.784190  3.135494  7.721349

[3 rows x 30 columns]
```

In the Listing 9-10, I scale the dataframe using natural algorithm and the output is displayed there. We are doing this in order to do feature scaling. If the data is not normally distributed and the mean and median vary significantly, then we can apply nonlinear scaling on search data. Here, I am not using box Cox transformation test for scaling; I am using a simpler approach using natural algorithm. You can apply box Cox testing on this data if you want using scipy package of Python.

In Figure 9-2, we see the correlation matrix of the samples data after applying natural log transformation. We can see that there is a significant change as far as the correlation among the features is concerned, and we see significant negatively correlated features—for example, LED bulbs with bread with a negative correlation of -0.87 and a negative correlation between fitness equipment and bread of -0.9252. This shows that our log transformation has worked and we are ready to move to the next step of identifying outliers. Although the output of the entire table is truncated due to maintaining brevity, in Table 9-2 you can run the command from Figure 9-2 to run the complete output of the correlation table.

Table 9-2. *Sample Correlation After Natural Log Transformation*

	Bread	Milk	Toasters	Movies	Popcorns
Bread	1	-0.567927	0.999984	-0.934429	-0.922904
LEDBulbs	-0.874226	0.896117	-0.871473	0.98982	0.993766
PackagedWater	0.987271	-0.429787	0.988152	-0.865889	-0.849917
Vitamins	-0.473998	-0.455546	-0.478957	0.129318	0.098425
Juices	0.235358	0.666292	0.240837	0.12622	0.157002
Butter	-0.130568	0.890186	-0.124972	0.475107	0.502236
Jelly	-0.106274	0.878774	-0.100663	0.453439	0.480931
Diapers	-0.570271	0.999996	-0.565627	0.825439	0.842591
Toasters	0.999984	-0.563275	1	-0.932405	-0.920717
Movies	-0.934429	0.823827	-0.932405	1	0.999517
Popcorns	-0.922904	0.841053	-0.920717	0.999517	1

Outlier Detection and Filtering

Listing 9-11 shows the code for outlier detection and then filtering it out of the data set.

Listing 9-11. Finding Outliers

```
#Identifying Outliers
#Using Counters
from collections import Counter
outliers_counter = Counter()

# For each feature finding out the data points with extremely high or low
values - Outliers
outliers_scores = None
```

```
for feature in log_data.keys():

    # Calculate Q1 (25th percentile of the data) for the given feature
    Q1 = np.percentile(log_data[feature], 25)

    # Calculate Q3 (75th percentile of the data) for the given feature
    Q3 = np.percentile(log_data[feature], 75)

    # Use the interquartile range to calculate an outlier step (1.5 times
    the interquartile range) step = 1.5 * (Q3 - Q1)

    empty = np.zeros(len(log_data[feature]))
    aboveQ3 = log_data[feature].values - Q3 - step
    belowQ3 = log_data[feature].values - Q1 + step
    current_outliers_scores = np.array(np.maximum(empty, aboveQ3) -
    np.minimum(empty, belowQ3)).reshape([-1,1])
    outliers_scores = current_outliers_scores if outliers_scores is None
    else np.hstack([outliers_scores, current_outliers_scores])

    # Display the outliers
    print("Data points considered outliers for the feature '{}':".
    format(feature))
    current_outliers = log_data[~((log_data[feature] >= Q1 - step) &
    (log_data[feature] <= Q3 + step))]
    display(current_outliers)
    outliers_counter.update(current_outliers.index.values)
```

Data points considered outliers for the feature 'Juices':

	Bread	Milk	BathSoaps	FrozenFood	Detergents	Chocolates	\
64	8.468003	7.112327	8.086410	8.222554	7.128496	7.043160	
73	9.898425	8.581482	9.072571	9.003562	6.638568	6.473891	
85	9.687630	10.740670	11.437986	6.933423	10.617099	7.987524	
123	9.320987	9.284427	9.084097	7.693482	7.588830	4.962845	
131	7.650169	6.378426	5.749393	5.846439	4.248495	5.736572	
133	9.152075	6.948897	7.118826	6.077642	5.545177	5.981414	
134	8.907612	7.540090	7.684324	6.579251	3.850148	6.285998	
186	8.009363	6.255750	6.749931	8.151910	6.855409	6.588926	

190	9.737197	8.740337	7.591357	8.900004	4.770685	4.158883
193	5.192957	8.156223	9.917982	6.865891	8.633731	6.501290
219	8.332068	5.905362	7.237059	7.743270	4.454347	4.867534
266	6.349139	9.186355	10.007036	7.705713	8.493310	7.848934
267	9.947169	7.108244	7.853993	8.287780	6.602588	8.196437
321	9.122055	7.548029	8.550048	7.906179	5.429346	7.014814
349	8.696343	9.591581	9.929204	7.603399	9.410666	6.098074
371	9.908724	7.542744	7.569928	9.007490	6.573680	6.672033
375	8.672657	7.279319	7.057898	6.391917	6.165418	4.248495
433	7.591862	8.076515	7.308543	7.340187	5.874931	7.278629

...

In Listings 9-11 and 9-12, I'm now moving on to identify outliers in our data set. I will be using the counter library from collections package, and then I use a for loop to pass between the keys of each feature to determine whether the data is within the interquartile range or data at the 75th percentile through 25th percentile. Anything that is 1.5 times of Q1 (25th percentile) and Q3 (75th percentile) is considered an outlier. We have used this approach in Chapter 3 as well, so the readers will recall that we have used the same approach to finding the outliers. Next, after determining the features, each feature is identified with its own set of outliers and the result is displayed out. Next, I print out the data points and more than one feature is considered an outlier.

Listing 9-12. Index Values with Outliers in Multiple Features

```
min_outliers_count = 2
outliers = [x[0] for x in outliers_counter.items() if x[1] >= min_outliers_
count]
print("Data points considered outlier for more than 1 feature: {}".
format(outliers))
Data points considered outlier for more than 1 feature: [29, 35, 38, 50,
64, 65, 66, 75, 81, 83, 85, 86, 87, 95, 96, 104, 109, 127, 128, 134, 135,
137, 145, 147, 154, 162, 163, 171, 179, 180, 183, 184, 187, 190, 193, 196,
199, 210, 218, 228, 229, 231, 232, 250, 267, 276, 278, 299, 304, 305, 315,
321, 322, 327, 331, 338, 353, 355, 357, 412, 420, 431, 433]
```

We see in Listing 9-12 that there are about 63 such data points that have outliers in more than one feature. In a production environment or in a commercial setup, you would now need to decide on what to do with these outliers. You could make three decisions: one is to not do anything with them, and the justification would be that we would lose 63 rows out of a total of 440 and hence keep them; second you could delete them in order to improve the accuracy of your model; or finally, you could replace these outlier values with mean or median values. In my case, I am going to remove them from the data set in the code given in Listing 9-13.

Listing 9-13. Getting Good Data by Dropping the Outliers

```
good_data = log_data.drop(log_data.index[outliers]).reset_index(drop = True)
```

Principal Component Analysis

I am going to now apply PCA, which is a technique used for reducing the number of dimensions as features. Listing 9-14 gives the output code for applying PCA and looking at its dimension value.

Listing 9-14. Applying Explained Variance on PCA

```
#   Apply PCA by fitting the good data with the same number of dimensions
as features from sklearn.decomposition import PCA
pca = PCA(n_components=len(good_data.columns)).fit(good_data)

#   Transform log_samples using the PCA fit above
pca_samples =pca.transform(log_samples)

# Generate PCA results plot
pcaOutput = pcaOutput(good_data, pca)
# show results
display(pcaOutput)
# Cumulative explained variance should add to 1
display(pcaOutput['Explained Variance'].cumsum())

Dimension 1     0.2925
Dimension 2     0.4495
Dimension 3     0.5200
```

```
Dimension 4      0.5760
Dimension 5      0.6255
Dimension 6      0.6706
Dimension 7      0.7132
Dimension 8      0.7528
Dimension 9      0.7900
Dimension 10     0.8237
Dimension 11     0.8566
Dimension 12     0.8853
Dimension 13     0.9108
Dimension 14     0.9266
Dimension 15     0.9416
Dimension 16     0.9546
Dimension 17     0.9662
Dimension 18     0.9739
Dimension 19     0.9811
Dimension 20     0.9867
Dimension 21     0.9897
Dimension 22     0.9924
Dimension 23     0.9947
Dimension 24     0.9969
Dimension 25     0.9980
Dimension 26     0.9989
Dimension 27     0.9998
Dimension 28     0.9998
Dimension 29     0.9998
Dimension 30     0.9998
Name: Explained Variance, dtype: float64
```

Now I am going to apply PCA by fitting the good data with an equal number of dimensions as features, and here I am going to use the PCA output function. I am importing the PCA from the decomposition library package sklearn, and the ultimate result is with an explained variance for each of the 30 dimensions. This is shown in Figure 9-4. We can clearly see that the explained variance is increasing with the increase in dimension, with dimension 1 being the lowest explained variance and dimension 30 having the highest explained variance.

Clustering and Biplot Visualization Implementation

Figure 9-4 provides the code to implement biplots.

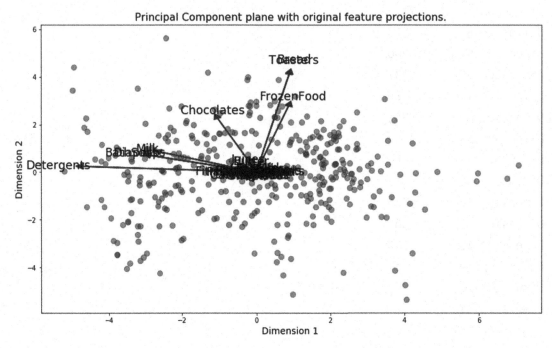

Figure 9-4. *Biplots of dimensions and features*

In Figure 9-4 we look at the biplot of dimensions and features. The biplot tells us that toasters and bread have a relationship between them and may be frequently bought together by customers of this retail chain. Similarly, there could be a relationship between bread and milk, which is appearing together near dimension 2.

In the last part of the code, I now implement clustering on PCA, the reduced data that shows output in tick marks for our selected samples. I am using the GMM for clustering and silhouette score library from a scalar matrix. In code Listing 9-15 we look at implementing clustering.

Listing 9-15. Implementing Clustering

```
#Import GMM and silhouette score library
from sklearn.mixture import GMM
from sklearn.metrics import silhouette_score
```

```
#Divided the logic into Clustering and Scoring functions
#Then Iterated through the clusters in the identified range

#This function creates Cluster using GMM
def clusterCreator(data, n_clusters):
    clusterer = GMM(n_components=n_clusters, covariance_type='full',
    random_state=45).fit(data)
    preds = clusterer.predict(data)
    centers = clusterer.means_
    sample_preds = clusterer.predict(pca_samples)
    return preds, centers, sample_preds

#Scoring after creating Clusters
def scorer(data, n_clusters):
    preds, _, _  = clusterCreator(data, n_clusters)
    score = silhouette_score(data, preds)
    return score
```

Here I have used cluster creator function, which initializes the GMM or the (Gaussian mixture models) in order to create clusters. The cluster projects are based on the data set from the retail domain and use the PCA samples to make sample predictions in the school function. I am scoring after creating clusters by calling the cluster to create a function and returning the silhouette score for the data and the predictions. In the for loop, I am running the clusters in ranges from 2 to 10 dimension and scoring them by creating the cluster output. After this, I am now fitting the Gaussian mixture models with the reduced data and then making predictions and finding out the centers of each dimension. After I have the data, I pass reduced data to make prediction centers and PCA samples to cluster output function, which we had seen earlier, in order to print the cluster dimensional data. Now we look a at Clustering results based on "channel" data in Figure 9-5.

```
#Iterate in the clusters and Print silhouette score
for n_clusters in range(2,10):
    score = scorer(reduced_data, n_clusters)
    print "For n_clusters = {}. The average silhouette_score is : {}".
    format(n_clusters, score)

n_clusters=0
```

```
# Resetting as due to loop run before we need to reset values again with 2
cluster components
clusterer = GMM(n_components=2).fit(reduced_data)
predictions = clusterer.predict(reduced_data)
centers = clusterer.means_
sample_preds = clusterer.predict(pca_samples)
# Display the results of the clustering from implementation
clusterOutput(reduced_data, predictions, centers, pca_samples)
```

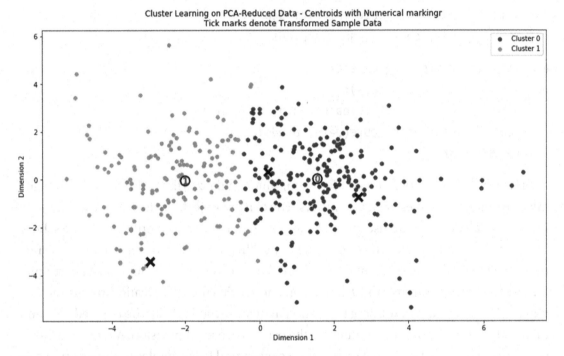

Figure 9-5. *Printing the cluster dimensions*

Now we need to develop the channel output that gives a clear understanding as to how the data has been transformed by calling the channelOutput function. In the code Listing 9-6 we can see Clustering results based on "channel" data.

```
log_centers = pca.inverse_transform(centers)

#   Exponentiate the centers
true_centers = np.exp(log_centers)

# Display the true centers
segments = ['Segment {}'.format(i) for i in range(0,len(centers))]
```

```
true_centers = pd.DataFrame(np.round(true_centers), columns = data.keys())
true_centers.index = segments
display(true_centers)
#Compare the True Centers from the Central values Mean and Median
#display(true_centers - data.mean().round())
delta_mean=true_centers - data.mean().round()
#display(true_centers - data.median().round())
delta_median=true_centers - data.median().round()
delta_mean.plot.bar(figsize=(10,4), title='Compared to MEAN', grid=True)
delta_median.plot.bar(figsize=(10,4), title='Compared to MEDIAN', grid=True);
```

```
# Display the predictions
for i, pred in enumerate(sample_preds):
    print "Sample point", i, "predicted to be in Cluster", pred
samples
```

```
# Display the clustering results based on 'Channel' data
redData=reduced_data
channelOutput(redData, outliers, pca_samples)
```

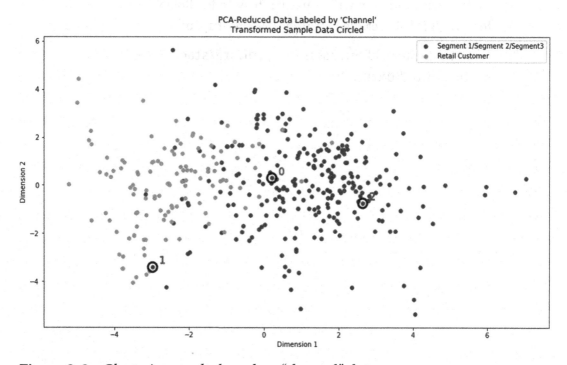

Figure 9-6.   *Clustering results based on "channel" data*

I have used GMM in this example, whereas I could have used the K-Means algorithm also. Compared to K-Means, GMM has many parameters that can be tuned. It is an expectation maximization algorithm. It is a fast algorithm and can be used on small sample data sets in comparison to K-Means. It uses Mahalanobis distance to center to compute clusters [2]. Choosing GMM as the sample data set is not large, and GMM will work well [2]. Did you notice that the red dots in the Figure 9-6 denote the various segments that may be associated with another retail customer chain? Can you think of ways they could be differentiating among themselves like what would be the profile of Segment 1, Segment 2, or Segment 3 customers? Would they be geographically based differentiation? This is something that you would need to sit with the customer management department and work out to see what those segments of customers signify to the business. With this, I close the sample implementation of machine learning in retail. In the next chapter, we will see two case study implementations of machine learning in retail operations.

End Notes

[1]   Biplots taken from the script on GitHub by Teddy Roland, `https://github.com/teddyroland/python-biplot`

[2]   Gaussian Mixture, `http://scikit-learn.org/stable/modules/mixture.html#mixture`

## CHAPTER 10

Case Studies in Retail AI

Disclaimer: The case studies in this book have been taken from real-life organizations. Care has been taken to ensure that the names of the organizations and the names of its employees are changed and do not resemble my clients in any way. The reader familiar with the healthcare industry will definitely find these situations very practical and insightful.

What Are Recommender Systems?

Recommender systems are used by online retailers to recommend products to people. Good examples of this implementation include Amazon.com's "Recommended for you," "People who bought X also bought," and "You may like." We see this implementation on other websites, like Netflix.com and Walmart.com, which have their own recommender systems, such as "Customers also considered," "Customers also bought these products," and "Customers also viewed these products." This is a straightforward implementation of machine learning techniques—more specifically, a technique known as collaborative filtering. In simple terms, this means that we are using machine learning techniques to learn about actions that a group of customers takes based on products or user information. It could also be called Group Filtering, wherein we try to see what actions and behaviors the users do collectively. Once the machine learning algorithm sees some patterns, an algorithm is built around it in order to look at your buying behavior and give a similar recommendation. The basic assumption is that people display similar buying behavior; for example, if one person bought a television and universal remote, then the second person who is buying a television is also likely to buy the universal remote. This example is nice because it does not talk about group behavior, but we can extend it by saying that our machine learning algorithm found that 70 percent of the users who bought the television are likely to buy the universal remote. Searching a pattern can be created by a recommendation system algorithm and can be used for giving the most

© Puneet Mathur 2019
P. Mathur, *Machine Learning Applications Using Python*, https://doi.org/10.1007/978-1-4842-3787-8_10

likely buying behavior patterns. The application of machine learning using collaborative filtering requires availability of large data sets spanning across various categories of buying behavior by customers. There is no limit to where this technique can be used. For instance, it can be used by a consumer products retailer, a high-end fashion online store, a financial products retailer, or a wholesale seller of mineral exploration products on an online website. The effort in collaborative filtering is to find groups of people who have similar interests, and the recommendations are made based on this. A user's actions and buying behavior are captured through purchase actions, ratings, feedback, etc. Collaborative filtering is used on items, products, and user-based recommendation systems. The items or products offered by a retail store form a base for creating an item-based recommendation system, and users' actions and preferences are used as a base for user-based recommendation systems. Usually, in practice, item- or product-based collaborative filtering is found to be more accurate than user-based collaborative filtering, as the major drawback with the user-based approach is that people's tastes change over time, and they may not like what they liked in the past. Consider this example: a person bought three science fiction novels some months back, and we pick up this pattern to recommend to other users who are buying a science fiction novel. Let's say the first user whose buying pattern we pick up suddenly changes her buying behavior and moves to romantic novels 3 months after her science fiction purchase. If the system picked up this pattern and gave a recommendation of romantic novels when a user selected a science fiction novel, the recommendation would go all wrong. In the case study in this chapter, I will be giving you based an example of item-based collaborative filtering. I am sure you will enjoy this case study, as it deals with the insides of an online retail store and what they go through to keep afloat and expand their business among cutthroat competition.

CASE STUDY 1: Recommendation Engine Creation for Online Retail Mart

Aystsaga is a retail chain in Europe that caters to a wide variety of customers in the middle class segment. It has more than 250 retail outlets in major cities of Europe, such as Zurich, Paris, etc. It makes more than US$ 300 billion in yearly revenue from its retail operations. The large closely held company has tough competition from online retail stores that are mushrooming all over the internet. In an effort to retain its number 4 position in the retail sector and to grow its revenue, Aystsaga has implemented an online retail mart.

Mr. Zacky Johannsen is the head and CEO of the Internet Operations of this company. He came up with an idea of floating an online retail division and announced the building of its internet retail store to online customers. While the online sales have been increasing ever since the launch of the online store in 2014, the other online retail stores have been eating into the share of revenue from rival online sales by offering better pricing and other customer-friendly features like recommendation engines, similar to the recommendations that show up on websites like Amazon.com. Mr. Zacky called for a report from its competition intelligence officer on the reason for the decline in sales this year and questioned how Aystsaga's competitors were doing better than Aystsaga. Zacky called for a discussion with Arnold Zaine, the head of the online retail division at Aystsaga, and asked him to come prepared with the following agenda:

1. Current state of Aystsaga's online sales

2. State of competition

3. Key things that need to be addressed in order to boost online retail sales

Arnold came to the meeting with a presentation, facts from which are reproduced in Table 10-1. Online sales numbers for Aystsaga show an increase, but revenue has been declining.

Table 10-1. *Aystsaga's Sales Figures*

Description	2014 US$ (Million)	2015 US$ (Million)	2016 US$ (Million)	Projected 2017 US$ (Million)
Total Sales	451	694	712	726.24
Revenue	132.3	165.5	135.2	108.9
Revenue %age	29.3%	23.8%	19%	15%

Arnold explained that although they could take consolation from the fact that the online sales have been increasing year after year, the revenue share has been decreasing sharply in comparison to sales. He attributed aggressive competitive strategies by rival online stores as the main reason for the decline in revenue, as Aystsaga had to offer products at reduced prices when the competition cut their profit margins to increase their sales. He also pointed to the fact that the rival stores had better programs to retain customer loyalty and drive repeat orders or make a customer increase their sales by recommending products that the customer was likely to buy on their websites. For example, the main competitor of Aystsaga was able to increase its customer recommendations through a machine learning-based online recommendation engine on its website, which it deployed the year prior. Arnold noted this is something that Aystsaga did not have on its website, and Aystsaga urgently needed to build a recommendation engine to help increase sales. A look at the repeat orders data in Table 10-2 tells us we need help in this area.

Table 10-2. *Average Sales Data for Aystsaga Online Retail Sales*

Description	2014 US$ (Million)	2015 US$ (Million)	2016 US$ (Million)
Total Sales	451	694	712
Average Sales per Invoice ($)	156	114	83

Arnold further mentioned that there was a decline of 27 percent in average sales from 2014 to 2015 and the same percentage in decline (27.2 percent) from 2015 to 2016. This reduction in average sales per invoice meant that each customer was ordering less than they did the previous year. This was not just a cause of concern but also meant that it needed to be looked at more closely regarding the reasons for such a decline. To understand why customers ordered less, a customer feedback survey was performed online asking about the various features of the website and the customer experience. The feedback ran for a length of 3 months during the Christmas season, when the sales were very high. The results of the survey are shown in Table 10-3.

Table 10-3. *Survey Results at Aystsaga*

Survey Results	
Total Users	551
Total Products	39

From the survey results table, we can see that it was presented to 551 users who rated a total of 39 products with a rating size of 1719 ratings. Arnold said that they had collected the survey data and needed help from machine learning engineers to build recommendation engines for their online retail store. They had identified the following questions that needed answers:

- Which were the products in the survey that had the highest ratings?

- Was there any brand loyalty behavior shown by the users? If so, then which was the topmost brand?

- Can we build a recommendation engine algorithm from the data to give accurate recommendations on similar products? If so, then what is the solution?

- What were the most popular products in the survey?

- What was the similarity score of the most popular products in the survey? (Give visualization in terms of graphical representation.)

I will now move on to giving the Python code to the questions raised by Arnold in the case study for their organization. Please note I have used aystsaga.csv as the dataset, which can be accessed from the website http://www.puneetmathur.me/Book9/aystsaga.csv. The Python code can also be downloaded from http://www.puneetmathur.me/Book9/aystsaga.py.

Let's load the data using Python first before we start to answer the questions from the survey (see Listing 10-1).

Listing 10-1. Loading and Fetching Data

```
# -*- coding: utf-8 -*-
"""
Created on Sat Jun 30 13:30:46 2018

@author: PUNEETMATHUR
"""
#Loading libraries
import pandas as pd

#Loading the retail dataset
survey=pd.read_csv("aystsaga.csv")

#Looking at the dataset one row
print(survey.head(1))
#Shape of the dataset Rows and Columns
print(survey.shape)

    product_id              product_name   user_id   rating
0           16   Dalmere Chocolate cup       894        3
(1719, 4)

#Looking at the columns in the dataset
print(survey.columns)
Index([u'product_id', u'product_name', u'user_id', u'rating'],
dtype='object')
```

The Python code first loads the data from aystsaga.csv and then shows the first row of data, which is product_id of 16 product_name "Dalmere Chocolate cup" rated by user_id 894 with a rating of 3. The survey.shape command shows us there are total of 1719 rows of ratings and 4 columns. Next, the code survey.columns shows us the 4 columns: product_id, product_name, user_id, and the rating of the product by the user given in the survey. Please note that the quantity bought by the user is not taken in this dataset since I want to keep it simple; however, in a retail store you would have columns running into the thousands, giving a lot more data like location, quantity, credit card used, etc., some of which would be very sensitive information. You may need to consult legal experts about using such data due to data privacy laws like GDPR (General Data Protection Regulation) of your country, similar to the one in European Union. Next let us look at the data types and also look to see if we have any missing values (see Listing 10-2).

Listing 10-2. Data Set Datatypes and Missing Values Check

```
print(survey.dtypes)
#Are there any Null values in the dataset
print(survey.isnull().any())
product_id        int64
product_name      object
user_id           int64
rating            int64
dtype: object
product_id      False
product_name    False
user_id         False
rating          False
dtype: bool
```

We can see from Listing 10-2 that all the columns except product_name, which holds the product's short description, are of int64 or numerical. We also see using the isnull(). any() function that there are no missing values in this dataset. Again I must inform you that this rarely happens in the real world. You will usually get a lot of junk and missing values as the data is migrated from one system to another, such as from Oracle to hadoop or csv to xml. You will need to treat them like I treated missing values before you proceed further. Since our data is clean, let's now create a pivot table in Table 10-4.

```
#Creating a pivot table for product ratings
productRatings = survey.pivot_table(index=['user_id'],columns=['product_
name'],values='rating')
#Peeking into the pivot table
productRatings.head(1)
```

Table 10-4. Creating the Pivot Table

product_name	Aeso napkins 10 PACK	Aeso napkins 20 PACK	Aeso napkins 40 PACK	Aeso napkins 50 PACK	Ajnin peppermint rolls 10	Ajnin peppermint rolls 5	Ajnin peppermint rolls 50	Ajnin peppermint rolls SINGLE	Ajnin peppermint rolls SINGLE CINAMON	Arutnev sea salt	...
user_id 1	NaN	NaN	NaN	NaN	NaN	NaN	NaN	4.0	NaN	NaN	...

product_name	Mudlok wheat bread	Neek corn chips	Noit house cleaner	Pitrez sweet cake	Rewop toothpaste	Serut nose wipes	Sirp mozzarella cheese	Spets stain remover	Thygie fruit juice concentrate	Yssbol Magazine	...
user_id 1	NaN	NaN	NaN	4.0	NaN	NaN	NaN	1.0	NaN	NaN	...

In the pivot table here, you will notice one row of feedback from the user with id 1, and she has rated the three products Ajnin peppermint rolls SINGLE, Pitrez sweet cake, and Spets stain remover with ratings of 4, 4, and 1, respectively. However, you will note there are NaN values for those product columns where the user has not rated. This will create a problem in interpreting our results so let us get rid of them in the next section of our code. In the next section, I implement the following use-case:

As a customer of Aystsaga's website, I should be able to get recommendations based on my current purchases so that I am able to make another purchase.

To implement this use-case it is important to assume that the customer has selected a particular product and then see what recommendations the system gives. So let's get started with implementing the next piece of code in Listing 10-3.

Listing 10-3. Choosing a Product and Showing Similar Products

```
##============================Customer chooses a
product============================================================
#Sample Product rating view assume here that a customer selected the
product 'Dalmere Chocolate cup'
#What recommendation are you going to give based on this selection
#Users who bought 'Dalmere Chocolate cup' also bought:
dalmereRatings = productRatings['Dalmere Chocolate cup']
dalmereRatings.head()
Out[233]:
user_id
1     5.0
3     NaN
4     NaN
6     NaN
7     NaN
Name: Dalmere Chocolate cup, dtype: float64

In [234]:
similarProducts = productRatings.corrwith(dalmereRatings)
#Dropping the NA values to get more meaningful data
similarProducts = similarProducts.dropna()
df = pd.DataFrame(similarProducts)
df.head(10)
```

```
Out[234]:
                                   0
product_name
Aeso napkins 10 PACK          1.000000
Ajnin peppermint rolls SINGLE 0.021653
Condsi Pen                    1.000000
Dalmere Chocolate cup         1.000000
Deur masscara                 0.188982
Dostixee potato chips         0.476342
Dothis Pins                   0.563854
Ega hair remover             -1.000000
Erutan shampoo                1.000000
Evol paper cups              -0.228218
```

In Listing 10-3, I have first assumed the product selected by the customer is Dalmere Chocolate cup. After this selection, in the background, ratings are selected for the particular product, which in our case shows that from the top seven users, user ID one has given rating of 5. For the other four users, the ratings are given as NaN, which means the users have not given any ratings for this product. In the next piece of code, I now make a correlation between product ratings, which was our pivot table comprised of index user id, and column product name and the values as ratings. The correlation between product ratings and the dalMere ratings, which is our data frame for Dalmere chocolate cup that we are assuming to be the product selected by the user. In the data frame using similar products, we get the correlation, and now I drop the NaN-values from the similar products data frame. After doing this in the next line of code, I look at the first 10 values of the data frame. We can see that the product Aeso napkins 10 PACK has the highest correlation of 1 with Dalmere chocolate cup. Similarly we have the product Condsi Pen, which also has a correlation of 1 with Dalmere chocolate cup. You can also see that Agar hair remover has a negative correlation of -1 with Dalmere chocolate cup. Although these results are good, they are not sorted so in the next piece of code, I solve these products. This can be seen in Listing 10-4.

Listing 10-4. Sorted Values of the Similar Products

```
similarProducts.sort_values(ascending=False)
Out[235]:
product_name
Aeso napkins 10 PACK              1.000000
Thygie fruit juice concentrate    1.000000
Dalmere Chocolate cup             1.000000
Condsi Pen                        1.000000
Erutan shampoo                    1.000000
Pitrez sweet cake                 0.798935
Dothis Pins                       0.563854
Yssbol Magazine                   0.500000
Dostixee potato chips             0.476342
Getty plastic cutlery set         0.335047
Fitre friendship band             0.272375
Deur masscara                     0.188982
Spets stain remover               0.076743
Ajnin peppermint rolls SINGLE     0.021653
Evol paper cups                   -0.228218
Rewop toothpaste                  -0.845154
Neek corn chips                   -1.000000
Ega hair remover                  -1.000000
dtype: float64
```

If you look at the results in Listing 10-4 closely, you will see that there are some spurious correlations as well, such as a high correlation for Condsi Pen and Everton shampoo—to name just a few. This tells us that although our method of doing correlation works, we do not have a 100 percent accurate result from the similar products. You will find when building search products for the production environment that your approach may give results but they may not be satisfactory to give any meaningful business advice. In such a case, you may need to take an alternative approach, such as aggregating product name and rating and then trying to implement and see the similarity between different products. So in order to refine our results, I will now implement code from Listing 10-5 onward to remove the spurious results.

Listing 10-5. Removing Spurious Correlation

```
#Now let us get rid of spurious results in the similarities
import numpy as np
productStats = survey.groupby('product_name').agg({'rating': [np.size,
np.mean]})
productStats.head()

productStats.sort_values([('rating', 'mean')], ascending=False)[:15]

#I am now getting rid of ratings size greater than 50 to create meaning
results which matter to the business
popularProducts = productStats['rating']['size'] >= 50
productStats[popularProducts].sort_values([('rating', 'mean')],
ascending=False)[:15]
df = productStats[popularProducts].join(pd.DataFrame(similarProducts,
columns=['similarity']))
df.head(15)
df.sort_values(['similarity'], ascending=False)[:15]
Out[241]:
```

product_name	(rating, size)	(rating, mean)	similarity
Aeso napkins 10 PACK	64	3.468750	1.000000
Dothis Pins	175	3.645714	0.563854
Dostixee potato chips	208	3.817308	0.476342
Getty plastic cutlery set	246	4.077236	0.335047
Fitre friendship band	198	4.292929	0.272375
Spets stain remover	127	2.574803	0.076743
Ajnin peppermint rolls SINGLE	256	3.875000	0.021653
Evol paper cups	90	3.888889	-0.228218

You can clearly see from the results in removing spurious correlation that we now get better results than the list of products that we got earlier. Here we have products with ratings similar to and rating size. In this piece of code, for variable in the product stats data frame, there is a size of greater than 50. In simple terms, I have selected only those products where the number of survey respondents or user ids are more than 50. I have also sorted the values in ascending order and then joined the popular products product stats with similar product data frames to create a new column known as similarity, which is nothing but the correlation value for each product with the chosen product. In the illustrated case, we have seen that there are the products like Aeso napkins 10 PACK, Dostixee potato chips, Getty plastic cutlery set, Ajnin peppermint rolls SINGLE, Evol paper cups, Dothis Pins, and Spets stain remover that help correlation or similarity score with our chosen product. Can you think of any correlation between these products as far as the buying behavior of any user of the online store in regards to why they would buy these products together?

If you look at the nature of products then you will understand that people buy things like plastic cutlery sets, napkins, potato chips, peppermint rolls, paper cups, pins, and stain removers when they usually have a party at home. From this perspective, the similarity between these products makes sense. We can visualize the bar plot for similarity as well in Figure 10-1.

```python
df['similarity'].plot(kind='bar')
ax = df['similarity'].plot(kind='bar')
x_offset = -0.03
y_offset = 0.02
for p in ax.patches:
    b = p.get_bbox()
    val = "{:+.2f}".format(b.y1 + b.y0)
    ax.annotate(val, ((b.x0 + b.x1)/2 + x_offset, b.y1 + y_offset))
```

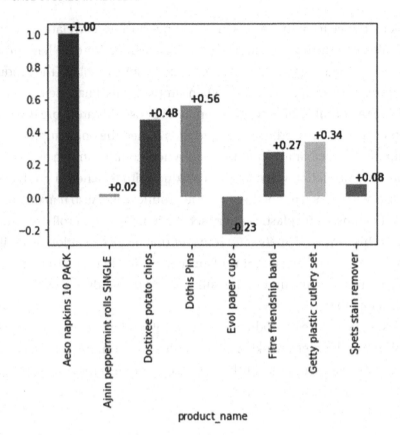

Figure 10-1. *Similarity score of products bought with product Dalmere chocolate cups*

I have used a bar plot in the code by using the plot function parameter equal to bar elaborate the access object from this plot with an x offset set of -0.3 and a y offset of 0.2. The highest similarities are between Aeso napkins 10PACK and Dothis pins and Dostixee potato chips. So we see that we get good results for our initial Dalmere chocolate cups selected by the user.

Let us now run this set of code for another product: Aeso napkin 10 PACK. We can see in Figure 10-2 all the results for selecting similar products. There is no change in code from what we have seen in the earlier Python code set. The only change is the product name and the subsequent results from the code:

```
#2nd Sample Product rating view
aesoRatings = productRatings['Aeso napkins 10 PACK']
aesoRatings.head()
```

```
#Now finding products with similar ratings
similarProducts = productRatings.corrwith(aesoRatings)
similarProducts = similarProducts.dropna()
df = pd.DataFrame(similarProducts)
df.head(10)

similarProducts.sort_values(ascending=False)

#Now let us get rid of spurious results in the similarities
import numpy as np
productStats = survey.groupby('product_name').agg({'rating': [np.size,
np.mean]})
productStats.head()

productStats.sort_values([('rating', 'mean')], ascending=False)[:15]

#I am now getting rid of ratings size greater than 20 to create meaning
results which matter to the business
popularProducts = productStats['rating']['size'] >= 50
productStats[popularProducts].sort_values([('rating', 'mean')],
ascending=False)[:15]
df = productStats[popularProducts].join(pd.DataFrame(similarProducts,
columns=['similarity']))
df.head(15)
df.sort_values(['similarity'], ascending=False)[:15]

#Visualization of similarities
df['similarity'].plot(kind='bar')
ax = df['similarity'].plot(kind='bar')
x_offset = -0.03
y_offset = 0.02
for p in ax.patches:
    b = p.get_bbox()
    val = "{:+.2f}".format(b.y1 + b.y0)
    ax.annotate(val, ((b.x0 + b.x1)/2 + x_offset, b.y1 + y_offset))
```

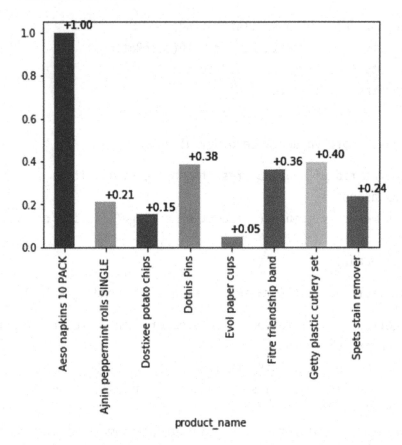

Figure 10-2. *Similar products to Aeso napkins 10PACK*

Now we look at the results and we see that there are no products with very high similarity scores like the one we saw in the chocolate cups product category. Here the highest similarity scores are for Getty plastic cutlery set and Dothis pins. Although the similarity scores are not high for these products, they still make sense because they are all used by the customers for meeting a single need—that of buying party products. This code will need to be tested with live audiences before being deployed into production. A short survey can be run with a few hundred customers to see if selection of these products and then the recommendations coming out of the code make sense regarding whether the customers buy the associated products. With this I conclude the solution for the first case study.

The second case study is a discussion-based case study that talks about a scenario of implementing talking bots for the retail chain group from Southeast Asia. A discussion-based case study is where the questions and the data are presented, but the solution is only discussed and no code is implemented. The purpose of giving a discussion-based case study is to help you, the reader, to develop a business mindset of giving solutions for different business problems. You can refer case study implementations of birds, which I have given in the healthcare section, for implementing your solution of the code.

CASE STUDY 2: Talking Bots for AMDAP Retail Group

AMDAP group has stores in Southeast Asia, Australia, and New Zealand. It is one of the largest retail concept stores in the region. It has taken nearly 20 years for its founder, Mr. Hun Hun Makawaki, to make the group reach the position where it is today. The Concept retail stores of the AMDAP group are unique and differentiate themselves by selling exotic international items to the local people through their stores. For example: In Thailand the stores sell exotic fruits from all over the world, such as kiwi, which are hard to get in the local market; in Australia and New Zealand, they sell wares from Thailand, Indonesia, and Malaysia as well as other countries. Their range of product varies from fruits and vegetables to clothes, and they also sell exotic packaged products such as cheese, sauces, deli meats, flowers, furniture, etc. The success of the group is told by the numbers, as it has 137 stores from the humble 2 stores that it opened in Thailand in 1998. It now has an annual sales turnover of 1.26 billion USD.

Since 2014 the group has seen a slow growth of its sales. It had implemented a pilot scheme by introducing sales kiosks around its stores to boost sales; however, as we can see in the Table 10-5, this did not give any significant results.

Table 10-5. *Sales Before and After Pilot Implementation*

Store sales before pilot	Store sales after pilot
$216 Million	$207 Million

Customers could walk up to the kiosk and look up a product or item that they wanted to search. The automated kiosk would then display the area, the price, and the alternate products that were available in that particular store. This requires the customer to type the keywords appropriately in order for them to search a product. The kiosk was run by a central store network that would inform the customer about the availability of a product being in stock. It would also give the customer a date when the product would be available in case it was out of stock. This was an intelligent system built with careful planning and good use of technology, but the experiment failed miserably because it did not lead to a rise in sales in the stores where it was implemented. After this, the company did another pilot where it bought a talking robot with an unlimited set of products on its list. The customers would walk up and ask about the availability of a product, and the robot would display its status on the screen and talk back to the customer. This experiment worked wonders for the store, and it saw a significant increase in sales by (35 percent). These numbers of the robot pilot are given in Table 10-6.

Table 10-6. *Sales of the Store After Introduction of the Talking Robot*

Store sales before pilot	Store sales after pilot
$231 Million	$311 Million

That is all I have for this chapter on case studies. I hope you enjoyed going through the case studies as much as I enjoyed presenting them to you. After the success of this pilot, Mr. Makawaki called a meeting with the store's head, technology head, CTO, and Customer Management head. The purpose was to find out why this robot pilot introduction was more successful than the kiosks that they had piloted earlier. Mr. Hun Hun Magawaki, who was the head of customer management department at aMDaP retail group, said that his team had carried out a survey of customers for both the pilots, and the results speak for themselves. In the survey, the customers were given questionnaires verbally as well as in written medium and were asked to read their experience and explain what they liked and did not like about the technology being implemented. The results are given in Table 10-7.

Table 10-7. *Customer survey feedback*

Top Survey Questions	Electronic Kiosk	Talking Robot
What did you like about this technology?	Easy to find out-of-stock items	Verbal response
What did you not like about this technology?	Need to type	Not a human response

Mr. Hun Hun Magawaki explained that 84 percent of the customers surveyed responded that they liked the electronic kiosk feature wherein it made it easy to find out-of-stock items, whereas the customers found the verbal response from the talking robot very interesting about the technology. The thing that they did not like about the technology implementation for the electronic kiosk was the need to type, as they found it laborious, and a whopping 84 percent of the respondents said that they did not like this technology. Whereas for the talking robot, 34 percent of the respondents said that the robot did not give a human-like response. Mr. Hun Hun Makawaki gave the recommendation to the founder of the organization that the company introduce technology similar to a talking robot, as people were more comfortable talking than typing.

The finance head, Mr. Gin Gin Nuchigiwa, then gave a brief report on the comparative implementation cost for each pilot. This is given in Table 10-8.

Table 10-8. *Cost Comparison Between Pilots*

Cost of e-Kiosk pilot (per unit)	Cost of Talking Robot pilot (per unit)
$70,000	$250,000

We can see that the e-Kiosk's pilot per unit cost was much less than the cost of a talking robot per unit for implementation. Looking at this, Mr. Hun Hun Makawaki, the founder, commented that it was cost-prohibitive to implement the talking robot; however, he asked the technology head office organization if there was a possibility of introducing talking kiosks, as they were fairly less in cost and would give the same talking experience to the customer as given by a talking robot. Of course the difference would be that a talking robot would have an appearance and could walk to the customer, but in the case of an electronic talking kiosk the customer would have to walk up to it. But he said that looking at the cost advantage of electronic kiosks, he would like to go with this option if it was possible to build it.

The main task for you is the following:

- What do you think are the reasons for the increase in sales for the second pilot where the talking robot was implemented? What do you think was the main reason the pilot became successful? Was it the novelty of the idea, or was it the ability of technology to talk like humans? Why did the store's customers like the talking robots more than the electronic kiosks?

- Do you think that after introduction of electronic talking robots, once the novelty of the idea wore off, the customer sales in the stores would again drop? Give your reasons for your opinion.

- Do you agree with Mr. Hun Hun Makawaki that implementing talking electronic kiosks was the best solution in these circumstances?

- What would be your Python code of implementation for talking kiosks with the following menu?

  - Search Product

  - Place Customer Complaint

  - Recommendations for You

  - New Offers

Now I discuss the answers to these four questions. Please remember that in a case study approach, there is no single right or wrong answer; however, you need to give one that would be acceptable to the business.

The first question on the reasons for the increase in sales for the second pilot on talking robots, in my opinion, is that humans find it easier to talk, as in a retail store environment, people are typically carrying some items or bags or something else with them that does not allow them to put away those things and then start typing. Also talking can be done hands-free, and it does not involve any kind of physical involvement of hands. So in the store, the best way to implement customer service through technology is to talk to them directly.

Regarding the second question, in my opinion there definitely would be an increase in sales due to the presence of talking robots, as when people hear about it, they will go to the store and shop. However, I do not think the novelty wearing off would lead to a major drop since the technology is helping the customer and providing better service by talking back to them. So I do not think that after the introduction of talking robots or kiosks there would be a major drop in sales. If the talking robots do not help the customers in identifying and removing their problems, then the novelty of the idea would definitely wear off. In such a case, this retail group should continuously take feedback on improving the talking technology.

The founder of the store did not want to spend money on a talking robot and found it cost-prohibitive for implementation in his organization, so he chose a middle path where he could give the customer the experience of a talking robot in an electronic kiosk, which cost much less in comparison. In my opinion, it is a wise decision to take a middle path where it saves resources for the organization in the interest of business. They can later look at implementing talking robots when they have funds to implement.

I told you that for question four I will not be giving you the Python code for implementation of this case study. However, you can take the Python code from the case study in the healthcare section and add a talking ability using Python libraries like Pi audio and implement both speech-to-text and text-to-speech for talking to the customer. You can take the recommendations for your section straight from the case study that we have just completed in Chapter 10 of this book and implement the answers with text-to-speech implementation. The same can be done to search products that give an output of available items in the inventory with their stock status and quantity. You can implement speech-to-text first for getting the name of the product to search and then text to speech to give the response on the status of the item. For placing a customer complaint, you can create a prebuilt menu where it asks for the customer's product name, the bill number, and other such details and then registers the complaint that the customer speaks into the electronic kiosk through its microphone. This simple implementation can help you to understand how to implement audio that would talk to the customer and explain to them the current offers that are running on key products. In this way you can implement a simple solution and understand how to deal with a situation in the retail environment in case you encounter it. I will be implementing audio capabilities through the Python libraries in the third section of Finance of in this book. In the case study Chapter 3 you can look up to see how Python libraries have been used to give audio capabilities to the programs.

End Notes

[1] Biplots taken from the script on github by Teddy Roland, `https://github.com/teddyroland/python-biplot`

[2] Gaussian Mixture, `http://scikit-learn.org/stable/modules/mixture.html#mixture`

## CHAPTER 11

Pitfalls to Avoid With Machine Learning in Retail

This chapter is about ideas in retail for which using machine learning technology would help the organizations to monetize them. I present to you just three ideas that, as per my research in the retail sector and after having consulted experts from the retail field, I conclude not just need more attention but are going to be the focus for the retail industry in the future. Some of the things that I tell you in this chapter may sound far-fetched and far from realistic but you will realize as we progress that these ideas are definitely going to take shape and are going to be implemented in the retail industry. Of course these ideas are good for any startup to pick up and start working on. It is not that there are no startups working on these ideas, but I am presenting you a fresh view of the ideas and how to monetize them as far as machine learning is concerned. The first idea is about Supply Chain Management, the second one is about Customer Management, and the third is about the use of IoT in Retail. While I tell you about these ideas, I will also tell you about some of the pitfalls and the dangers that exist in the current state where these ideas stand.

Supply Chain Management and Logistics

It is important to understand that in the retail sector the most underutilized area for machine learning is supply chain management; hence, it holds a lot of scope for implementation. It is underutilized because it involves logistics or physical movement of goods or products. This is where the key area of implementation in machine learning

© Puneet Mathur 2019
P. Mathur, *Machine Learning Applications Using Python*, https://doi.org/10.1007/978-1-4842-3787-8_11

is not only lagging behind but needs a lot of focus for gaining advantage from things such as GPS tracking of good or services. Why just track and report reschedules and schedule misses? Why not be predictive by using machine learning? This is a pitfall that an organization should avoid while implementing their machine learning applications. If you look at it from a retail perspective, then the arrival of particular goods is linked to sales of those goods to the customer on time. If the GPS traditional tracking systems just report and then the retail organization's team keeps taking corrective measures to bring back the missed schedule goods, then it costs more money. Instead of this approach, they should become more proactive and predict goods that are likely to miss the schedule with prescriptive actions that will enable the business to keep its logistics deliveries on schedule, leading to massive savings in terms of time and missed sales. For creating such a predictive model, massive supply chain management data is required, with a lot of historical background. The model needs to learn what leads to a missed schedule, which types of goods are prone to have missed schedules, and is there a pattern? Sometimes the reasons for a missed delivery schedule lie beyond the retail organization's boundaries and are due to external parties. Even in such cases, there should be data that is collected with regards to failed deliveries from external organizations and analyzed to find out if there is a pattern in this. Data from procurement or the purchasing department can help in all this analysis and model building. For example, I was working for a client whose 5 percent revenue was being lost annually due to late delivery schedules by its suppliers. After analyzing the data, I found that most of the supplies were failing from a particular location inside the country, as all the suppliers in that area were delivering key products for sales after the scheduled delivery period more than 50 percent of the time. After further investigating with the suppliers, the retail organization found out that this was due to heavy traffic congestion on the highway, as the deliveries were being made through one of the world's most notable national highways. This was leading to an average delay of 2.6 days. The retail organization then started exploring alternate routes for delivery that would not go through the high-traffic area and would be able to reach the warehouse destination faster. An alternate route was found that would take 7 more hours to reach the destination and was not as congested as the highway. This saved them 14 hours of delay on a single side delivery. With this new arrangement the goods were delivered on time and the loss due to missed schedules was substantially reduced. Sometimes you need to have a questioning attitude from the findings when you start to see patterns of problems.

Another area of supply chain management is cost control. This is a constant challenge for the supply chain manager to effectively control the cost, as it keeps rising due to rise in fuel/freight costs, use of new technology such as GPS tracking, etc. This is again a bad pitfall to avoid since it involves increasing of product handling and transportation costs. A key part of the supply chain management lies in handling inventory and the cost efficiency involved with it. Applying machine learning to increase inventory management efficiency and reducing the cost of handling the inventory should be the top most tasks. Although this topic is a good candidate for a case study to make you understand better, I will try to give you some tips on how I have done this implementation for some of my clients. A simple inventory process is given below in Figure 11-1

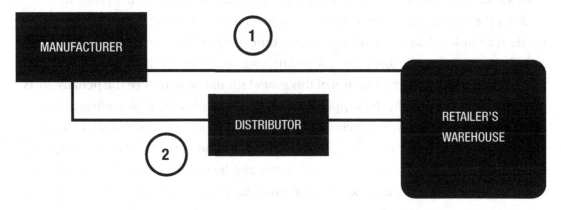

Figure 11-1.   *The inventory process*

Inventory Management

Before we begin to look at inventory management, I will show you a diagram that causes the scenarios through which goods move to the retailer's warehouse. In the first scenario, the goods move directly from the manufacturer to the retailer's warehouse; in the second scenario, goods move from the manufacturer to the distributor and then go to the retailer's warehouse. In the diagram, to simplify, this process of movement of goods from the manufacturer to the retailer's warehouse is the major theory of supply chain management inventory control. If there is delay in the delivery of goods from the manufacturer to the distributor, it leads to delays for the retailer as well. To compensate for these delays, retailers put penalty fees in their contracts. Although this can limit the retailer's revenue loss, it cannot compensate for the retailers loss of goodwill in front of its customers. Goodwill is not tangible. Over a period of time, the supplies coming late to the retailer causes revenue losses long-term.

The supplies coming into the retailer's warehouse constitute a retailer's inventory. If inventory is not matched to the sales of products, then it will lead to dissatisfaction due to nonavailability of product. Any machine learning model that needs to be built for increasing efficiency and reducing the cost of inventory has to take into account cost and time variables. The cost variables include prices, products they are ordering, donations, unit pipeline costs, and unit penalty costs. The sales and time variables include projected sales units for a particular item in stock, stock review intervals, average transportation time for the product, and the average time it is stored in the warehouse. The inventory model should try to predict based on data the projected goals for the arrival time interval and recommendation on the unit of inventory that needs to be ordered based on transportation time of a product. Some companies follow inventory principles, like just in time inventory management. All those principles can be incorporated in this model. The aim of this model should be to reduce the penalty costs that are being increased by the suppliers and ultimately reduce the late deliveries that are taking place in the inventory control system. To build such a model you will need a massive amount of data not just from the retail organization but also from the suppliers who are external parties. Some information may also be required from external parties, like transporters, clearing agents, and other such agencies.

Customer Management

Now let us look at customer management. Customer management involves creation of customer-centric processes. It starts from acquisition of a new customer to gaging their needs and catering to them. It also includes activities like customer care, listening to customer grievances, giving refunds for faulty products, giving out promotional products, or exchanging items for customers who have bought products.

Customer Management is extremely important if there is any kind of customer involved in recruitment. I would like to give you another example from my client-run job placement service that deals with selling their recruitment services through their website. The management of the company wanted to automate the entire recruitment process. The automation was to replace all human activity by calling up the people who had purchased their services online. From when the customer purchased the recruitment service to the stage of landing a job offer, everything happens automatically without any human intervention. When this automation was launched, it showed an initial increase in retail revenue at the company due to its ad campaign; however, a few weeks after launch, the entire revenue of the website started declining drastically. Even increased advertisement campaigns did not yield any significant upside. I reviewed their entire process, looking at how the online service worked before and after automation. Machine learning was used heavily as Natural Language Processing was required to understand and match resumes of candidates with job descriptions. Once they found the job listings, they were sent to the candidate's e-mail ID. After a few days the automated system would call the candidate and request them to check their e-mail. The customer would then call the automated IVR system and gave feedback on the forwarded listings. The candidate's preference would be stored and analyzed for the system to learn better. This loop of sending job listings would continue until candidate selected a job listing to which they would like to apply. The system then sends an automated e-mail to the company recruiter informing them of a potential candidate. The system would also call the recruiter to inform them every week about job listing e-mails.

The entire process looks fantastic in theory; however, one important lesson to be learned was that humans like to talk to humans in a natural manner.

This fact came about when the company, at my insistence, carried out a customer feedback survey on the new automated system. The customers clearly called out the rival company's services were much better because there was a human being calling them to understand their preferences.

On getting a clear message from the customers, I asked the client to remove automation from some of the processes. Now we had humans working with machines to get feedback from the customers. The moral of the story is that humans are not yet ready for 100 percent automation. Humans prefer some interaction with human beings in the entire machine learning implementation. We ran another survey after introducing human interaction back to the customers, and the results were much better. The revenue of the company also saw an astounding jump. Any organization should implement machine learning only if it does not lead to dissatisfaction. Customers are key to any business, and this mantra cannot be forgotten.

Let us now look at another client scenario where they had customer-centric processes in their customer management divisions. Every company that faces consumers directly for selling its products requires some kind of feedback or survey in order to gage the customers' response or feeling about its processes. You can see this happening through survey forms online on the company's website or through e-mails to the customers. In some cases, feedback and surveys are done through chatbots as well. You are familiar with some of the automated feedback implementations done by some big names, and you will notice after experience in their customer care automation that sometimes it is very irritating. For example, when you start to interact with the customer care department of the retail organization through e-mail, you receive an automated response stating that your request has been registered and you will receive a response within a certain time frame.

You hope to hear after this that a human will respond to your issue and that response may or may not resolve your problem. Now you notice that immediately after you send your e-mail there is an automatic feedback e-mail that comes back to you asking for your feedback on the resolution provided. If the response by the customer care executive does not solve your problem, even then the feedback e-mail comes to you asking for your response. This is known as dumb implementation of machine learning, where the machine is automating the process of taking feedback from customers without checking if the response given is sufficient or not. Ideally there should be machine learning applications that should be intelligent enough to understand if the response e-mail given by the customer service executive is going to actually solve the customer's problem or not. If the customer's problem is not solved, then it should not send an e-mail to get feedback from them. Think about a time as a customer when you were already frustrated with a problem in the company's product or services and on top of that you received an e-mail from a customer executive that did not solve your problem, but you then received an e-mail asking for your feedback. It will lead to an even more frustrated and agitated customer implementing a down automation level in your processor. This is why I am inviting people to implement real intelligent automated systems rather than just dumb automation.

Instead of increasing customer satisfaction, this kind of dumb automation will lead to customer dissatisfaction. So we need to be cognizant of this pitfall while implementing machine learning in the retail industry. I want you to look at this differentiation between dumb and intelligent use of machine learning for automation in Table 11-1. The figure shows that dumb machine learning implementation uses just event-based automation, like when we saw automated feedback e-mail generation being sent to customers blindly. However, an intelligent machine learning implementation would do this based on certain rules being made, such as whether the customer resolution has been appropriately given by the customer executive. Dumb implementation is blind and does not do any analysis before implementation. However, intelligent implementation uses analytics before its implementation. In the implementation, there are no pre-checks before an event is triggered; however, in intelligent machine learning implementation, there are a lot of pre-checks before something takes place. The term implementation makes sense less than 50 percent of the time for dumb automation, whereas an implementation that is intelligent in nature make sense more than 50 percent of the time. The implementation uses a low level of intelligence; however, intelligent implementation emulates human intelligence and analysis for executing any kind of automation. Table 11-1 is going to guide you in your implementation of machine learning within your organizations or machine learning projects.

Table 11-1. *Dumb vs Intelligent Machine Learning Implementation*

Dumb Machine Learning Implementation	Intelligent Machine Learning Implementation
Event-based automation	Rule-based automation
Blind Automation	Analytics-based automation
No pre-checks before automation	Lot of pre-checks before automation
Makes sense <50% of the time	Makes sense >50% of the time
Low level of intelligence	Emulates human intelligent analysis for execution

Internet of Things

We now move on to the next topic, which is IoT (Internet of Things). This advancement in technology has seen rapid implementation along with use of machine learning by providing devices and services that are intelligent. There has been early adoption of IoT in retail by companies like Walmart, where they use RFID in their stores in refrigeration units to alert the need for proactive maintenance and put temperature sensors inside those units. However, such implementation has not been successful. There is a dramatic shift in the implementation of IoT for retail by targeting customer care then looking at increasing operational efficiencies [1].

The main implementation is to enhance the customer experience online or inside the store. One implementation example is where IoT is being used by creating smart pushcarts that track the shopper's or customer's footfall inside the store and communicates the places where a customer has stopped and the areas inside the store where the customer has had maximum footfall. This kind of data collection helps in using machine learning to find out how customers move inside the store and to enhance the display and promotional offers for the items that are being sought after most by the customers. Customer footfall data not only helps in creating optimal displays but it also helps in finding out why customers are frequenting a particular promotional offer or not and to correlate it with the success and failure of product promotion. If there are maximum footfalls for a promotion given by the smart pushcart, then it indicates customer interest in the product. If there are no or light footfalls for an area of the product where the promotion is taking place, then it means that the product offered to the customers is not exciting them to even stop by and have a look. This is an intelligent use of machine learning with IoT to enhance customer experience. 1 say to most of my clients that any retail organization that uses IoT for enhancement of the business should look at the ROI it provides. For example, if you have technology being used for a plantation organization to monitor trees by putting sensors inside them and with data being collected in a cloud storage centrally, the organization would have to think about if it is worth putting so much technology investment into monitoring of trees. Does it provide any cost efficiency or revenue enhancement due to this investment?

In retail, a smart application of IoT with machine learning could be where the IoT devices at each store location track movement of people near a popular product and pop-up a display right near the product that caters to the particular customer with a discount offer. This does not require usage of any mobile device or any app in order to interact with the user. The IoT device communicates with the cloud storage and uses machine learning to find out if the customer's location inside the store is a hot promotional region or not. If it is a hot promotional region, then it displays on the screen a promotional offer video that enables the customer to buy the product. Such a usage of IoT requires huge investment by the retail organization. The investment would be in the IoT devices stationed at each key store location and then in the collection devices that collect data from inside each location of the store and transmit it to the centralized cloud storage. On receiving analysis and patterns from the machine learning application, the smart display device would need to turn on and show a particular promotional offer, so there is a requirement for a huge investment in technology for this kind of setup to exist. If we ignore the ROI from creating such a smart promotion network, then after a while this kind of investment would be dumped by the management. And accurate estimation and monitoring as well as tracking for the increase in sales due to implementation of a smart promotional network would need to be done to categorize it as a success or failure.

This is one pitfall that retail organizations should avoid when they implement machine learning in their retail stores.

There is also a tendency among the retail organizations to track their employees' movements and their utilization for enhancing customer experience. In one case there is a retail organization that uses tracking devices on the employees' ID cards to track their movements inside the store and to report back on where they are currently located. The technology allows us to do this now. The motive of the organization is to correlate between the customer's movements and the employees' movements to find out if the employees are actually serving the customers inside the retail store. A preliminary look at this does not make it look bad; however, tracking employees' movements and then linking it to their performance appraisals could make the use of this technology go a bit too far. Certainly it can help increase employee utilization and increase their productivity, but it could also demoralize the employees to think that they are being monitored and their salaries are going to depend on where they are moving inside the stores. We need to avoid this pitfall where we are making the technology interact with humans, as they are sensitive to how technology is being used to track and monitor them.

We have looked at three different scenarios in this chapter and their implementation in the retail sector, and we have also discussed the major pitfalls that hinder the growth of an organization and the proper implementation of technology inside it. I am sure the scenarios are going to help you decide on improving the implementation of machine learning in your projects as well.

End Note

[1]   Nikki Baird, Apr 24, 2017, 10:46am IoT in Retail: `https://www.forbes.com/sites/nikkibaird/2017/04/24/five-retail-iot-use-cases-when-retailers-finally-get-around-to-iot/#65bf88226255?`

## CHAPTER 12

Monetizing Retail Machine Learning

In this chapter, I am going to put forward some innovative ideas that can be monetized using machine learning. I will also show you some examples where a similar approach has been used and has succeeded.

The three areas for monetizing are the following:

- Connected retail stores

- Connected warehouses

- Collaborative community mobile stores

In a way, as I will explain further, the concepts of connected retail stores and connected warehouses are linked to each other. We will, however, look at them separately to understand them in greater detail and then see how they can work together.

Connected Retail Stores

In order for us to understand what I mean by connected retail stores, let us first understand what a connected retail store is not. I see this misconception with a lot of big companies as well.

- A connected retail store is not about just extending digital capabilities to your existing brick and mortar store.

- A connected retail store is not just about adding RFID tags to your products and carrying out an analysis of consumer behavior.

© Puneet Mathur 2019

P. Mathur, *Machine Learning Applications Using Python*, https://doi.org/10.1007/978-1-4842-3787-8_12

- A connected retail store is not using Bluetooth or online means of sending products and offers to the customer as they shop.

- A connected retail store is not using phone calls to make offers to customers while they shop inside the store.

After looking at what a connected retail store is not, let us now look what a connected retail store should be and whether we have any examples to emulate or learn from. Let us look at a diagram of a truly connected store in Figure 12-1.

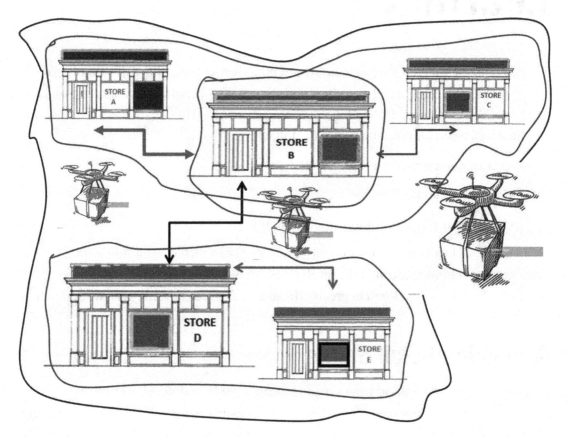

Figure 12-1. *Connected stores diagram*

In this example diagram, I show you a group of five connected retail stores belonging to a single retail organization in any city. The red line denotes the city limits, and the blue lines denote stores in the same community or locality. Central to this connected stores theme is the concept that each retail store has a lot of movement of goods and services every day.

Customers walk into any or all of those stores in various parts of the locality in a city. If you are familiar with the retail industry then you would know that not all the stores have the same amount of sales for any given product. For example, in Figure 12-1 we could have Store A selling more of frozen products than Store E and Store B selling a lot more milk and bread than Store C. There could also be a situation where during some seasonal cycles, for example, Store D starts selling more sweets and chocolates than any of the stores. This sudden spurt in demand for certain products in certain localities causes the stock in that particular store to go off the shelf. In order to take care of these sudden demands by the consumers, we can have prediction models; however, the logistics involved in moving goods from warehouses to stores, which is the current model of operation in all the major stores in the world, is going to change because of this new concept of connected stores.

Let us now take an example of how a connected store system would work. Let's assume that during the festive season, two stores (Store E and Store A) are seeing lower shelf sales levels of chocolates and sweets. Store E knows that in the past week there has been a lot of demand for chocolates and sweets, and hence in the coming week it is likely to run out of stock. In the case of a connected store, the store manager automatically raises a request to the central retail store system to get more sweets and chocolates based on the predicted demand for the next week. In a traditional retail store organization, this demand would go to the central warehousing system, and then the central warehousing system would fulfill the demand of individual stores slowly as and when the stock arrives. Consider that the demand for chocolates and sweets has gone up only in two stores in the entire city. There are three more stores, and stores that have excessive stock on their shelves that the consumers are not buying at the moment. Now it makes sense for the store manager to requisition the central retail store system and get the stock for the coming week immediately from stores B, C, and D.

However, there would be logistical challenges in moving goods across different stores in different localities, so a machine learning algorithm can be developed that can look at the distance between the stores based on their geographic locations and then calculate the nearest store that has excess of shelf volume of the particular product demanded by the requisition store manager. In our case, in Figure 12-1, we can see that Store B is closest to Store A. So it makes sense to get the demand for chocolates and sweets fulfilled between Store B and Store A by moving some of the excessive products from Store B to Store A. It is for the local store algorithm to decide how much excessive stock there is in Store B, and after determining that excessive quantity, it then accepts the requisition request from Store A and prepares its delivery drones to push the excessive products from its store shelves. This is just one example of how this system can function. However, once this system is automated and built, it would actually save millions of dollars for organizations that have multiple stores around the city. Merchandise would be moving from store to store based on algorithmic sequences and machine learning models that predict the most efficient quantities that need to be retained in a particular store. The major advantage of having such a connected store system is the reduction in stale or near-expiring goods on the store shelves. Another advantage is meeting the demand just in time, thereby increasing customer confidence in the store and also leading to an increase in revenue and customer loyalty. This system would also reduce the cost of warehousing a product not just in the organization's warehouses but also in the retail stores.

These are some of the great benefits that a connected store system can look to implement as a result of implementing the latest technologies, such as machine learning and artificial intelligence. I could not find any great implementation of this type of connected store with any of the retail chains such as Walmart, Macy's, or others. One company that is using drones, machine learning, and artificial intelligence is Amazon, and the Amazon go stores [1] that have opened in the past few years do use drones for delivery; however, it is not very clear in the public domain whether they use this concept of moving products between various retail stores by harnessing the power of drones. The difference between what I am talking about in terms of a connected store and what has been implemented with Amazon go [1] is the front-end and the back-end of a store. Amazon go talks about no lines and no checkouts; however, I am not talking about that customer experience. I am talking about the back-end operations of the store to create the efficiency and the predictability in the current retail store operations so that they reduce cost and increase their revenue in the long-term.

Connected Warehouses

Now we come to the next concept: connected warehouses. This concept of connected warehouses is also part of the back-end system of retail store operations. The idea that I am going to give here is also related to the previous idea of connected stores; however, here I am talking about connecting different warehouses of a retail store operation of any organization. In this machine learning and AI operation, I am showing how different warehouses of a company can be connected internally based on certain criteria.
Let us take any big retail company like Target or Walmart; they have different stores

within a city, and to service them there is a network of warehouses that are not visible to the customers. Some of the warehouses reside at the back of the retail store and some of them are outside of the city limits or the suburban areas. The purpose of such a network of warehouses is to be able to service the retail stores within a particular city's limits. Any given company can have warehouses situated outside of city limits as the requirement for cheap land is met there; however, in the back-end operations we know that if we do not manage the number of goods and services stored in the respective warehouses, then the entire retail system will become inefficient and will cost the company a huge amount of dollars to maintain. Most of the organizations of this size do have internal inventory management systems; that is not what I am talking about here. I am talking about connecting different warehouses of the same company in a city or across multiple cities in a way that the machine learning-based and the AI-based systems predict the demand for particular goods and services within each locality of the city based on seasonal demands or any random spike in demands for particular goods and services. Now look at Figure 12-2 to understand the Connected warehouses diagram.

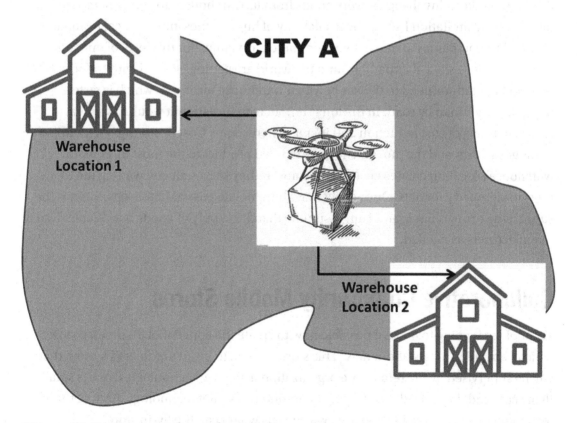

Figure 12-2. *Connected warehouses diagram*

To understand this system better, I will now explain, with the help of an example, how the entire system can work. Let us assume in Figure 12-2 that there are two warehouses of a given organization on the outskirts of the city. In location one warehouse, there is a demand for frozen products that is predicted to go up by a substantial number in the next month. In the other warehouse, there is a predicted demand for home cleaning items that is the predicted to go up in the next month. The machine learning and AI system would look at the current stock levels in each of those two warehouses, then look at the predicted demand for the next month for each of those warehouses, and then draw up the number of excessive items that are there and transmit to respective locations. If it sees that warehouse location two has a higher quantity than required for frozen items, then it would order the system to move items from location two to location one for the excessive quantity of products. Again the way the transportation would happen could be based on the use of huge drones that are capable of carrying high volumes of goods. Again I do not see a practical application of this concept being directly used for warehouses. We know that Amazon is using this for operations involving delivery goods from its warehouses to consumers. One technological limitation I see is the availability of huge drones and the legal formalities required by companies to make them commercially viable. But this level of operation will have to start since the roads around the world are getting clogged with traffic and the retail operations need to deliver between warehouse locations, which is faster through the air than by road. In the long run, such an investment would give great results in terms of cost reduction and increase in revenue. Cost of storing low-demand items goes down and the movement of demanded product to the most in-demand warehouse's location creates customer loyalty, as they see a reduced waiting time for the most in-demand products. One aspect that I have not discussed in this operation is the supply side of operations, and I am assuming that the supply of goods is available from manufacturers as needed.

Collaborative Community Mobile Stores

Technology is going to make it possible now to create the concept of fly-in retail stores, which I am going to talk about now. This store is going to be an automated system that will be supervised by the retail store organization using two technologies: one is small flying cars and the second is self-flying or autonomous pilot technology. Both of these technologies, when married together, will give us what I call the fly-in store.

Before I start to enumerate and discuss how you can monetize this concept, let's first look at the need for this concept itself. We know there are three major problems in today's modern society where people have to work more hours at their workplaces, and this trend is increasing daily all around the world. The other trend is that of traffic on the roads, which is also increasing and clogging the roads during peak hours and at other times, making it a nightmare for people to go out and do their retail shopping. The third is the problem that a store does not collaborate in a particular community or a locality with the residents who reside there.

Let us look at how the fly-in store can help a large retail organization address all these three pains of the consumer that often lead to lower sales.

People are getting busy, and they need places to shop near their workplace or their homes, where they spend most of their work or personal lives. On weekdays they do not get the time to go out frequently to malls or other retail stores; hence, they need something that is available for shopping very near their workplaces or their homes. A fly-in store will definitely help address this problem because it can self-fly itself into any location where there is a concentration of people, like large office complexes or large apartment complexes. This ability of a store, wherein the consumer does not go out to the store but the store comes to the consumer, is actually going to turn the retail game around through its implementation. This is an idea that is waiting to be implemented, and the retail chain that implements it first is going to reap major revenue sales increases.

The second problem that a fly-in store is able to address is people not coming to the store because of the high amount of traffic on the roads. The fly-in store moves into designated communities, where the local people can come and shop at their convenience, which is a big plus for them. Imagine if a person comes to work and is greeted by a fly-in store that gives them the products that they have been asking for from local grocery stores or fashion stores near their apartment complex. The store could also fly into large local parks and park itself there to allow the nearby citizens to come and shop. This added convenience of shopping nearby is going to make this idea a great success. With this, we are turning the problem of clogged streets due to traffic into a plus for the retail store, as it is now closer to the consumer and is able to deliver goods at times that are more convenient to them. Another advantage with this fly-in store is that a car can also come and park itself near major business centers, which have a concentration of employees working in them. During free times (e.g., lunch breaks and coffee breaks), the employees of such business centers can shop at their convenience.

Again the advantage here is that they do not have to wait through the traffic in order to buy things for their homes. Of course, this may not work for bigger items like household electronics but it will definitely work for things like home groceries, etc.

We already know that the malls in the US are closing down and one of the major causes of this trend is lack of time for people to go to them. With the implementation of the fly-in store, the store goes to the people instead of people coming to the store. In order for a smooth implementation of this technology, we need to have small self-driving or flying cars that can evade traffic and move into any locality, as required by the central theme of a retail organization.

The third problem that this self-driving fly-in retail store is going to address is that of community-based collaboration. Let me explain this a little further with regards to what I mean by the community- or locality-based collaboration. We are primarily talking about two entities—one is the retail store organization and the second is the local community of residence. The residence can belong to any major community in any city; however, if you take any mall or retail store, then they hardly interact with the local residents and they do not communicate with them or their local needs.

I emphasize this local community collaboration because I have seen from the retail data that the local community or local residents often have different needs for products at different times than do localities around other parts of the city. For example, a store located in a more affluent locality may need to stock different types of high-end products and even products of exotic types than a store based in a less affluent locality. Every retail store understands this difference, and they spend their time merchandising accordingly. This is just an example based on the division of economic criteria; however, this division of consumers and localities is not just limited to their financial backgrounds but can be segmented into seasonal demands such as the high demand for items of a particular kind in a particular season due to change in weather conditions. This is where we need the help of machine learning and artificial intelligence to mine data based on the local needs of consumers and predict their demand for certain goods when such patterns reoccur. This data needs to be drilled down and made available to the retail organizations geographically for each locality in a city. Of course a retail store may not target all the localities of a city and can choose to target and sell their products in a particular locality where they find the demand for their products is going to be high.

One more aspect of the locality or community collaboration that is currently missing in the major retail organizations is the ability to harness locality-based demand data for products. Let me further explain what I mean by this by taking an example. Let's say a major retail store in the US wants to sell its products to residents of the Malibu, which is one of the most premium communities in Los Angeles where a lot of celebrities live, and the store needs to harness data on the major items demanded by the celebrity residents of this community and not just the seasonal or any pattern-based demand, which is unique for this community. For finding such information regarding the likes and dislikes of people in a locality or a community, the data will need to harness local social media data for residents of that locality. Once it has feedback on the likes and dislikes of the residents of this community, the data can now look to target and advertise about an upcoming fly-in retail sales event that it wants to conduct at this community. Again social media advertising can be used to make the citizens aware and to generate awareness about the event. It is this change in the way retail organizations are going to sell products in the future that is going to bring major dividends in terms of high revenue, with targeted demand being met with targeted supply. The store may no longer sell "everything" but only that which is demanded by the residents of a particular community. The retail store is now collaborating with the local community and is looking at their local needs and meeting them with frequent fly-in retail events.

Of course when a retail store organization is focusing its sales on a particular community that it thinks is appropriate for a fly-in event, then it would also have to interact with the local residents through local community billboard advertising or sending its community workers to various community centers, where the residents congregate for events in order to let them know of any event that is going to happen in the future. This is apart from the social media campaign that would be targeted to the residents, and when the fly-in events are launched it would help make them a big success.

This need not be restricted to fly-in cars; we can also have self-driving mobile bus retail stores that are modified to give ambient retail experience to the consumers. One example of this technology implementation is Robomart [2], which is waiting for legal hurdles to be removed before it can become operational.

End Notes

[1]   Amazon Go stores: `https://www.amazon.com/b?ie=UTF8&node=16008589011`

[2]   Robomart- Self Driving Retail Store: `https://www.youtube.com/watch?v=FJMC40vkTTQ`

## CHAPTER 13

Overview of Machine Learning in Finance

A few years back I was approached by the financial client from the Southeast Asia region to help them with their machine learning effort since they were newly implementing it in their industry and they had become stuck with the practical implementation of the machine learning algorithm in their financial advisory services domain. During the implementation, I studied the financial industry around the world in order to get a better grip on what was required in order to implement this assignment.

Even today the implementation of machine learning and artificial intelligence in the field of the financial industry holds a lot of scopes.

In a very broad sense, financial services [1; `https://en.m.wikipedia.org/wiki/ Financial_services`], as defined by Wikipedia, is comprised of businesses that manage money. These include credit unions, banks, credit card companies, insurance companies, accountancy companies, consumer finance companies, stock brokerages, investment funds, and individual fund managers. Of course, in our discussion, I am not going to talk about the government-related financial services.

As far as the segmentation of the financial services market is concerned, I will be using the following broad segments that are described in Table 13-1.

The clear differentiation in the business approach can be seen from Table 13-1.

259

© Puneet Mathur 2019
P. Mathur, *Machine Learning Applications Using Python*, https://doi.org/10.1007/978-1-4842-3787-8_13

Table 13-1. *Different Segments of Financial Industry, Broad Classification*

Type	Focus	Services and Differentiation
Consumer Finance	Providing personal loans, indirect financing, including lease and sales financing, credit card issuers, pawn shops, and payday loan providers	Provide unsecured loans to individuals for both commercial and personal purposes. They operate in the subprime category and provide loans to individuals with bad credit history
Capital Markets	Undertake activities, including trading, brokerage, strategic advisory, portfolio management, asset management, and investment advice	Primarily work as intermediaries, either to provide or manage capital, thereby satisfying financial goals of institutions and individuals
Diversified Financial Services	Providing financial services, such as financial advisory firms, investment research companies, stock exchanges, and credit rating companies	A majority of their revenue is derived from one particular area of expertise and specialized activity

In Table 13-1 the market segmentation of the financial services industry [2; `http://media.lockelord.com/files/upload/advisenIndustryReportDivFinConsFinCapMrkt.pdf`], which is based upon the financial services industry, subprime and credit crisis weighs heavy, according to a 2008 edition report by John W. Molka III, CFA Senior Industry Analyst and Editor. We first look at the consumer finance section, which is a group of companies providing personal loans, indirect credit card issuers, pawn shops, and payday loan providers. This list does not include mortgage and lending companies. The main item that these companies deal with is unsecured loans to individuals. Of course, all the statistics given in the report are based on the US; however, the percentages are applicable for all the developed countries. For example, the consumer finance companies hold 23 percent of the consumer credit as of 2007, and this can be applied to other developed economies as well. While this statistic looks dated by more than 10 years, it gives us an idea of how much share the consumer finance companies hold in the consumer credit in a nation's economy.

Next in the segment are capital markets, which are comprised of organizations undertaking stock trading brokerages, strategic financial advisory portfolio management, asset management, and professional investment advice. These companies are intermediaries, and they work for the goals of other financial institutions or individuals.

These companies include investment banking and trading in stocks, bonds, derivatives, and commodities. It also includes asset management firms that manage large funds for individuals and institutions around the world. The increasing trend in the sector is the rise in investment banking and securities dealings and that of securities brokerages. The largest services category is investment banking and security dealing, which comprises 41 percent of the total segment business. An increasing trend in the segment is the rise of mutual funds and investments, and this trend can be seen both in the developed and emerging markets.

Which is essentially the companies involved in financial advisory investment research, stock exchanges, rating, and credit rating. This is a market where there are top 10 players, like Citigroup, Berkshire Hathaway, Goldman Sachs, Morgan Stanley, JP Morgan Chase, and Merrill Lynch. The next is the diversified financial services segment.

Now that we have looked at the broad segmentation in the financial industry [2], we will now look at some of the key segments and the value proposition that they provide.

Financial Segments

In the drill-down financial statements diagram in Figure 13-1, we can see the categorization of financial industry into banking and nonbanking segments.

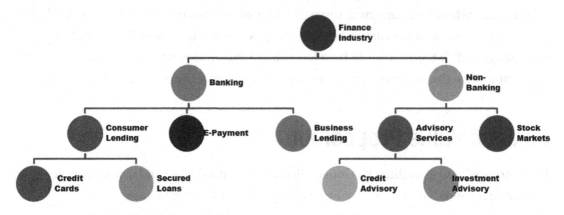

Figure 13-1. *Financial segments*

The banking segment is comprised of consumer lending, which is a very structured form of business where the creditworthiness of the consumer is ascertained through the creation of credit profiles of the consumer. If the credit profile is found to be risky, then the rescue level is ascertained, and only then is the lending possible in the segment. Next is the business lending, which is also a very structured form of lending to commercial organizations for their investment and growth. Although this type of business lending also has a lot of variations, I am not going to go into them now. The third type of banking segmentation is that of e-payments. Both the consumer and the business make electronic payments through the electronic payment banking systems, which are local to each country. The consumer lending can further be divided into credit card lending and secured loans lending. Credit cards are issued by banks only when the creditworthiness of a person is ascertained so that they can perpetually use the credit and then repaired within the given stipulated period. Secured loans are given only when the creditworthiness of an individual is ascertained with respect to the assets that they hold and the liabilities that they have against various loans that they might have taken in the past.

In the non-banking space, we divide the segment into advisory services and the stock markets. In advisory services we again divide our segment into credit advisory services and investment advisory services. The credit advisory services are related to the credit ratings of agencies, banks, countries, and companies. There are various credit rating agencies that operate all over the world and they fall in this segment category. Investment advisory is concerned with management and advice on the funds held by various individuals and organizations. This includes portfolio management services and other such financial advice given by various agencies. Stock markets involve a segment of portfolio management services and brokerages that can be the regulated stock exchanges and unregulated stock exchanges, like the ones used by blockchain technology (e.g., bitcoin). We will be referencing this drill-down version of our segmentation of the finance industry in this finance section throughout this book.

Finance Value Proposition

Value proposition, as defined by Google dictionary, is marketing and innovation, service, and features intended to make a company or product attractive to customers.

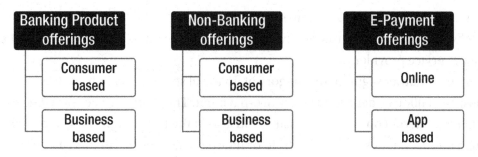

Figure 13-2. *Finance customer value proposition*

The finance-based services that are offered by organizations have a different values proposition for consumers and businesses for both banking and financial services. This is depicted in Figure 13-2.

In a typical financial organizational setup, there are some common departments like consumer services and business and investment services. Especially in the consumer services division, it is further divided into general consumers and premium customers or privileged customers. The financial institution like a bank or a financial advisory or portfolio management company differentiates between the consumers in this way and offers its different level of services accordingly. We will now look at how machine learning is being applied in some of these departments. An important thing to note is that the customer generally faces only the marketing department or the customer support department, and the rest of the department works in the back end. However, in the financial services industry, there is an increasing trend to have a dedicated relationship manager for privileged or premium services customers.

In Figure 13-1 we already saw the type of services under non-banking segment, mainly comprised of advisory services (both credit and investment) and the services related to the capital of the stock markets. It is important to understand here that both credit and investment advisory services can be for personal individuals as well as for other companies, organizations, or institutions. The consumer-based are the advisory services provided to individuals as customized or tailored for the needs of that individual. These types of credit advisory services are premium services meant for the privileged people of the society. The focus is to provide credit information such as rating, bankruptcy status, financial analysis, fraud alert, and other services in this category. The investment advisory services are provided in the form of portfolio management, asset management services, and fund management services for individuals. It is upon the individual to buy both advisory and management services from that particular provider or to buy advisory services from one provider and the investment management service from another provider. Usually, consumers or individuals who have high net-worth generally prefer to get investment advisory and management services from the same financial service provider.

There is another segment or category of financial services that have value proposition falling under the category of e-payment. These are services provided online through the internet on various websites and also in the form of app-based services through mobile phones such as Android or iPhone. The offerings in this category of e-payment or online payment financial service providers [3; `https://en.wikipedia.org/wiki/List_of_online_payment_service_providers`] is more oriented toward country-based providers, and there are very few providers who can actually call themselves global. Prominent in this category are providers like Paypal, Payoneer, Apple Pay, Amazon Pay, and Google Pay, who are from the US but have a major global presence. PayU is another that has a good global presence; however, we have some regional ones, such as Trust in the European Union and Alipay in China. This list is not exhaustive; however, there are many more that have deep regional and local presence.

The reason for such a thin growth in the global players of this segment is the fact that financial services are a highly regulated industry. The major central banks around the world regulate and bring out norms, guidelines, and proposed laws for regulating these types of services. Any major operator who wants to become a global operator has to have not just the understanding but the capability to implement regulations in major countries around the world where it wants to operate. The global players that I have listed have been able to meet these norms, and hence they have been able to build a global base.

There are some service providers that have only an online presence; however, there are some that have an app-based mobile presence as well, such as Alipay from China, which has both mobile and online payment platforms. Payoneer provides e-wallet services or digital payments services, which allow customers to send and receive funds into their bank accounts or reload them into prepaid debit cards. This company focuses more on business-to-business payments across the world. It is now known as the backbone of the business-to-business digital transaction system globally. Similar to Payoneer is PayPal, which allows online money transfers as a replacement to checks and money orders. Paypal, however, does not focus just on business-to-business but also on business-to-consumer transactions as well.

Before I wrap up the value proposition section, I would like to mention the recent developments that have happened in the e-payments category, which have been the advent of blockchain technology that have brought virtual currency like bitcoin and ethereum. These currencies have not been accepted by major countries and their central banks as a mode of payment and have been banned in some countries like South Korea and India. I don't want to go into the controversy of these e-payment services; however, you should be aware that there are a lot of startups around the world that have cropped up and are providing digital payment services in these blockchain currencies as well. Prominent among them is Payza, which allows bitcoin money orders and transfers to credit or debit cards via bitcoin or altcoin. In my opinion, this perception that a lot of illegal transactions happen through the blockchain type of currencies will get moderated in the near future and will come under the regulations in major countries around the world. Blockchain technology that is peer-to-peer or consumer-to-consumer is more trusted by the users since there is no centralized server or centralized institution that is controlling the entire system. The decentralized financial framework, in my opinion, is the future that is waiting to happen once the technological understanding deepens with the regulators around the world and people adopt the technology in spite of the regulations and the warnings given by various governments.

The Process of Technology Adoption in the Finance Sector

Figure 13-3 depicts the process of technology adoption taken from this book's healthcare section.

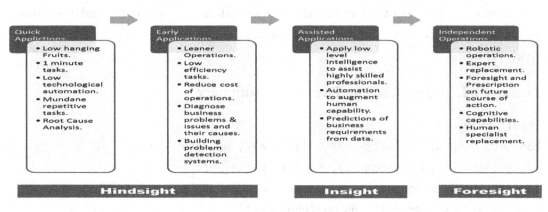

Figure 13-3. *Process of technology adoption*

> **Descriptive Analytics:** This field of analytics is invoked to know
> the answers to questions for projects that have already happened
> in the past, such as what is the status of X financial transaction in
> the past?

Traditionally the finance sector has been using descriptive analytics to produce reports about its customers for any given services category, and this has had a big impact with the top management while making various decisions, such as whom to target for any new financial product, how do we make strategy change decisions against competitors, and how is our service perceived by the end customers? All these questions are very well-answered by descriptive analytics. This is beside the trend of putting together the five-number summary for any data to the management [4; https://en.wikipedia.org/wiki/Five-number_summary]. For example, for comparison of financial data sets between the spending patterns of the millennials and the baby boomers generations, five-number summary may tell us about how the minimum spending pattern and maximum spending pattern differ between these generations. It then becomes easy for the top management to customize their financial services offerings to them specifically. Unless descriptive analytics is used, it will not be possible to take out such information.

Product-wise sales reports, product-wise discount reports, and store-wise and product-wise sales reports are some of the examples where descriptive analytics has been used traditionally. This trend is not going to go away. We will see the use of descriptive analytics in the retail sector. However, we will also see the emergence of other analytics that I talk about in the next section. I give you an example of how to use the five-point summary of financial data in the short example Python code in Listing 13-1. Since this is an example, I will be taking not more than 10 rows of data; however, in the real world this would be comprised of data for millions of users. All values for spending are in US $ and yearly value.

Listing 13-1. Python Code for Five-Points Summary

```python
import numpy as np
bboomers = np.array([14230, 345, 1912, 472, 63, 861, 270, 713])
fivepoints= [np.min(bboomers), np.percentile(bboomers, 25,
interpolation='midpoint'), np.median(bboomers),np.percentile(bboomers, 75,
interpolation='midpoint'),np.max(bboomers)]
for fivepointsummary in fivepoints:
print(fivepointsummary)
```

Output:

63

307.5

592.5

1386.5

14230

```python
import numpy as np
millennials  = np.array([12519, 845, 912, 72, 93, 615, 70, 538])
fivepoints= [np.min(millennials ), np.percentile(millennials ,
25, interpolation='midpoint'), np.median(millennials ),np.
percentile(millennials , 75, interpolation='midpoint'),np.max(millennials)]
for fivepointsummary in fivepoints:
    print(fivepointsummary)
```
Output:

70

82.5

576.5

878.5

12519

After running the Python code in Listing 13-1, we see the output that the minimum average yearly spending by baby boomers in our data set is 63, that the 25th percentile happens at 307.5, the median lies at 592.5, the 75th percentile is at 1386.5, and the maximum that a baby Boomer generation spends in our data set is $14,230 yearly. In the second code snippet for Listing 13-1, we see the minimum that millennials spend is $70, and the 25 percentile stands at 82.5, the median is at 576.5, the 75th percentile is at 878, and the maximum spend is at $12,519 yearly. In a simple comparison like this, an excellent guide to determine who is spending more for example, in our data set the baby boomers generation is spending the highest; however, they are also spending the lowest, so the dispersion is higher in the case of baby boomers than the millennials. Baby boomers spending appears in both max and min function in Listing 13-1. You will find this kind of a scenario in practical datasets. The Key thing is to know how to interpret and analyze it. The median values speak a lot about how the spending of the baby boomers and millennials in our data set is structured, and the median value for the baby boomers is pretty low, at 82.5, in comparison to the baby boomers, which is at 307.5. This means that the baby boomers are indeed higher spenders, with the midpoint line much higher in our data set.

Diagnostic Analytics: We know that this type of analytics is used to know the root cause of a phenomenon, such as a project success or a failure. Why did the X fraud happen? What was the root cause of this fraud to happen in our financial systems? What was the root cause that our financial systems did not catch the money laundering transactions? All such questions can be answered using diagnostic analytics. All forms of financial risk assessment come under diagnostic analytics. A practical implementation is a tool by Pricewaterhouse Cooper known as Halo [5; `http://halo.pwc.com/`]. This tool works on accounting journals and ledgers and has the capability to flag higher-risk transactions. Of course, this is not an online real-time solution since the effort is only to diagnose and point out the financial risks. Accounting is about old transaction records, and that is what a tool like a halo tries to extract information from a client's systems and discover to bring forth high-risk transactions with their patterns and trends. It also gives out information on process inefficiencies in the accounting process, like eliminating duplicate accounting journal entries, etc. This is especially useful for a large financial organization because of the high volume of transactions that happen during a particular period in various departments.

Predictive Analytics: We have seen in the healthcare and retail sections of this book that this type of analytics is used for determining the outcome of an event in the future, such as a financial transactions success or failure, financial budget overrun, or a budget slippage for an organization such as a bank or a company. This analytics is something that brings about the actual ability to avoid situations in the future—for example, by using predictive analytics we can predict if a particular type of financial transaction is going to succeed or fail. There could be various parameters that the machine learning model code takes into account for analysis before coming to such a conclusion. However, the whole purpose is to give a sense to the top management on the direction that the financial side of the business is going to take. Even this does not solve the problem, but it merely tells or acts as a warning signal of a failure or a deviation from the plan in the future related to finances. When we apply predictive analytics, then we get a lot more fields of finance that come into play, such as cost accountancy, managerial economics, and decision support systems. Giving out predictive costing reports based on past cost accountancy data is something that I have implemented for one of my clients. This helps large financial businesses stay on track with their cost budgets and ensure the right flags are raised in case the actual cost is predicted to increase as a result of prediction by a machine learning model. In management accounting or economics, as it is known in the academic circles, the focus is on what-if scenarios, such as $x million invested in pqr and abc projects and which one is better. And why? What if we invested the $x million in acquiring a certain startup? What would be the ROI on that investment in comparison to putting in the above two projects? All such complex decision-making questions are very easily answered by building machine learning models based on past data and applying them based on principles of management accounting.

Prescriptive Analytics: We now know that in this field of analytics the maximum value of analytics is achieved as it builds upon the prediction made based on predictive analytics, and it prescribes actions that should be taken for the future. In prescriptive analytics, it uses machine learning to build a future plan of action that is based on past failures in financial transactions in similar situations, such as failed financial transactions, and it gives out specific activities that need to be carried out in order for the financial transaction to be a success. In the financial sector, prescriptive analytics is now truly able to do course corrections even before the failures happen. Every financial organization around the world is striving to make a breakthrough in this field of analytics; however, there are very few successes as of the time of writing this book. I say this because if you take the case of business cycles, although it is known from the domain of macro-economics that they occur roughly 8 to 10 years, nobody is still able to predict when they would really happen again. The prescriptive part starts when there is an accurate prediction made; then the actions that need to be taken even before this happens come after that. For example, a global financial conglomerate bank creates a machine learning model to predict the onset of the next global financial recession with an accuracy of 92 percent; however, this is not enough. The top management needs to know what steps they need to take so that the impact on the organization is nearly minimal. Building and creating such a system would need a huge amount of data and many years of a model building-testing-feedback cycle in order to arrive at production. There are organizations that are trying to build models to predict the crash and boom cycles in capital markets; however, due to the involvement of such a high amount of data and environment variables, there is no breakthrough yet.

End Notes

[1]   Financial Services. `https://en.m.wikipedia.org/wiki/Financial_services`

[2]   John W. Molka III, CFA Senior Industry Analyst and Editor 212-984-2753, FINANCIAL SERVICES INDUSTRY SUBPRIME AND CREDIT CRISIS WEIGHS HEAVY, `http://media.lockelord.com/files/upload/advisenIndustryReportDivFinConsFinCapMrkt.pdf`

[3]   List of Online Payment Service Providers, `https://en.wikipedia.org/wiki/List_of_online_payment_service_providers`

[4]   The Five number summary, `https://en.wikipedia.org/wiki/Five-number_summary`

[5]   Halo software by Price waterhouse Coopers, `http://halo.pwc.com/`

## CHAPTER 14

Key Technological Advancements in Finance

Scenario 2027

In the not so distant future in the year 2027, 27-year-old Godson is working from his community office near his house. This is the age when the concept of dedicated office space has given way to community offices. These are the advanced versions of the co-working spaces that became popular about a decade back. People no longer have to travel to dedicated offices but have to just travel to their nearest community office close to them in order to work. Godson is an entrepreneur and has his own investment company. As he walks into his office, he is greeted by his drone personal assistant robot, which informs him about his priorities for the day. Godson asks the drone PA to come up with his stock market monthly report. The drone PA links up with Godson's TradeBot, which is the investment robot taking care of all the financial transactions. The TradeBot gives out the report to the central drone PA through trusted link-up technology. The report shows Godson's investments in the stock market nosedived by 5.2 percent last month due to a crash in the market. The TradeBot informs Godson in the report that this loss is curtailed due to the stop-loss limits that he had put in place for all his shares, and his loss today would stand at 12.8 percent had he not put those limits in the system. The TradeBot advises Godson to make changes in his stock market portfolio and add and drop a few stocks that, as per TradeBot's prediction system, would go up by 25 percent in the next 3 months. The Bot gives its reasons with the analysis of news from various channels and the effect they are going to have on this new suggested portfolio The TradeBot is fully automated and does not need any human intervention to trade on the stock market. However, for certain things like stock selection and assigning limits and percentages to investments, there is a manual override in the system that allows it to take

© Puneet Mathur 2019
P. Mathur, *Machine Learning Applications Using Python*, https://doi.org/10.1007/978-1-4842-3787-8_14

human input from Godson. The TradeBot is owned by Godson's stockbroker, who gives a salary to the TradeBot out of the commission it earns from Godson's stock trade.

This is the future of finance, which is going to move from algorithmic trading to automated bot-based transactions. Do you think it is possible in the future?

Today it may sound far-fetched, but in the near future this is going to turn into reality. Take a gander at a portion of the innovation progressions that have been made and this will guarantee you that what's to come will enable us to do things all the more productively with the utilization of innovation that resembles man-made brainpower machine learning and robotics. Smart trading bots that are given in Scenario 2027 can use not just algorithmic trading but build stock trading models by creating a simple machine learning-based deep neural network to identify if a stock in the portfolio is nearing expected profitability or losing value. It can also have algorithms to determine the likely rise and fall of shares based on any given news. The robotic trading bot would help hold the stock until the desired profitability level is reached.

Another application we saw was that of bots talking to each other through some link-up secure technology. This is going to be a major challenge in the future as every company that is creating a bot is doing so in silos. Once the bot technology becomes mainstream and people start adopting them, there will be an urgent need to make the bots talk to each other. So a common interface and language would be needed that would have its own standards and benchmarks. Any company that is going to build a bot will have to adhere to those standards much like we have the HTML protocol that every browser follows in order to give a similar user experience. These bot protocols would do the same for the "bot world." The ability of the trading bot to trade without human interference is going to amaze the people in the future. We already have the algo trading software that does automate the task of stock trading to quite an extent. However, it is not a totally automatic service. Human override is very common in this current system. Machine learning models that predict the extent of market movement in advance based on news coverage is something that is going to be a reality for the trading bots of the future.

Narrow vs Broad Machine Learning in Finance

As we found in the healthcare segment that there is a pattern that there is all of a sudden a monstrous development of limited machine learning technologies as opposed to expansive applications, this pattern is likewise found in the finance sector.

In a 2017 study spanning financial consumers across the globe [1; https://www.accenture.com/in-en/insight-financial-services-distribution-marketing-consumer-study].

We can clearly see the profile of the new financial consumer. There is the emergence of three distinct consumer profiles or personas: 1) the nomads; 2) the hunters; and 3) the quality seekers. The nomads are people who are digitally active but price their data and treat data as currency. The data that we are talking about is their own personal data. These nomads are aware of the value of their data, and they want the financial institutions to offer them personalized services in exchange for their data. The hunters are those financial consumers who are always in the search for the best price for the financial services. They are kind of hybrid customers who operate both in traditional provider environments like traditional banks, credit cards, etc., and they also operate equally well in the digital environment. The quality seekers are loyal traditional customers of the financial service providers who like to stay with a brand if there is value in it, and they look for service excellence. This consumer is not price-sensitive; however, they do value their data and hence data privacy is very important to them. The study also showed That each country has a different profile of these three financial consumers; for example, in the US the nomads are at a height of 46 percent, the hunters are at 14 percent, and the quality seekers are at 40percent in comparison to a small country like Singapore, where the nomads are at 41 percent, the hunters are at 16 percent, and the quality seekers are at 43 percent. In Brazil the nomads are at 62 percent, the hunters are at 9 percent, and the quality seekers are at 29percent. Brazil is leading as far as the nomad's financial consumer segment is concerned. Canada has the least amount of nomads and the least amount of hunters and has the highest value of quality seekers, where the nomads stand at 20 percent, the hunters stand at 23 percent, and the quality seekers stand at 55 percent. This also points to the fact that Canada has an aging population problem and that's why there are very few nomads and more quality seekers who are traditionally brand-loyal. This study not only points to segmentation of financial consumers, but it also points to the changing trends in the society at large. The nomads represent the new generation that is more or less the migrating population that is willing to move from one location to the other in search of jobs that are nothing but freelance work available online and offline. The hunters are middle-aged people who are witnessing the change from traditional financial services to digital financial services. And the quality seekers are the older generation that wants to stick to the brands that they are aware of and have faith in due to their old association and their good customer service levels. This is a customer who is going to stick to a brand for a longer time.

The Current State of Finance Institutions Around the World

In Figure 13-1 you can see that we have three types of financial segments. The first is consumer finance, whose focus is providing personal services such as loans, indirect financing, leases, self-financing, credit cards, pawn shops, and payday loan providers. Providing loans to individuals with bad credit history is not permitted and hence they may not exist globally. Consumer finance caters to the large part of the population of any country.

And here the focus is to take activities related to a stock market trading advisory to clients and their assets (portfolio management) and give out various investment advice (asset management services). Stockbrokering is a very localized activity and we have not seen any global stockbrokers who operate in major capital markets. The next is diversified financial services, which focuses on providing corporate financial advisory doing investment research for companies and stock exchanges and the credit rating agencies. This diversified financial services providers are a niche market, and they concentrate on providing advisory services and financial services to premium corporate and personal customers.

Importance of Machine Learning in Finance

The finance sector is different from most of the other sectors because it depends on people and their behavior. The financial sector gives out services to customers and so it is different from other sectors that offer products such as retail. Machine learning has come to assume a necessary part in numerous periods of the financial system, from approving advances to overseeing assets and resources. A major area where machine learning is being extensively used is fraud detection. Consolidating more available processing power, web usage becoming more common, and an expanding measure of profitable organization information being put away on the web produces a "flawless tempest" for information security hazards. While past money-related misrepresentation location frameworks depended vigorously on unpredictable and hearty arrangements of principles, current fraud detection goes after an agenda of risk factors–it effectively learns and aligns to new potential (or genuine) security dangers. Machine learning in fraud detection is used extensively, yet similar standards remain constant for other information security issues. Machine learning frameworks can identify one-of-a-kind exercises or practices ("abnormalities") and ban them from security groups. The test for these frameworks is to stay away from false-positives–circumstances where "dangers" are hailed that were never hazards in any case.

Another great use of machine learning is in the loan and insurance underwriting business. Loan and insurance underwriting could be depicted as an ideal occupation for machine learning in the financial sector, and in fact, there is a lot of stress in the business that machines will supplant an extensive swath of the guaranteeing positions that exist today. Particularly in organizations such as enormous banks and traditional open-market protection firms, machine learning calculations can be prepared on a huge number of cases of shopper information (age, work, conjugal status, etc.) and monetary loan or protection results (did this individual default, pay back the advance on time, get in a pile up, etc.?). All such questions are being answered through application of machine learning.

The hidden patterns that can be evaluated with calculations and consistently broken down to recognize patterns that may impact loaning and guaranteeing what is to come (Are an ever-increasing number of youngsters in a specific state getting in auto collisions? Are there expanding rates of default among a particular statistic populace in the course of the most recent 15 years?) are hot topics for extracting results from loan and insurance data. These outcomes have a huge substantial yield for organizations; however, at the outset are costs fundamentally saved for bigger organizations with the assets to employ information researchers and the monstrous volumes of information over a wide span of time to prepare their calculations.

With sources returning to the 1970s, algorithmic exchanging (here and there called "Computerized Trading Systems," which is apparently a more precise depiction) includes the utilization of complex AI frameworks to settle on, to a great degree, quick exchanging choices.

Algorithmic frameworks regularly make a large number of exchanges every day, leading to the expression "high-recurrence exchanging," which is thought to be a subset of algorithmic exchanging. Most mutual funds and money-related organizations don't straightforwardly unveil their AI methods for dealing with exchanging (in light of current circumstances). However, it is trusted that machine learning and profound learning are assuming an undeniably essential part in aligning trading decisions live and online.

Now I take you through a survey done online with experts from the finance industry used to find out, through the Delphi Method, which segments of the industry would fall under the level of technology adoption. This survey is very similar to the survey done in the retail and healthcare section of this book. The key segments identified in a preliminary survey by the finance experts are stock market investments, banking, financial advisory and management services, accounting, and electronic payment services. The purpose of carrying out this survey was to bring to the reader a clear understanding of where the technology adoption maturity lies in each area of finance. The experts were dispersed across organizations with brick and mortar financers, online financers, and hybrid organizations.

Some of the key areas where finance has machine learning applications are:

Finance Segments for Survey:

1. **Stock market investments**

2. **Banking**

3. **Financial advisory and management services**

4. **Accounting**

5. **Electronic payment services**

Stock market investments are increasingly becoming automated in nature. These stock exchange companies typically exchange on exceptionally powerless connections that are revealed because of research from a quantitative investigator (once in a while referred to as a "quant"), who is persuaded of the legitimacy of the relationship. While these relationships are powerless, the scale at which these quant exchanging firms work can make every one of these individual systems worth many thousands, millions, or much more. Be that as it may, there is space for the speediest firm to make the trade to exploit this relationship. In this manner, quant firms intensely upgrade their procedures for speed. With the low idleness, they can beat any other person to the correct exchange, since just the speediest players will get the benefit. Since their systems are improved for speed and dependability, the machine learning methods they utilize are normally exceptionally basic. Also, in view of this heartless rivalry for gainful exchanges, quant firms are staggeringly shrouded and defensive of their protected innovation in the area of algorithmic trading.

Banking is an area where utilization of machine learning procedures are applied to rich informational databases and can help battle financial frauds, save time and cash for clients, and computerize back-office capacities. One of the central uses for machine learning in managing a customer account in the banking world has been to battle fraud and hacking attempts and enhance consistency. In a perfect world, the innovation is suited to the issue, as machine learning calculations can search gigantic databases and informational collections to detect unusual financial transactions.

In the area of **financial advisory and management services,** resource and riches administration firms are investigating potential AI answers for enhancing their speculation choices and making utilization of their troves of chronicled information. Resource administration for computerized resources (like a venture portfolio) or appropriated modern resources (like production line apparatus or an armada of transportation trucks) are applications where voluminous information about the advantages (like the verifiable execution of a specific reserve or the authentic upkeep information for an armada of trucks) is as of now being recorded, making them ready for robotization through AI. Unsupervised learning methods connected to monetary information, news, modern sensor information, or even web-based social networking information, hold the guarantee to advise venture choices in new and energizing ways, conceivably giving speculation firms an edge in the market.

Accounting and bookkeeping programming is getting more intelligent, and it is now performing errands that before required human mediation. Redundant, manual, and dull assignments are disposed of with the goal that accountants and entrepreneurs would now be able to invest less energy in staying up with the latest and would have additional time for other essential tasks. Bookkeeping applications learn receipt coding practices and propose where exchanges ought to be distributed. For example, if the business assistant ordinarily assigns an item to a specific deals account, next time that the business representative adds that thing to a receipt, the bookkeeping application will consequently distribute it to the correct record. It additionally takes a gander at mistakes that clerks and bookkeepers settle. For example, if the entrepreneur apportions something to the off-base record and the bookkeeper settles the mistake, the bookkeeping application will accept the bookkeeper's determination as the correct one.

Bank compromises are robotized. Once more, innovation gains from past designations and records decisions and after that makes the correct suggestions for new bank exchanges.

Banks utilize AI chatbots to enable clients to determine normal inquiries. Chatbots from bookkeeping programs, like Xero [2; https://www.xero.com/us/why-xero/benefits/online-accounting/], let you question the most recent monetary information, like how much cash is in the bank, when a specific bill is expected, and who owes you cash, and it can even associate clients with Xero [2; https://www.xero.com/us/why-xero/benefits/online-accounting/] counselors from their registry. More such applications of accounting and bookkeeping are being developed that are not offline but are online real-time auditors. Furthermore, this innovation will likewise influence inspectors sooner rather than later. At present, reviewers just examine a select sample of transactions. They utilize huge groups of bookkeepers who work extra time to finish audits by the due date. The immense measure of transactions that course through organizations restricts the number of exchanges that auditors can assess physically.

Machine learning calculations will process and survey the information, perceive peculiarities, and assemble a rundown of exceptions for evaluators to check. Rather than investing the majority of their energy checking information, auditors can apply their abilities to examining and concluding the explanation for an abnormal transaction registered in the journal or the ledger.

The last segment is the **electronic payments industry,** which is disrupting all the notions of how transactions used to happen with banks traditionally. Global electronic payment companies are now comfortable with machine learning, essentially in accordance with charge card exchange checking, where learning calculations assume imperative parts in close ongoing approval of exchanges. Given the present fast development of information catch and moderate elite figuring, McKinsey sees numerous close and long-haul chances to grow the utilization of machine learning in installments. These incorporate everything from utilizing web-sourced information to more precisely foreseeing borrower wrongdoing, utilizing virtual partners, or enhancing client benefit execution. In card issuing, machine learning is having a significant effect. This is particularly valid in card collections, where McKinsey has seen 10 percent to 15 percent upgrade in recuperation rates and 30 percent to 40 percent improvement in accumulations proficiency. To limit misconduct, backers can utilize singular record design acknowledgment innovations and create contact rules and methodologies for accounts that are as of now reprobate. Following a record misconduct, guarantors permit a concise time window (for the most part 90 days) before they discount the receivables and turn to gather over to outsider suppliers. This short period is a perfect time for guarantors to apply accumulation procedures that draw vigorously on the abilities of machine learning. A key advantage of AI is that it can help installments organizations significantly enhance operational proficiency; cases include diminishing handling times and human mistakes and giving client bits of knowledge and expanded robotization. In this sense, AI is pushing organizations to rethink and rebuild working models and procedures. For instance, it can bolster organizations in handling enormous volumes of information to produce monetary reports and fulfill administrative and consistence necessities, such as forms that would regularly require vast quantities of individuals performing redundant information preparation. Truth be told, AI's transformative power is having such a momentous effect on the financial administration's industry that it is anticipated to supplant up to three-fourths for every penny of outsourced money-related administrations employments inside 15 years (KPMG). This could have enormous ramifications on organizations hoping to decrease operational costs, empowering them to create and support different territories of their business.

So far we have looked at the importance of machine learning applications in each of the chosen sectors. Now let us look at the survey and its research methodology.

> **Research objective:** The primary objective of this research is to use expert opinion in finding out and mapping two parameters of artificial intelligence and machine learning: (1) the current technology maturity level of AI and machine learning in the key areas of the finance industry, and (2) the technology adoption process inside the finance industry.
>
> There were initially 25 key areas identified by the expert groups in the first iteration. These areas were then reiterated with the expert group to find out among them the most important areas that would evolve in the future. The expert group was able to narrow this down to five areas in finance that would be important for the finance industry to advance further. The research study does not provide the results of this iterative selection of the key areas, but it starts from the point where the experts have selected these **five key areas**. I have already discussed in this chapter those five areas, starting from stock market investments to electronic payment services.
>
> **Research sample:** The group of experts that was selected were from a total population of 160 experts. The experts were comprised of finance professionals who had worked in the industry for more than 20 years at positions involving stock exchange firms, banking experts in and finance institutions, director of a finance facility, chief executive officer of a finance organization, or academic professors who had worked on research in the finance industry with accepted and published papers. I have covered all the experts from each of the areas in finance such as supply chain management, customer care, merchandising,

CEOs, and AI experts—to name just a few. A total of 45 such professionals were shortlisted for this study. There were no absentees nor attrition in this study.

Information needed: In order to make decisions and to support them, various secondary data like published papers on the state of machine learning and AI in finance were provided. Some examples are those of Pricewaterhouse Coopers or other financial institutions. The required information in order to create a map between the two parameters mentioned earlier was based on the experts' understanding of the current state of technology implementation in the five areas starting from stock market investments to electronic payment services. To assist the decision making of the experts, explanations on the levels of technological maturity and the phase-wise identification of technology was provided to them; beyond this, there was no other information provided, so care was taken not to create a bias in the minds of the experts. The information needed for this study was contextual, theoretical, and expert knowledge. There was also a requirement for the experts to use their tacit or inherent knowledge, which they possess as being associated with the finance industry for so long.

Research Design Overview

The primary steps involved in this research are the following:

1. Define objectives of the research.

2. Find experts who are willing to help in this research study.

3. Design questionnaires that gather information and involve less writing effort by the experts.

4. Administer the questionnaires to the experts.

5. Gather responses to the questionnaires and analyze them to see if consensus has been achieved.

6. Iterate and administer more questionnaires until the experts reach a consensus on a particular key area.

7. Once a consensus is reached, move on to the next key area and iterate the questionnaire until a consensus is reached. Until consensus is reached, more information is provided based on the previous responses provided by the experts.

8. Analyze and create a map of the technical maturity levels and phases of adoption of AI and machine learning.

Data Collection Methods

Literature regarding finance was not a data to be collected for this study. The test study that was conducted, which I already mentioned earlier, was that of taking expert help in narrowing down from 16 to 5 key areas that are going to be important for the future of finance industry. This is an important thing because in our study we are using expert judgment on what is going to be the focus of finance industry based on their past experience. We have used the Delphi Method of study from a paper by Chittu Okoli and Suzanne De Poweski ("The Delphi Method") as a research tool example regarding design considerations and applications [3; `https://www.academia.edu/399894/` `The_Delphi_Method_As_a_Research_Tool_An_Example_Design_Considerations_and_` `Applications`].

The questionnaire method was used for data collection from the experts through e-mail online administration of surveys.

Data Analysis

During a particular iteration when the data was collected, Microsoft Excel software was used to record the expert's response in a tabular format. For any given key area, a graph was made to check if there was a consensus reached, and if the graph showed sufficiently well that there was consensus then the iteration was stopped. So the data analysis was done manually with the help of computer software. The mapping of technology maturity and phases of technology adoption was undertaken using Excel software to create a technology map graph. This was also done with the help of the computer software program Microsoft Excel.

Ethical Considerations

It is possible that bias could have slipped into the study had we not made sure that the results and the responses of the experts were kept anonymous and did not affect the outcome of this study. So due care was taken in order to ensure that the experts were not known among themselves. As I have already mentioned, there are in the finance industry two groups of people: those who like technology and those who do not like technology. We did not do an expert selection based on these specific criteria, so this study could very well be biased on such grounds, and we have not tested for this.

Limitations of the Study

Qualitative research has as its biggest limitation that of not being able to exactly quantify the outcome of the future, and this is very much applicable to our study. However, by using categorical variables in our questionnaires, we have tried to take the quantitative analysis of our outcome as well. Mapping of the technological adoption and understanding of the technological maturity is not something that a normal human being can do unless they have been associated with the industry, and that is why we chose experts to carry out the study; however, it is possible that some of the experts may not have sufficient knowledge or exposure to the advances in artificial intelligence and machine learning. We acknowledge that this could be a limitation to the study.

Examining the Study

We already know from Figure 1-1 from this book that there are four phases of technology adoption. In Figure 14-1 we look at this mapping.

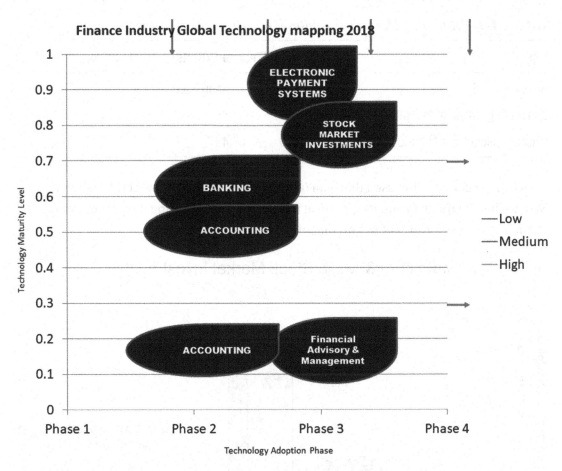

Figure 14-1. *Finance industry technology adoption phases*

From Figure 14-1, there are two axes: the x-axis represents the technology adoption phase as outlined in Figure 1-1, and the y-axis represents the technology maturity level. **The maturity application level is divided into low, medium, and high. Low means the technology is at a research stage and is not in production yet. Medium means the technology has been implemented in production with some hits and misses and needs more research to move to mainstream production. High means the technology is well-researched and is ready to move into production or is being used in a production environment,** such as finance stores, etc.

Table 14-1 and Figures 14-2 through 14-8 present data in with analysis of the Delphi Method research.

Table 14-1. *Data on Delphi Method Research Used in the Study*

Topic	No of Finance Experts		No of Iterations
Delphi Method	Invited	Shortlisted	
Current Application of AI & ML in Finance	160	45	3
Future Application of AI & ML in Finance	160	45	5

We have already discussed this data in the methodology section of this chapter. Now we look at the data and its graphical representation regarding the parameter of technology maturity level of AI and machine learning in finance.

State of AI & ML in Stock Market Investments

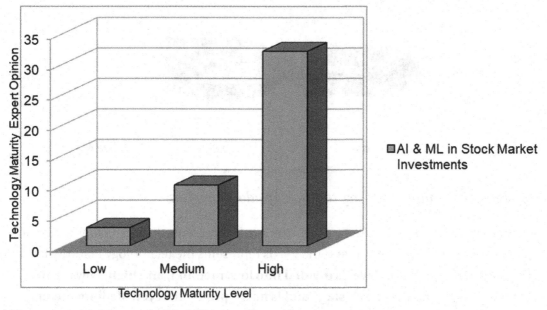

Figure 14-2. *States of AI & ML in stock market investments*

In stock market investments, the parameter technology maturity levels of AI and machine learning in the finance industry is at the high end. This is ratified by our experts from the financial industry. This means that our experts say that stock market investments have technology implemented and it is being used in mainstream production to the extent that it can replace the human expert. Here is the stock market, the human being in between the market, and the trader is the broker, and the broker's function has been completely automated and is in production now.

Another aspect of the stock market is giving advice to the traders and investors on the stock market using buy and sell signals, and even that has been fairly automated by use of machine learning and artificial intelligence. A good example of this is on the website stocksrank.com [4; `https://www.stocksrank.com/?gclid=EAIaIQobChMI683Yht-o3QIVipOPChOM-AfsEAMYAyAAEgKF8fD_BwE`], which gives trading signals from a robot analyst that monitors the markets and puts the trends in front of its customers. The use of machine learning and AI is very important because of the gargantuan scale of data that is produced by the stock market for all the stocks every second of the trading hour. It is not humanly possible to analyze and find out trends from such a high volume of complex data and find out the trends and patterns. This is why machine learning and AI have been successful in giving advice for stocks that was not previously possible for any human to find out.

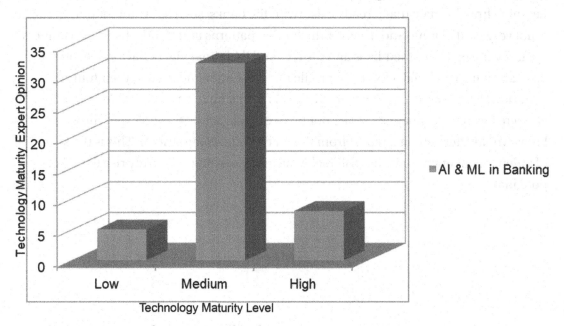

Figure 14-3. *State of AI & ML in banking*

Now let us look at another area, which is banking. Our experts tell us that here AI and machine learning are in the medium stage of technological maturity, with 71 percent of our experts sharing this opinion. We can see in Figure 14-3 that the rest of the experts say it is high (18 percent) or low (11 percent). The medium level of technological maturity means that the experts say this technology is not yet moved into mainstream production and has a few hits and misses here and there.

The McKinsey report [5; https://www.mckinsey.com/industries/high-tech/ our-insights/an-executives-guide-to-machine-learning] points out that in Europe, more than 12 banks have replaced traditional statistical modeling with machine learning modeling, which has resulted in a 10 percent increase in sales of new products, 20 percent savings in capital expenditure, a 20 percent increase in cash collections, and 20 percent decline in charge. The various banks have implemented recommendation engines, and they have also built micro-targeted models that forecast whether a consumer is going to cancel their service or is going to default on their loans. They also devised mechanisms based on this on how to intervene if this is going to happen. We can see from this important report as to how machine learning is making business sense to the banks in Europe. With such strides, machine learning is indeed going to play at center stage in transforming the bank's revenues and operations in the long run. Learning from big data that already exists with the banks, such as customer transactions, is not very hard to mine and discover the hidden patterns and trends that the customers are throwing up about their likes and dislikes and their financial behaviors. Using such data, any bank can build a financial profile of a consumer and predict their future behavior. However, the next level of operations of machine learning and AI in banking is where it can really not just predict but take concrete actions, as an expert human being would after getting a report from the machine learning system. This is the stage of independent operations that will make machine learning in AI truly rise to its full potential.

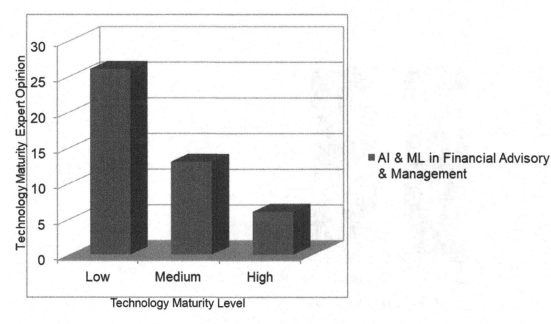

Figure 14-4. *State of AI & ML in financial advisory and management*

Now we look at the state of AI and machine learning in the area of financial advisory and management. Our financial experts, after five iterations, revealed that the application of AI and machine learning in this area was very low, with 58 percent of our experts saying so and 29 percent of experts saying it was medium. The majority of our experts said that the technology in this area is at a research stage and has not yet moved into production. There are various companies in this area that are trying to develop machine learning applications for asset management and investment advisory services; however, there is one company known as Swiss Finance Technology Association that has done some research on wealth management using digital technologies like machine learning and AI [6; `https://swissfinte.ch/machine-learning-digital-wealth-management-part-1/`].

Including client segmentation customer experience enhancement for the client and product onboarding or matching of financial products that are specifically suited for a particular client profile using machine learning and artificial intelligence. This technology is again in the research stage and is not in production, so our experts have correctly identified this area as a low technology maturity level.

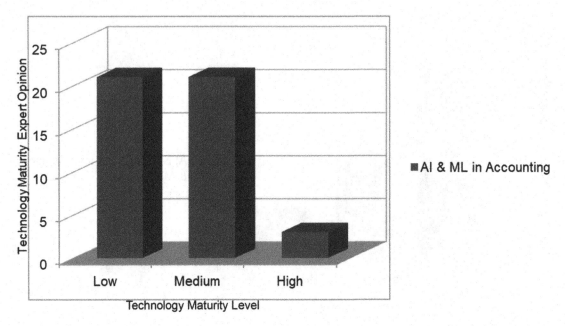

Figure 14-5. *State of AI & ML in accounting*

Now we look at another key area—that of accounting. In Figure 14-5, we can clearly see that our experts are tied between low and medium technology maturity levels, with 47 percent of experts saying that technology maturity level is at each of these levels. The low maturity level of technology, as we already know, means that it is at a research stage and not yet moved into production. The medium level means the technology has been implemented in production with some hits and misses and needs more research to move into mainstream production. The frontrunner in this research is PWC [7; `https://www.pwc.com/us/en/services/audit-assurance/financial-statement-audit-innovation.html`] or Pricewaterhouse Coopers, the accounting firm that has created software known as hello based on machine learning, and this software is enabled for tech-enabled audits. However, this is not fully automated software and does require human intervention for it to work. The audit is not done real-time but the data is provided on a monthly or annual basis as the client decides to do so.

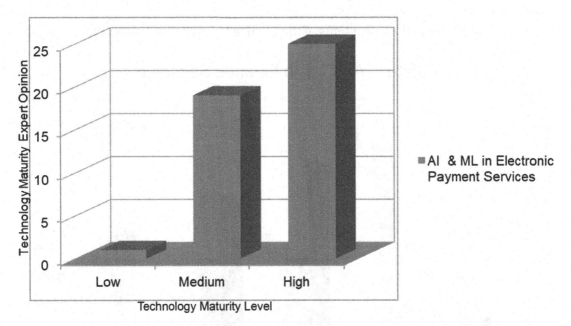

Figure 14-6. *State of AI & ML in electronic payment services*

The last application in our study is that of AI and machine learning in the area of electronic payment services. The expert opinion about the application of AI and machine learning in electronic payment services is that it has reached high maturity level. This means the technology in this area is well-researched and is ready to move into production or is already being used in the production environment. Our experts were very quick in reaching this decision after just 3 iterations, and 56 percent of them said that it was at a high maturity level; 42 percent said it was at the medium level. In this chapter I have shown you that machine learning is being used for fighting fraud of all kinds, and here in the electronic payments industry the online transactions for payments have a very high degree of machine learning usage for fighting fraud and making real-time decisions to evaluate a huge number of transactions that are taking place online. The machine learning applications here are able to improve their accuracy and are able to detect nonintuitive patterns in the human beings, identify fraud, and avoid false-positives. This is told in the Visa companies [8; https://usa.visa.com/dam/VCOM/global/support-legal/documents/webinar-machine-learning.pdf] webinar on machine learning in payments industry held on May 24, 2018. We know that Visa is a major player in the payments industry, and it has started using machine learning for making accurate business decisions by implementing machine learning algorithms in their processes.

Overall this is how all the segments of the finance industry stack up on the bar graph.

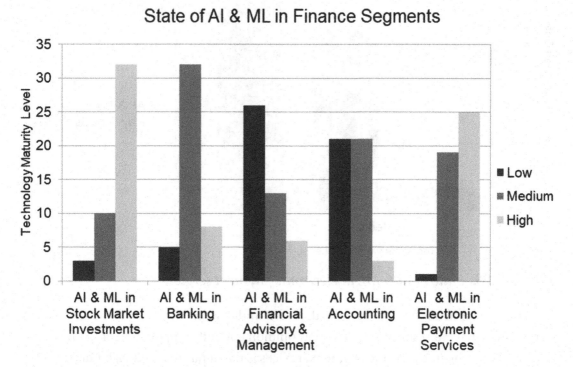

Figure 14-7. *States of AI & ML in finance segments*

Phases of Technology Adoption in Finance, 2018

Now we move on to the second parameter of our research study, that of phases of technology adoption in finance. I have already discussed in Chapter 1 that there are four phases, from the quick applications phase to the independent operations phase. After analyzing, we can see this from Figure 14-8.

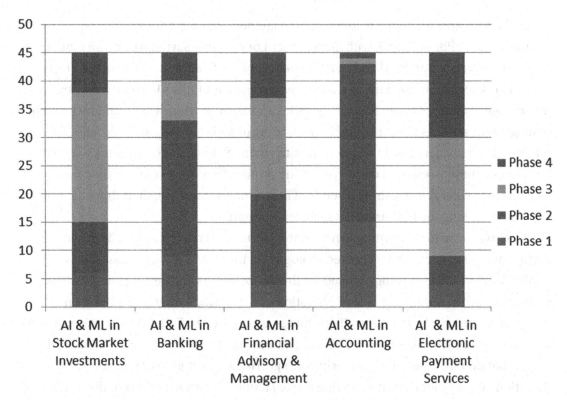

Figure 14-8. *Phases of technology adoption in the finance industry, 2018*

We can clearly see that stock market investments is categorized as a Phase 3 implementation. This is the stage where we get insights by using assisted applications where low-level intelligence is used to assess highly skilled professionals, and automation is used to augment human capability and predictions of business requirements from data. The stock market applications like algorithmic trading or Robo-assisted trading is a very good example where skilled traders are getting augmented by using machine learning in their operations.

In the next area of banking, our experts put the phase implementation as a Phase 2 level, with 53 percent of our experts saying so. Phase to Phase to provide hindsight and is an early applications stage where Lena operations and low-efficiencytires are used to reduce cost of operations and diagnose business problems and are used for building problem detection systems. We know that major banks around the world have implemented fraud detection systems, and they have extensively used machine learning to reduce the cost of operations by using chatbots and even using robots in banking operations. This is primarily seen in the customer-facing roles of the banks.

In the next area of financial advisory management, our experts say that the technology is at Phase 3 level, with 38 percent of our experts saying so, and 36 percent of our experts also putting AI and machine learning applications in this area at Phase 2 Level. However, this is not a tie, and hence we will go with Phase 3, which has a higher percentage of our experts. In Phase 3-assisted applications the advisory and investment management services are using machine learning to assist skilled professionals, like relationship managers and investment management experts, in determining a match between the best assets for a customer for the profile. They are also using machine learning to predict the investment needs of individuals by creating their financial profiles and then targeting the best financial services for them.

Next, we move to accounting, where our experts are very clear, with 62 percent saying that the application level of technology is in the Phase 2 stage. Phase 2 is early applications where technology is used for linear operations and getting low-efficiency tasks done and to reduce the cost of operations, such as audit operations done on financial statements by machines. Technology is also used to find out business problems and issues and their causes, such as finding out the past transactions in the financial ledger that pertain to money laundering or high-risk items, and to create problem detection systems; for example, finding money laundering transactions in the journal or ledger of a company is an example of the use of early applications.

The last area is that of electronic payment services, and 47 percent of our experts feel that it is in Phase 3 of operations, which is assisted application, where low-level intelligence is used to assist highly skilled professionals in this field, and automation is used to augment human capability, as it is not possible for a human being to scan millions and billions of transactions happening throughout the globe in the payment system.

With this, I end presentation of the study that took me more than 3 months to implement along with the experts from the finance industry, and I do hope that it will provide the reader with a concise view of where the finance industry stands with respect to its applications and adaptation of AI and machine learning.

End Notes

[1]   2017 GLOBAL DISTRIBUTION & MARKETING CONSUMER STUDY, Accenture LLP US, https://www.accenture.com/in-en/insight-financial-services-distribution-marketingconsumer-study

[2]   Why Xero, https://www.xero.com/us/why-xero/benefits/
      online-accounting/

[3]   The Delphi method as a research tool: an example, design
      considerations and applications, Chitu Okoli*, Suzanne D.
      Pawlowski a John Molson School of Business, Concordia
      University, GM 209-23, 1455 Boulevard de Maisonneuve Ouest,
      Montre'al, Que'., Canada H3G 1M8 b. Department of Information
      Systems and Decision Sciences, Louisiana State University,
      Baton Rouge, LA, USA. Accepted 8 November 2003. Available
      online 27 March 2004, https://www.academia.edu/399894/
      The_Delphi_Method_As_a_Research_Tool_An_Example_Design_
      Considerations_and_Applications

[4]   Stocksrank.com website, https://www.stocksrank.
      com/?gclid=EAIaIQobChMI683Yht-o3QIVipOPChOM-
      AfsEAMYAyAAEgKF8fD_BwE

[5]   An executive's guide to machine learning, By Dorian Pyle and
      Cristina San José, McKinsey Quarterly June 2015, https://www.
      mckinsey.com/industries/high-tech/our-insights/an-
      executives-guide-to-machine-learning

[6]   Machine Learning in Digital Wealth Management (Part 1) By
      johnhucker, 13 December 2017, https://swissfinte.ch/machine-
      learning-digital-wealth-management-part-1/

[7]   Financial statement audit Tech-enabling the audit for enhanced
      quality and greater insights, pwc USA, https://www.pwc.com/
      us/en/services/audit-assurance/financial-tatement-audit-
      innovation.html

[8]   Machine Learning in the Payments Industry 24 May 2018 John
      Steensen, https://usa.visa.com/dam/VCOM/global/support-
      legal/documents/webinar-machine-learning.pdf

## CHAPTER 15

How to Implement Machine Learning in Finance

The three most promising areas in finance are:

- **Algorithmic stock trading**

- **Automated robo-advisors**

- **Fraud detection and prevention**

In the finance industry, the topmost item that has huge potential is applying machine learning to algorithmic stock trading. Although algorithmic stock trading is an automated version of manual stock trading, I will say it lacks artificial intelligence that machine learning can provide in forecasting and predicting, rather than analyzing and actioning in the form that it is today. To give you an example of what I mean, let us look at how a retail trader trades in the stock market around the world. To keep the discussion simple, I am talking about cash trading, rather than about derivatives options trading. On any typical day, a retail stock investor will ideally study the news about a company and check its fundamental and technical analysis positions and then make a decision to sell or buy the stock. If, for example, the trader is following a Commodity Channel Index (CCI) technical indicator then they would look at the CCI showing an oversold signal to start buying and overbought signal to start selling.

While this is a simple example, experienced traders use many more technical indicators than just the CCI, such as stochastics oscillator and Bollinger bands indicator—to name just a few. The algorithmic trading in its current form has successfully automated the use of technical indicators and incorporated it into

© Puneet Mathur 2019

P. Mathur, *Machine Learning Applications Using Python*, https://doi.org/10.1007/978-1-4842-3787-8_15

automated trading systems. However, this is not artificial intelligence or machine learning. There is hardly any prediction being done here if we look closely. It is just automation of what a human would do when the market goes up or down and then taking action based on the price movement. There is hardly any prediction happening here. For example, there is no model being built in this system to predict what the price of the stock would be in the next 1 hour, 1 day, 1 week, 1 month or prediction of stock price movement for any other such time period. If a model is built around this, then combining it with algorithmic trading will give fantastic results. So the application of machine learning in the stock market for prediction of stock prices or the indices adds some intelligence to it, and then using perspective analysis a complete system that gives recommendations on actions to be performed by the algo trading system will give it sufficient intelligence to take advantage of price movements.

Another area in finance that holds a lot of potential is that of financial and investment advisors. There is a lot of scope for implementation here. Let us take an example: a person has a million dollars to invest. However, the problem that any investor faces in spite of the rise in information access to all is that of choosing the best investment option that would give capital appreciation over time. Here the investor uses their gut feelings and friend networks or human advisors to give them advice on where to invest and where not to invest. This, however, is a very naïve process of making investments of large sums. It is anybody's guess as to how many of those investments fail and succeed. However, if we use existing data from the capital markets about prices and other factors that affect them, then we can build a prediction model and be sure that the investments will not fail over time. By this I do not mean the current robo-operations like Alexa by Amazon that can only tell you about the current market scenario; I mean creation of a robotic advisor that not only creates a notional portfolio but also gives its owner the prediction based on past data, such as stock prices, collectible art prices, commodity prices, oil prices, etc. This robotic financial advisor will not only have the ability to create machine learning models but also harness them and make recommendations about its owner's portfolio. Based on changes in the market prices, it alerts its owners sufficiently in advance regarding the recommended changes in their investment portfolio.

Fraud detection and prevention is another area that needs to be upgraded. Although there are applications of machine learning and artificial intelligence in this area, they are not sufficient enough to prevent fraud from happening globally. Fraud detection systems need to use machine learning by finding the patterns that the money launderers and other hackers use to misuse the system. Hacking attempts lie in the area of cyber-security; however, transactions related to money laundering and fraud are hard to detect. The main reason for this is that the system recognizes the users as legitimate users and hence do not flag them. However, by using techniques like outlier detection and combining it with other fraud detection algorithms, a robust system can be built that does not allow such transactions in real time. Giving out a red flag for a transaction that has already happened cannot help in any way other than by making criminal charges against the users of the systems who may have fled by the time the fraud is detected. However, by creating machine learning models such as the one we saw in Chapter 14 of this book, we can easily detect and prevent such transactions from happening in real time.

Implementing Machine Learning Life Cycle in Finance

Now we will look through an implementation of machine learning in the finance industry. Here I am going to use the supervised machine learning technique to show you how to implement on accounting data set. The data set used in this example is fictitious but is based on electronic payments ledgers commonly used by any organization and is suitable for you to understand how machine learning can be implemented in the field of accountancy.

Now let us look at the data set that is going to be used in this chapter, look at the data dictionary, and understand it before starting to work on it. Columns in the data set are described here.

- **Record No:** This is the record number of the ledger transaction in the digital payments register.

- **Transaction No:** This is the unique transaction number provided by the payment gateway on successful completion of the payment transaction.

- **Fiscal Year:** This is the financial year in which this transaction has taken place.

- **Month:** This entry gives the month in which the transaction takes place.

- **Department:** Department columns include finance, human resources, learning and development, legal, marketing, procurement, research, strategic planning, and transportation department of a company are presented here.

- **Account:** The account column represents account number with the company order in its ledger. This is internal to a company.

- **Expense Category:** Expense category represents the type of expense that the company is doing while making the payment to a vendor.

- **Vendor ID:** This is signed by the payment or procurement system to a vendor to whom payment is being carried out.

- **Payment Method:** This column tells about the type of payment method used, such as automatic clearinghouse check or a wire transfer.

- **Payment Status:** Payment status is confirmation on the payment transaction that has been reconciling, not just with the bank but also with the internal procurement committee. Paid inside means payment has been approved and confirmed by the bank and also the payment has been approved by the procurement committee within the organization.

- **Payment Date:** This is the actual payment date the transaction has happened.

- **Invoice ID:** This is the invoice ID of the invoice that has been generated against which the payment transaction is happening.

- **Invoice Date:** Represents the date the invoice has been generated.

- **Amount:** Actual amount of payment transaction that has happened.

- **Red Flag:** The column value of 1 means that the amount of transaction is lower than the 25th quantile of the amount column and the payment status is paid unreconciled. A Red Flag transaction requires further investigation. The value to represent the transaction is higher than the 75th quantile and has a status of faith and reconcile. This shows that it needs further investigation. A value of 0 means that the transaction is within the 1.5 times 25th quantile and hence it is deemed as legitimate.

In this data set, I am going to use supervised learning techniques with specific classifiers to classify a transaction that is legitimate.

This data set is in the form of a flat file, PaymentsLedger.csv, which is available at the following URL: http://www.PuneetMathur.me/Book009/.

Starting the Code

Let us now jump into implementing unsupervised learning on this data set.

> **Information: All the code used in this exercise is tested for compatibility with Python 2.7 in Anaconda environment. It should work on 3.x as well; however, it has not been tested.**

In Listing 15-1, export the Python libraries like String IO and numpy in order to start working.

Listing 15-1. Importing Basic Python Libraries

```
#Importing python libraries
import pandas as pd
from io import StringIO
import os
import numpy as np
os.getcwd()
```

In Listing 15-2 I load the data set from flat files and then look at the data set loaded into the dataframe.

Listing 15-2. Loading and Checking Data Set in Memory

```
#Reading data set from flat files
fname="C:/PaymentsLedger.csv"
openledger= pd.read_csv(fname, low_memory=False, index_col=False)

#Check the data Loaded into memory
print(openledger.head(1))
```

```
   Record No  TransactionNo  Fiscal Year  Month Department  Account  \
0          0        1095300         2018      1    FINANCE    54050

   Expense Category Vendor   ID        Payment Method      Payment Status  \
0  Food And Beverages       59169  Automated Clearing House  Paid-Unreconciled

  Payment Date     Invoice ID  Invoice Date  Amount  RedFlag
0   07/21/2017  DDSM100367442    07/19/2017   10.08        1
```

Next, in Listing 15-3, I transfer the data in a standard Pandas dataframe and then look to check if the data set has loaded properly. Then I look at the shape of the data set, which tells us that the 7500 rows and 13 columns. We also look at the names of columns, which are the same as the data dictionary we discussed at the beginning of this section. I use the dtypes property of the dataframe to look at the data types of the columns that have been loaded as well.

Listing 15-3. Loading Pandas Dataframe and the Column Datatypes

```
dfworking= pd.DataFrame(openledger)
#Look at the first record
print(dfworking.head(1))
#Check the shape size and columns in the dataset
print(dfworking.shape)
print(dfworking.columns)
dfworking.dtypes
   Record No  TransactionNo  Fiscal Year  Month Department  Account  \
0          0        1095300         2018      1    FINANCE    54050

   Expense Category Vendor   ID        Payment Method      Payment Status  \
0  Food And Beverages       59169  Automated Clearing House  Paid-Unreconciled

  Payment Date     Invoice ID  Invoice Date  Amount  RedFlag
0   07/21/2017  DDSM100367442    07/19/2017   10.08        1
(7293, 15)
Index([u'Record No', u'TransactionNo', u'Fiscal Year', u'Month', u'Department',
u'Account', u'Expense Category', u'Vendor ID', u'Payment Method',
u'Payment Status', u'Payment Date', u'Invoice ID', u'Invoice Date',
u'Amount', u'RedFlag'],
      dtype='object')
```

```
Out[20]:
Record No              int64
TransactionNo          int64
Fiscal Year            int64
Month                  int64
Department            object
Account                int64
Expense Category      object
Vendor ID             object
Payment Method        object
Payment Status        object
Payment Date          object
Invoice ID            object
Invoice Date          object
Amount               float64
RedFlag                int64
dtype: object
```

Next, in Listing 15-4, I look to see if we have any missing data to understand if we need to treat it before starting to pre-process the data.

Listing 15-4. Finding Empty Rows in the Dataframe

```
dfworking.isnull().any()
#Counting the Number of Null rows in each Column of the dataframe
dfworking.isnull().sum()
Out[21]:
Record No           False
TransactionNo       False
Fiscal Year         False
Month               False
Department          False
Account             False
Expense Category    False
Vendor ID           False
Payment Method      False
Payment Status      False
```

```
Payment Date       False
Invoice ID         False
Invoice Date       False
Amount             False
RedFlag            False
dtype: bool

Out[22]:
Record No              0
TransactionNo          0
Fiscal Year            0
Month                  0
Department             0
Account                0
Expense Category       0
Vendor ID              0
Payment Method         0
Payment Status         0
Payment Date           0
Invoice ID             0
Invoice Date           0
Amount                 0
RedFlag                0
dtype: int64
```

After having checked the null values in the dataframe, we find that there are no empty or null columns. In the real world, however, this is never the case, so you may need to deal with and treat the missing values in various columns. Before we move on, let me introduce you to some of the functions that I am going to use in this machine learning model building. The first Python function is distribution. I am going to use this function to create distribution plots to see and compare them and to look at results between algorithms. I will also use this to establish the benchmark predictor algorithm as well. Let us look at the code in Listing 15-5.

Listing 15-5. Distribution Function

Visualization Functions which will be used throughout this model

```python
import matplotlib.pyplot as pl
import matplotlib.patches as mpatches
from time import time
from sklearn.metrics import f1_score, accuracy_score

def distribution(data, transformed = False):
    """

    Visualization code for displaying skewed distributions of features
    """

    # Create figure
    fig = pl.figure(figsize = (11,5));

    # Skewed feature plotting
    for i, feature in enumerate(['Amount','Month', 'Fiscal Year']):
        ax = fig.add_subplot(1, 3, i+1)
        ax.hist(data[feature], bins = 25, color = '#00A0A0')
        ax.set_title("'%s' Feature Distribution"%(feature), fontsize = 14)
        ax.set_xlabel("Value")
        ax.set_ylabel("Number of Records")
        ax.set_ylim((0, 2000))
        ax.set_yticks([0, 500, 1000, 1500, 2000])
        ax.set_yticklabels([0, 500, 1000, 1500, ">2000"])

    # Plot aesthetics
    if transformed:
        fig.suptitle("Log-transformed Distributions of Continuous Census
        Data Features", \
            fontsize = 16, y = 1.03)
    else:
        fig.suptitle("Skewed Distributions of Continuous Census Data
        Features", \
            fontsize = 16, y = 1.03)
```

```
    fig.tight_layout()
    fig.show()
#End of Distribution Visualization function
```

The distribution function input parameter is the same, and the second parameter is informed to explain whether the required dataframe needs to be transformed. This is for applying log transformation later. In the first line of the function, I create a figure by using the Matlab figure function with the figure size of 11 and 5. After this, I create a featured plot in a for loop, which enumerates through the columns amount month and fiscal year. Please note that these columns are numeric in nature. After that, I add each of these columns as a subplot to the figure and then I create a histogram with the data feature of 25 films and provide a title for the feature distribution, setting the x-label and y-label values as x-ticks in the white x-values and label. After the for loop has finished creating the figure, the next check is for the second input parameter. If a log transformation is required, a confirmation is required, then a separate figure supertitle is affixed with log-transformed distributions; otherwise it is the skewed distribution of continuous census data features. So I am using this function to create log-transformed distributions and a skewed distribution. After this is completed, the figure is used with the type layout, and it is shown on the screen. A simple function really works well for showing professional grade work for both transformed distributions and skewed distributions.

Feature Importance

Next we look at feature importance function known as feature_plot() in Listing 15-6.

Listing 15-6. Feature Importances Function

```
# Plotting Feature Importances through this function
def feature_plot(importances, X_train, y_train):

    # Display the five most important features
    indices = np.argsort(importances)[::-1]
    columns = X_train.columns.values[indices[:5]]
    values = importances[indices][:5]
```

```
# Creat the plot
fig = pl.figure(figsize = (9,5))
pl.title("Normalized Weights for First Five Most Predictive Features",
fontsize = 16)
pl.bar(np.arange(4), values, width = 0.6, align="center", color =
'#00A000', \
       label = "Feature Weight")
pl.bar(np.arange(4) - 0.3, np.cumsum(values), width = 0.2, align =
"center", color = '#00A0A0', \
       label = "Cumulative Feature Weight")
pl.xticks(np.arange(5), columns)
pl.xlim((-0.5, 4.5))
pl.ylabel("Weight", fontsize = 12)
pl.xlabel("Feature", fontsize = 12)

pl.legend(loc = 'upper center')
pl.tight_layout()
pl.show()
#End of Feature Importances function
```

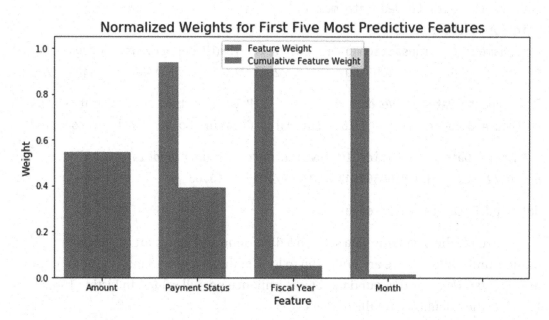

Figure 15-1. *Normalized Weights for First Five Most Predictive Features*

The feature_plot function takes in the first parameter as Feature importances the second parameter as X_train and the third parameter y_train. First, I created a sort of all the important features from the end of the importances variable, and then I took the column name from x_train and the values from the importance variable into the values variable. After this, I created a bar diagram with values that were extracted from the importances variable; these are just five because we want to look at the top five important features here.

Looking at the Outliers

We now look at the outliers in the data set. I would like to remind the readers from the previous two sectors of healthcare and retail that we had defined outliers as those values that are less than 1.5 of the lower quantile and 1.5 times greater than the upper quantile of the amount column. The lower quartile is 0.25 and the higher quantile is 0.75.

Listing 15-7. Load the Data Set

```
fname="C:/DATASETS/data.ct.gov/PaymentsDataset.csv"
openledger= pd.read_csv(fname, low_memory=False, index_col=False)

#Verify the data Loaded into memory
print(openledger.head(1))
   Unnamed: 0  TransactionNo  Fiscal Year  Month Department  Account  \
0           0        1095300         2018      1    FINANCE    54050

      Expense Category Vendor ID           Payment Method      Payment Status  \
0  Food And Beverages     59169  Automated Clearing House  Paid-Unreconciled

   Payment Date    Invoice ID Invoice Date  Amount  RedFlag
0    07/21/2017  DDSM100367442   07/19/2017   10.08        1

data= pd.DataFrame(openledger)
```

To decode the payments data set into a dataframe and then start looking at the outliers and explore it, we are not going to look at data types and look at them in the area figures. We know that our data set is to enhance no null values. In Listing 15-8, I provide the calculation for the outliers.

Listing 15-8. Finding the Outliers in the Payments Data Set

```
#Total number of records
n_records = len(data.index)

#Number of records where payments are below 1.5 times of upper Quantile-
upper Outlier Limit

l=data[data['RedFlag'] == 2].index
n_greater_quantile = len(l)

#Number of records where payments are above 1.5 times of lower Quantile-
lower Outlier limit
l=data[data['RedFlag'] == 1].index
n_lower_quantile = len(l)

#Percentage of Payments above Upper Outlier limit
p=float(n_greater_quantile)/n_records*100.0
greater_percent =p

#Percentage of Payments above Lower Outlier limit
p=float(n_lower_quantile)/n_records*100.0
lower_percent =p

# Print the results
print "Total number of records: {}".format(n_records)
print "High value Payments above 1.5 times of 75th Percentile: {}".
format(n_greater_quantile)
print "Low value Payments below 1.5 times of 25th Percentile: {}".format(n_
lower_quantile)
print "Percentage of high value Payments: {:.2f}%".format(greater_percent)
print "Percentage of low value Payments: {:.2f}%".format(lower_percent)

Total number of records: 7293
High value Payments above 1.5 times of 75th Percentile: 366
Low value Payments below 1.5 times of 25th Percentile: 748
Percentage of high value Payments: 5.02%
Percentage of low value Payments: 10.26%
```

Before I explain the outlier, I would like to tell you that outliers for determining fraud or money laundering transactions is just one of the many techniques used for fraud detection. I am using a very simple setting and data set and simplest techniques for determining whether a transaction is fraud or not so that you can understand how we use and build a machine learning model for determining such types of transactions. In the n_ records variable, I take the length of the number of records in the data frame. Next, I set the boundaries for the lower and upper outlier limits. The whole idea is to hang out the number of records or transactions that are falling within the upper or the lower outlier limits. We know from the data dictionary description that the Red flag column value of 2 means that a record is falling in the upper outlier limit. Similarly, the Red flag of 1 means that the transaction is falling below then the poor people favorite the variables n_lower_quantile used to find out the number of rows which meet the lower. Similarly the variable n_lower_quantile used to determine how many payment transactions or records in the payment ledger fall in the lower outlier limit. After that it calculates the percentage of payment that falls in the greater outlier limit and the lower outlier limit. The results are meant to interpret statements using this variable. You can see that there are 366 high-value payments about the upper outlier limit and 740 transactions in the lower outlier limit. The transactions above the higher outlier limit are about 5 percent of the total transactions and the ones that are lower than the lower outlier limit are 10.26 percent of transactions.

Listing 15-9. Preparing Data

```
# PREPARING DATA
# Split the data into features and target label
payment_raw = pd.DataFrame(data['RedFlag'])
type(payment_raw)
features_raw = data.drop('RedFlag', axis = 1)
#Removing redundant columns from features_raw dataset
features_raw.dtypes
features_raw=features_raw.drop('TransactionNo', axis=1)
features_raw=features_raw.drop('Department', axis=1)
features_raw=features_raw.drop('Account', axis=1)
features_raw=features_raw.drop('Expense Category', axis=1)
features_raw=features_raw.drop('Vendor ID', axis=1)
features_raw=features_raw.drop('Payment Method', axis=1)
```

```
features_raw=features_raw.drop('Payment Date', axis=1)
features_raw=features_raw.drop('Invoice ID', axis=1)
features_raw=features_raw.drop('Invoice Date', axis=1)
features_raw=features_raw.drop('Unnamed: 0', axis=1)
features_raw.dtypes
type(features_raw)
Fiscal Year        int64
Month              int64
Payment Status     object
Amount             float64
dtype: object
```

Preparing the Data Set

Now that we are done determining that we have a substantial percentage of transactions in our data set that fall under the category of fraud or are a Red flag, we can now proceed to prepare our data set by splitting into a feature and target label. This is done in Figure 15-2. You will notice that I have dropped quite a few useless features, such as department, account, category ID, payment method, payment date, invoice date, and Invoice ID, in order to keep only those that are important for our model building. These columns are important in our model building process. The model building is an iterative process most of the time, and hence if I find later that some of the features are required, may have been wrongly selected, or are not giving sufficient accuracy, then I can consider adding some of the columns like department, expense category, and others back.

In Figure 15-2, I show the distribution for three columns: amount, month, and fiscal year. Please note that all these columns are numeric. The distribution function will not work with non-numeric columns.

```
# Visualize skewed continuous features of original data
distribution(data)
```

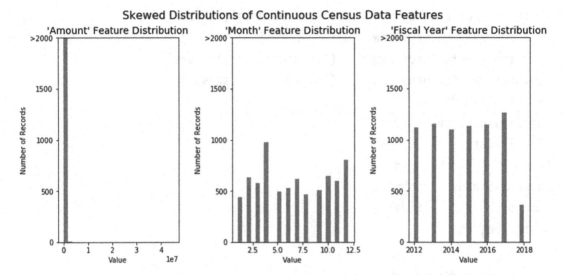

Figure 15-2. *Visualizing the numeric columns*

In Figure 15-2, I have used distribution data to show the distribution of the amount, month, and fiscal year, and we can see clearly that none of them are anywhere near the normal distribution curve. So these are highly skewed distributions that will need to be transformed. The first transformation that I would apply on these features is the log transformation. Remember that the distance from mean can only happen on the numeric features, and hence we are picking up the three columns or features that we have seen in the visualization in Figure 15-2. After applying the log transformation, the next step would be to apply the scale on these features in order to have to remove the high variations in magnitude of each of these features—for example, if the amount has a variation from 0 to greater than 2000, however month goes up to only 8000 records and so is the case with the fiscal year. Moreover, the amount is measured in dollars, month is measured from 0 to 12, and the fiscal year is measured from year to year. So if we do not apply a scaler, then we would be comparing or using features that are not uniform, and it would be like comparing apples and oranges. In Figure 15-3, we will see both the transformation of our data into log transformation and application of a minmaxscaler on the numeric data set, as features in the data set have very different scales and contain some very large outliers. These two characteristics lead to difficulties in visualizing the data, and more importantly, they can degrade the predictive performance of many machine learning algorithms. Unscaled data can also slow down or even prevent the convergence of many gradient-based estimators [1].

```python
# Log-transform the skewed features
#Replacing Null values with zero due to software data entry problem
#Known issue in software user screen takes null values there is no check.
import warnings
warnings.filterwarnings("ignore")
features_raw.isnull().sum()

skewed = ['Amount','Month', 'Fiscal Year']
features_raw[skewed] = data[skewed].apply(lambda x: np.log(x + 1))
features_raw.isnull().sum()
features_raw.fillna(0, inplace=True)
features_raw.dtypes

# Visualize the new log distributions
distribution(features_raw, transformed = True)

#Normalizing Numerical Features
# Import sklearn.preprocessing.StandardScaler
from sklearn.preprocessing import MinMaxScaler

# Initialize a scaler, then apply it to the features
scaler = MinMaxScaler()
numerical = [ 'Amount','Month', 'Fiscal Year']
features_raw[numerical] = scaler.fit_transform(data[numerical])
```

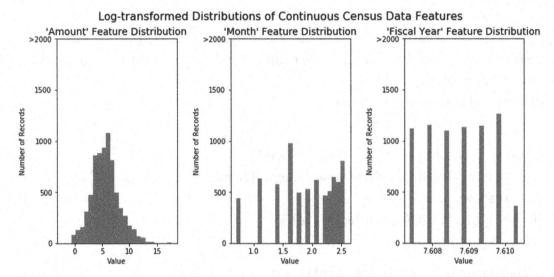

Figure 15-3. *Applying log transformation and scaler on payments data set*

If you compare between Figure 15-2 and Figure 15-3, then the graphs clearly show the effect of log transformation and scaling, where in Figure 15-3, after applying the transformation, the amount feature is almost normalized and the month feature has also changed a bit, but very little change can be seen in the fiscal year feature.

Encoding Columns

Next, I am going to encode one column that is a payment status column, and the reason for doing that is because Python scikit learn library needs numerical values for categorical variables as well. In the payment status column, we have only two values: one is "Paid-Reconciled" and the second is "Paid-Unreconciled". In Listing 15-10, I am hot-encoding "Paid-Reconciled" to a value of 0 and "Paid-Unreconciled" to a value of 1. And then that I look at how many features we have after the encoding is done.

Listing 15-10. *Applying Hot Encoding*

```
# Encoding the 'Non-Numeric' data to numerical values
#Payment Status column
d={"Paid-Reconciled": 0, "Paid-Unreconciled": 1}
features_raw['Payment Status'] = features_raw['Payment Status'].map(d)
```

```
# Printing the number of features after one-hot encoding
encoded = list(features_raw.columns)
print "{} total features after one-hot encoding.".format(len(encoded))
4 total features after one-hot encoding.
```

Splitting the Data into Features

In the next section of the code (given in Listing 15-11), I am going to split the data into features and Red flags by using the train test split function from the SKlearn package.

Listing 15-11. Dividing the Data into a Training Set and Test Set

```
# Importing train_test_split
from sklearn.cross_validation import train_test_split
payment_raw.columns
# Splitting the 'features' and 'RedFlags' data into training and testing sets
X_train, X_test, y_train, y_test = train_test_split(features_raw, payment_
raw, test_size = 0.2, random_state = 0)
X_train.columns
X_test.columns
y_train.columns
y_test.columns
# Showing the results of the split
print "Training set has {} samples.".format(X_train.shape[0])
print "Testing set has {} samples.".format(X_test.shape[0])
Training set has 5834 samples.
The testing set has 1459 samples.
```

Evaluating Model Performance

After this split, I am now going to carry out model performance evaluation by first using a benchmark classifier naïve-Bayes and then calculating its accuracy score and importing five other classifiers, comparing the results among them. You can see the results in Listings 15-12 and 15-13.

Listing 15-12. Scoring the Benchmark Predictor

```
#Evaluating Model Performance
#Establishing Benchmark performance indicator Naive Bayes
#Naive Predictor Performace
from sklearn.naive_bayes import GaussianNB
#from sklearn.metrics import accuracy_score, fbeta_score
from sklearn.metrics import accuracy_score, f1_score, precision_score,
recall_score, classification_report, confusion_matrix
NB = GaussianNB()
NB.fit(X_train,y_train)
pred = NB.predict(X_test)

#Calculating Accuracy Score
#Calculating Beta Score
accuracy_score(y_test,pred)
print(f1_score(y_test,pred, average="macro"))
print(precision_score(y_test, pred, average="macro"))
print(recall_score(y_test, pred, average="macro"))
0.8064675486756182
0.7243305924520346
0.9656357388316151
```

We see that the F1 Score, Precision score, and Recall scores for the benchmark
predictor are quite good at 0.80, 0.72, and 0.96, respectively. Now that we have the
score for the benchmark predictor or classifier naïve Bayes, let us apply this on the
other classifiers, such as Decision trees, Logistic Regression, SGD (Gradient Descent),
Extratrees Classifier, and Random Forest Classifier in the code given in Listing 15-13.

Listing 15-13. Initial Model Evaluation

```
# I AM GOING TO DO INITIAL MODEL EVALUATION NOW
# Importing the three supervised learning models from sklearn
from sklearn.naive_bayes import GaussianNB
from sklearn.tree import DecisionTreeClassifier
from sklearn.linear_model import LogisticRegression
from sklearn.linear_model import SGDClassifier
```

```
from sklearn.ensemble import ExtraTreesClassifier
from sklearn.ensemble import RandomForestClassifier

# Initialize the three models
clf_A = GaussianNB()
clf_B = DecisionTreeClassifier(max_features=0.2, max_depth=2, min_samples_
split=2,random_state=0)
clf_C = LogisticRegression(random_state=0)
clf_D = SGDClassifier(loss="hinge", penalty="l2")
clf_E = ExtraTreesClassifier(n_estimators=2, max_depth=2,min_samples_
split=2, random_state=0)
clf_F = RandomForestClassifier(max_depth=2)

# Calculate the number of samples for 1%, 10%, and 100% of the training data
#Defining function since percent is required 3 times

# Collect results on the learners
learners=["Naive Bayes","Decision Tree","Logistic Regression","SGD
Classifier","ExtaTrees Classifier","RandomFores Classifier"]
cnt=0
columns=['learner','train_time','pred_time','acc_train','acc_test','f1_score']
learningresults= pd.DataFrame(columns=columns)
results = {}

for learner in [clf_A, clf_B, clf_C,clf_D,clf_E,clf_F]:
    #print(learners[cnt])
    results['learner']=learners[cnt]
    #Fitting the learner to the training data using slicing with 'sample_size'
    start = time() # Get start time
    learner.fit(X_train, y_train)
    #Calculating the total prediction time
    end = time() # Get end time
    results['train_time'] =  end - start
    start = time() # Get start time
    predictions_test = learner.predict(X_test)
    predictions_train = learner.predict(X_train)
    end = time() # Get end time
    results['pred_time'] = end - start
```

```
    results['acc_train'] = accuracy_score(y_train, predictions_train)
    results['acc_test'] = accuracy_score(y_test, predictions_test)
    beta=0.5
    results['f1_score'] = f1_score(y_test,pred, average="macro")
    print(results)
    learningresults.loc[cnt]=results
    cnt=cnt+1

#Looking at the plots to determine the best Classifier for our Dataset
print(learningresults)
learningresults.columns
learningresults.plot(kind='bar', x='learner',
legend='reverse',  title='Classifier Algorithms Compared- Accounts Payment
Dataset',figsize=(10,10), fontsize=20)
```

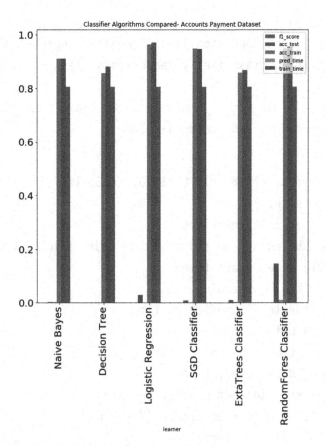

Figure 15-4. *Comparing the results from classifiers*

Before we proceed in our model implementation further, I would like to discuss the results of learners data set that stores the train_time for training time and pred_time for prediction time, acc_train for accuracy during training, and acc_test for accuracy during test as well as f1_score for the f1 score. These are presented in Table 15-1.

There are various approaches to selecting the best learner or classifier for your model. Different data sets and different business situations in which the model is applied can determine which learner is best for you. For example, just using a blanket parameter for model selection like the lowest training time is not necessarily good, as it may be the learner with a low accuracy during a test or an f1 score. Also if you are selecting a learner for a model that will be applied on a batch offline process such as monthly reports or other such overnight processes, then your aim may not be the lowest training and prediction times. If the business people want a higher accuracy in testing with the lowest prediction time, then your selection of learner in our case would be SGD Classifier. The context in which you are applying the model is more important and drives the model selection criteria.

Table 15-1. *Comparing the Learners or Classifiers*

Learner	train_time	pred_time	acc_train	acc_test	f1_score
Decision Tree	0.001	0.001	0.857045	0.880055	0.806468
Naïve-Bayes	0.002	0.002	0.910525	0.910898	0.806468
SGD Classifier	0.009	0	0.947377	0.946539	0.806468
ExtraTrees Classifier	0.01	0.002	0.858759	0.867032	0.806468
Logistic Regression	0.028	0.001	0.96349	0.971213	0.806468
RandomForest Classifier	0.146	0.011	0.948234	0.956134	0.806468

In Table 15-1, the f1 score by all the classifiers is same as 0.8064, so it cannot be considered for making a selection. I have used Logistic Regression, which is the best classifier in terms of least training time and highest accuracy for the test data set. In Listing 15-14, let's use this model to do hyper-parameter tuning using GridSearch cross-validation.

Listing 15-14. Tuning the Model Using GridSearch Cross-Validation Method

```python
# Import 'GridSearchCV', 'make_scorer', and any other necessary libraries
from sklearn.metrics import make_scorer
from sklearn.model_selection import GridSearchCV
from IPython.display import display
import pickle, os.path
from sklearn.linear_model import LogisticRegression
from sklearn.metrics import fbeta_score

def getscore(y_true, y_predict):
    return fbeta_score(y_true, y_predict, beta)

best_clf = None
beta=0.5

#Initialize the classifier

clf_C = LogisticRegression(random_state=0)

# Create the parameters list you wish to tune
#parameters = {'n_estimators':range(10,20),'criterion':['gini','entropy'],'
max_depth':range(1,5)}
parameters = {'solver':['newton-cg', 'lbfgs', 'liblinear', 'sag',
'saga'],'C':range(1,10),'max_iter':range(50,100)}

# Make an fbeta_score scoring object
scorer = make_scorer(getscore)

# Perform grid search on the classifier using 'scorer' as the scoring method
#grid_obj = GridSearchCV(clf_C, parameters, scoring=scorer)

#do something
grid_obj = GridSearchCV(clf_C, parameters)

#grid_obj = GridSearchCV(clf_C, parameters)

# Fit the grid search object to the training data and find the optimal
parameters
from datetime import datetime
```

```
startTime = datetime.now()

grid_fit = grid_obj.fit(X_train, y_train)
CV_lr = GridSearchCV(estimator=clf_C, param_grid=parameters, cv= 5)
CV_lr.fit(X_train, y_train)
print(datetime.now() - startTime)

    # Get the estimator
best_clf = grid_fit.best_estimator_

# Make predictions using the unoptimized and model
predictions = (clf_C.fit(X_train, y_train)).predict(X_test)
best_predictions = best_clf.predict(X_test)

# Report the before-and-afterscores
print "Unoptimized model\n------"
print "Accuracy score on testing data: {:.4f}".format(accuracy_score(y_
test, predictions))
print "F-score on testing data: {:.4f}".format(fbeta_score(y_test,
predictions, beta = 0.5,average='micro'))
print "\nOptimized Model\n------"
print "Final accuracy score on the testing data: {:.4f}".format(accuracy_
score(y_test, best_predictions))
print "Final F-score on the testing data: {:.4f}".format(fbeta_score(y_
test, best_predictions, beta = 0.5,average='micro'))
```

0:39:21.351000

```
Unoptimized model
------
Accuracy score on testing data: 0.9712
F-score on testing data: 0.9712

Optimized Model
------
Final accuracy score on the testing data: 0.9925
Final F-score on the testing data: 0.9925
```

As you can see, I implemented GridSearch cross-validation over the best-selected classifier, Logistic Regression, and it took about 39 minutes and 21 seconds for it to come up with the results. The results of the optimized model are really good, with an accuracy score and F-score of 0.9925, which is a significant improvement from the unoptimized model accuracy score of 0.9712 and F-score of 0.9712 as well. In the Listing 15-15, I now print the final tuned parameters that are going to be the ones we use for our prediction model.

Listing 15-15. Tuned Parameter for Logistic Regression Prediction Model

```
# Print the final parameters
df = pd.DataFrame(grid_fit.grid_scores_).sort_values('mean_validation_
score').tail()
display(df)
print "Parameters for the optimal model: {}".format(clf.get_params())
                                                  parameters  \
2098      {u'C': 9, u'max_iter': 69, u'solver': u'sag'}
2099      {u'C': 9, u'max_iter': 69, u'solver': u'saga'}
2100   {u'C': 9, u'max_iter': 70, u'solver': u'newton...
2086      {u'C': 9, u'max_iter': 67, u'solver': u'lbfgs'}
2249      {u'C': 9, u'max_iter': 99, u'solver': u'saga'}

    mean_validation_score                                cv_validation_scores
2098           0.985087  [0.9881808838643371, 0.9845758354755784, 0.982...
2099           0.985087  [0.9881808838643371, 0.9845758354755784, 0.982...
2100           0.985087  [0.9881808838643371, 0.9845758354755784, 0.982...
2086           0.985087  [0.9881808838643371, 0.9845758354755784, 0.982...
2249           0.985087  [0.9881808838643371, 0.9845758354755784, 0.982...
Parameters for the optimal model: {'warm_start': False, 'oob_score': False,
'n_jobs': 1, 'min_impurity_decrease': 0.0, 'verbose': 0, 'max_leaf_nodes':
None, 'bootstrap': True, 'min_samples_leaf': 1, 'n_estimators': 10,
'min_samples_split': 2, 'min_weight_fraction_leaf': 0.0, 'criterion':
'gini', 'random_state': None, 'min_impurity_split': None, 'max_features':
'auto', 'max_depth': 2, 'class_weight': None}
```

We can see that the optimal model parameters that are relevant are bootstrap:True, which means that the GridSearch cross-validation was able to apply bootstrapping on the model in order to get optimum results. For more information about how bootstrapping helps in model tuning, read the research paper from IEEE (https:// ieeexplore.ieee.org/document/6396613/). The other important parameters are n_ estimators: 10, max_depth:2.

Determining Features

After having found out the tuned parameters for the logistic regression prediction model, I am now going to get into feature importance for the top five, which will help us determine how our features help us in our prediction model. You can see this piece of code in Listing 15-16 using the feature_plot() function, which we had seen earlier in our code.

Listing 15-16. Extracting Feature Importances

```
# Now Extracting Feature Importances
# importing a supervised learning model that has 'feature_importances_'
from sklearn.ensemble import ExtraTreesClassifier
from sklearn.feature_selection import SelectFromModel
from sklearn.metrics import fbeta_score

# Training the supervised model on the training set
model = ExtraTreesClassifier()
model.fit(X_train, y_train)

# TODO: Extract the feature importances
importances = model.feature_importances_

# Plot
feature_plot(importances, X_train, y_train)
```

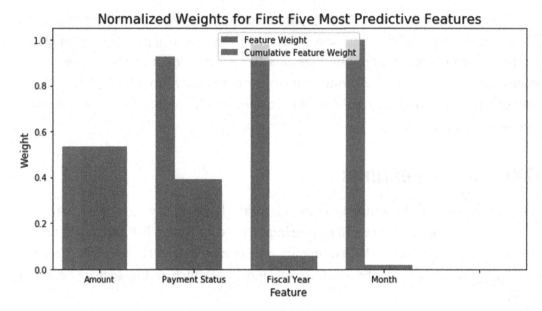

Figure 15-5. *Feature selection using the classifier*

As expected, amount turns out to be the most important feature in our model, followed by payment status. Please remember that our fraud in this data set is based on these two columns in the Red Flag column. The outliers that are greater than 1.5 times the 75th percentile and have a payment status of unreconciled are considered to be potential fraud or money-laundering transactions. Similarly the lower limit of fewer than 1.5 times of 25th percentile and transactions that have a payment status of unreconciled are considered to be potential fraud or money-laundering payment transactions. We can see from the graph that fiscal year and month do not have any significant impact on our prediction model and have low feature weight. Now that we have seen the best two features, let us select these features so that our model can be finally completed. This is done in Listing 15-17.

Listing 15-17. Feature Selection and Model Implementation

```
# Feature Selection
# Import functionality for cloning a model
from sklearn.base import clone
best_clf= clf_F
```

```
# Reduce the feature space
X_train_reduced = X_train[X_train.columns.values[(np.argsort(importances)
[::-1])[:5]]]
X_test_reduced = X_test[X_test.columns.values[(np.argsort(importances)
[::-1])[:5]]]

# Train on the "best" model found from grid search earlier
clf = (clone(best_clf)).fit(X_train_reduced, y_train)
best_predictions = best_clf.predict(X_test)
# Make new predictions
reduced_predictions = clf.predict(X_test_reduced)

# Report scores from the final model using both versions of data
print "Final Model trained on full data\n------"
print "Accuracy on testing data: {:.4f}".format(accuracy_score(y_test,
best_predictions))
print "F-score on testing data: {:.4f}".format(fbeta_score(y_test, best_
predictions, average="macro", beta = 0.5))
print "\nFinal Model trained on reduced data\n------"
print "Accuracy on testing data: {:.4f}".format(accuracy_score(y_test,
reduced_predictions))
print "F-score on testing data: {:.4f}".format(fbeta_score(y_test, reduced_
predictions, beta = 0.5, average='macro'))

Final Model trained on full data
------
Accuracy on testing data: 0.9561
F-score on testing data: 0.6537

Final Model trained on reduced data
------
Accuracy on testing data: 0.9548
F-score on testing data: 0.6523
```

We do not have such great results between the final model and full data that includes all the four features and those compared to the reduced data. So, in my opinion, we can retain the full data set, and there is no need to discard the other features, such as month and fiscal year.

The Final Parameters

The final parameters to our model are given in Listing 15-18.

Listing 15-18. Parameters for the Optimized Model

```
# Print the final parameters

print "Parameters for the optimal model: {}".format(clf.get_params())
Parameters for the optimal model: {'warm_start': False, 'oob_score': False,
'n_jobs': 1, 'min_impurity_decrease': 0.0, 'verbose': 0, 'max_leaf_nodes':
None, 'bootstrap': True, 'min_samples_leaf': 1, 'n_estimators': 10,
'min_samples_split': 2, 'min_weight_fraction_leaf': 0.0, 'criterion':
'gini', 'random_state': None, 'min_impurity_split': None, 'max_features':
'auto', 'max_depth': 2, 'class_weight': None}
```

With this we come to the end of the Implementation of Machine Learning in Payments data set. The implementation is pretty much similar to the approach you saw in the healthcare and retail segments of this book; however, here we have used payments transaction data set, which required us to tweak some of the ways in which we defined what is a money-laundering transaction. Please remember this is a very naïve and simplistic approach to detecting frauds. In the real world the models and the data become much more complex, such as adding complexity of nationality, ip address, or location, etc.

End Note

[1] Need for applying Scaling: http://scikit-learn.org/stable/
auto_examples/preprocessing/plot_all_scaling.html

## CHAPTER 16

Case Studies in Finance AI

Disclaimer: The case studies in this book have been taken from real-life organizations. Care has been taken to ensure that the names of the organizations and the names of its employees are changed and do not resemble my clients in any way. The reader familiar with the finance industry will definitely find these situations very practical and insightful.

CASE STUDY 1: Stock Market Movement Prediction

RISEGOINVEST, a leading Investment Advisory company and fund manager, has seen its funds rise many-fold since the time it was established in the year 1997, when the US security markets outperformed global peers by more than a decade and the best performance so far was by Dow Jones Industrial Average with a rise of 20 percent. Its founder and Chairman, Jimiki Takasata, established this company with an aim to establish a significant investment pipeline to the emerging markets like Asia, the Middle East, and Africa. He had the vision to understand that the developed countries would see stunted growth and that the emerging markets would see the next phase of exponential growth and offer opportunities that the developed economies did not provide. At that time he was a lone wolf in the herd where he was asking his investors to start looking for the developing and emerging markets. However, in the first year he was able to get a fund together in excess of $600 million. This showed that people had faith in his capabilities as an investor and his vision was shared among many at that time.

© Puneet Mathur 2019
P. Mathur, *Machine Learning Applications Using Python*, https://doi.org/10.1007/978-1-4842-3787-8_16

Since that early growth stage the company had grown exponentially and in the year 2017 had investment funds exceeding 92.5 billion dollars worldwide. Mr. Takasata had established a great team of investment advisors who were not only experts in their fields but were professionals who could spot an investment trend that was going to happen around the world. They had spotted the rise of emerging economies like India and China in the early years of 2000 and had started to push large investments for their major clients, giving them major returns, even during the global recession years. This had earned the company a good reputation and had been the main reason for growth in its investment customer base. With all the growth and the trends there were some investment opportunities that were missed by the fund managers and investment advisors at RISEGOINVEST. For example, it had failed to foresee the rise in investment opportunities in countries of Africa. It also had failed investments for many of its clients in securities markets in Hong Kong, Malaysia where it had burnt its fingers heavily.

There was also a rise in competition from competitors managing emerging market funds more efficiently. Due to competition, the investors were demanding more from the emerging market fund managers and advisors. One such major investor was Mr. Parakeet. He had his personal funds invested with Mr. Takasata's company to the tune of $850 million. He was a very important customer for the company, as he had been investing with them since 2003. It was more than a decade-old relationship. Mr. Takasata's investment advisor, Jim Catzat, who was managing Mr. Parakeet's account, reported to Mr. Takasata what he described as an "unusual conversation" that he had with his client. In a quarterly meeting with Mr. Parakeet, he had asked Jim to give him very accurate reports on stock markets from the emerging nations—especially India, where he had major investments. Mr. Parakeet wanted the daily and weekly advisory reports on his investments in stock markets in India to accurately predict the movement of the stock market and individual stock prices where he had investments. Jim informed Mr. Parakeet that the current reports gave alerts about his stocks and that this was based on the various fundamental and technical analysis that his company did for him and was reflected in the reports that were sent to him every day and every week. Mr. Parakeet said, "I need you to fine-tune your reports to such an extent that you predict to me the stock market movement or the stock price movement on what it is going to be tomorrow or the next trading day." Jim said this was impossible to achieve as it was impossible to predict stock prices, as they were based on various factors and none of those factors starting from macro- to micro-indicators were themselves very predictable. To this Jim replied, "I am giving you 1 month's time. If you do not have such a system, develop it and give me reports with at least 80 percent accuracy levels on stock prices in India, or else I will look to move my funds to some other company."

After being informed by Jim, Mr. Takasata explained that this was a large client and that word-of-mouth was extremely essential, so if this customer was dissatisfied then the word would go out to other clients as well, and they could also move their funds to other fund managers. He asked Jim to check with the company's computer scientist, Kazy Korone, to see if there was a computer model available to predict stock market prices.

Jim set up a meeting with Kazy to find out from her whether such a thing was possible to build in the first place and whether it could be done in 4 weeks, which is what the client had given them. Kazy told him that with the use of machine learning, it was possible to build such model that could predict stock prices. However, it required data from the Indian stock market from the past 10 years. She asked him to give her a week's time to build a prototype to demonstrate the prediction of stock prices based on the closing price of the stock in the last trading day.

Questions for the Case Study

1. Do you think it is possible to build a machine learning prediction model for any given stock and predict its price for the next day?

2. What data would you need to build such a prediction model? Define the common data features, such as stock name, closing price, opening price, etc.

3. What sources would give you the most accurate stock market data for an emerging market like India? Would that data be free or would you need to pay for it?

4. After you have collected the data from its source, what approach would you take to define the machine learning prediction model?

5. List out one or two algorithms that you would use in your model using the approach that you defined in question 4.

6. What will be your actual Python-based machine learning solution?

Proposed Solution for the Case Study

A solution for this case study will try to answer each of the questions in a way that is acceptable to both the business people and machine learning professionals. Please remember that no solution is the ultimate solution for a given problem, and it is possible that in this case study approach you may come up with your own unique solution. The purpose of giving this solution is in order to make you understand the way in which a professional solution is arrived at for a given business problem; important thing is that the time frame in which the solution is required to be given. However, in order for you to understand the business problem fully I will ask you to develop a full-fledged solution for this case study problem by using some of the processes and principles that I showed you in the healthcare and retail sections of this book.

Answer 1

I definitely think that it is possible to develop a chain model for predicting the price of a stock for the next trading day. I am sure because price is nothing but numeric data, and it is generated every second of every minute when the stock taking is happening in the stock market. There are various algorithms that can be used to predict the stock market price, and most of them are regressors.

Let's get a good look at a basic regressor since building the prototype is very short. Then we can look at improving it later when a full-fledged solution is being built.

Answer 2

As per me, the following features would be required along with the target predictor, which is the price:

Date: Date on which the stock has been traded.

Open: The opening price of the stock on that date.

High: The highest price of the stock on that date.

Low: The lowest price of the stock on that date.

Last: The last traded price of the stock on that date.

Close: The closing price of the stock on that date.

Answer 3

As of the time of writing this book, there are currently the following free data sources for getting National Stock Exchange and Bombay Stock Exchange data.

Yahoo using Pandas datareader library: In Listing 16-1, I give you a sample code that can be used to download any stock price historical values using this Python script.

Listing 16-1. Simple Python Script to Get Stock Market Data

```python
# -*- coding: utf-8 -*-
"""
Created on Sun Dec  3 23:32:32 2017

@author: PUNEETMATHUR
"""

import numpy as np
import pandas as pd
#import pandas.io.data as web
from pandas_datareader import data, wb

sp500= data.DataReader('^GSPC', data_source='yahoo', start='1/1/2000',
end='1/12/2017')
#sp500= data.DataReader('^GSPC', data_source='yahoo')
sp500.ix['2010-01-04']
sp500.info()
print(sp500)
print(sp500.columns)
print(sp500.shape)

import matplotlib.pyplot as plt
plt.plot(sp500['Close'])

# now calculating the 42nd Days and 252 days trend for the index
sp500['42d']= np.round(pd.rolling_mean(sp500['Close'], window=42),2)
sp500['252d']= np.round(pd.rolling_mean(sp500['Close'], window=252),2)

#Look at the data
sp500[['Close','42d','252d']].tail()
plt.plot(sp500[['Close','42d','252d']])
```

This script gets data for Standard and Poor's 500, for example, and then charts it by storing the data in the Pandas dataframe. However, this data is not very accurate, as it contains values for holidays and Saturdays as well, when we know for sure the stock market is closed. So we have a data source from Yahoo, but it is not accurate. So then I show you another source that has free and accurate data: Quandl.com. This data can be mined free of cost without many restrictions. You need to register on their website and get a free api key to make it work here: `https://www.quandl.com/data/NSE-National-Stock-Exchange-of-India`.

Now once you have registered and you get your free api key from Quandl, you can download the data directly using their Python api.

Before you start using the script in Listing 16-2, you will need to install the Quandl package by using the pip installer. Now I show you in Figure 16-1. Data download of a sample stock using quandl free Python library.

Listing 16-2. Loading Data from Quandl

```
pip install Quandl

# -*- coding: utf-8 -*-
"""
Created on Sat Sep 22 23:43:13 2018

@author: PUNEETMATHUR
"""

import quandl
quandl.ApiConfig.api_key = 'INSERT YOU API KEY HERE'

# get the table for daily stock prices and,
# filter the table for selected tickers, columns within a time range
# set paginate to True because Quandl limits tables API to 10,000 rows per call

data = quandl.get_table('WIKI/PRICES', ticker = ['AAPL', 'MSFT', 'WMT'],
                        qopts = { 'columns': ['ticker', 'date', 'adj_close'] },
                        date = { 'gte': '2015-12-31', 'lte': '2016-12-31' },
                        paginate=True)
data.head()
```

```
# create a new dataframe with 'date' column as index
new = data.set_index('date')

# use pandas pivot function to sort adj_close by tickers
clean_data = new.pivot(columns='ticker')

# check the head of the output
clean_data.head()

#Below script gets you Data from National Stock Exchange for a stock known
as Oil India Limited
import quandl
quandl.ApiConfig.api_key = 'z1bxBq27SVanESKoLJwa'
quandl.ApiConfig.api_version = '2015-04-09'

import quandl
data = quandl.get('NSE/OIL')
data.head()
data.columns
data.shape

#Storing data in a flat file
data.to_csv("NSE_OIL.csv")
#A basic plot of the stocks data across the years
data['Close'].plot()
```

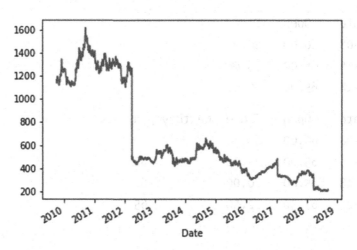

Figure 16-1. *Data download of a sample stock using quandl free Python library*

You will notice that in the first part of the code I am giving you an example of how to get stock market prices using Quandl library for a few stocks like Apple, Microsoft, and Walmart. I also show you how to clean up the data and show it in a presentable form after cleaning it up. In the second part of the quote I show you how to get the data from Quandl for the National Stock Exchange (NSE). Here I am using one stock from a company known as Oil India Limited, and I am searching its data and storing it in a file and then showing the plot for it. You will also notice that the stock has data from 2009 to 2018. So this is a very good free source of data for the stock market. This is the source I recommend to all my readers to give a solution for this case study.

Answer 4

My approach to solving this problem is to first get data about a company from Quandl by the method shown in Answer 3. After using the Python script, store the data in a flat csv file and then clean up data with null values. Sort the data with the date column. Do exploratory data analysis by looking at visualizations year-wise and month-wise. Calculate simple moving average on the stock, as it is a good indicator for gaging stock performance. There are only going to be three columns that I am going to use primarily for this prediction model: ['Date', 'Open', 'Close']. However, I will be creating a derived value column from the opening price for the next day and add it to the previous day's price. So I create a new feature ['NextDayOpen']. Let me illustrate this with an example in Listing 16-3.

Listing 16-3. Example of Adding Next Day Open Column Values

	Date	Open	Close
5909	1991-02-08	60.00	60.00
5908	1991-03-15	65.00	75.00
5907	1991-03-18	65.00	70.00

	Date	Open	Close	NextDayOpen
5909	1991-02-08	60.00	60.00	0
5908	1991-03-15	65.00	75.00	60
5907	1991-03-18	65.00	70.00	65
5906	1991-03-20	67.50	72.50	65

We can see from Listing 16-3 that the original dataframe that has only three columns (Date, Open, and Close features) now has an additional NextDayOpen feature as well. This is nothing but the previous day's opening price carried over to Next Day Open feature. The first one is blank because it does not have a previous Open value. In effect now the NextDayOpen column becomes our target variable or predictor. This is what we have to predict for the next day. This concept is fundamental and key to understanding how this prediction model works.

After this is done, create a model based on linear regression to predict the stock price for the next trading day. Although this is a simple prototype model for prediction, when moving it to production we would need to try out a few other regressors like decision trees, etc. I leave that to you to try on your own and select the best model for your production environment.

Answer 5

I would use linear regression to build a prototype model. The reason for doing so is because in the case study there is very little time to build a given model and linear regression techniques offer the quickest was to implement and get results. The only part that may not work well is the accuracy level of the prediction model; however, if you are in a hurry, then there are tradeoffs to be made.

Answer 6

Now I present to you my version of the solution that we discussed in Answer 5 above of this case study. You will see the code in Listing 16-4 onward. I am assuming that you have loaded the data using Python scripts given in Figure 16-1 and have stored it in a csv file.

Listing 16-4. Loading Data

```
# -*- coding: utf-8 -*-
"""

Created on Sun Dec 17 20:30:01 2017
@author: PUNEETMATHUR
I am creating this script to predict next day Opening Price based on
Today's Closing Price for any given stock
"""
```

```
import numpy as np
import pandas as pd
import os

#Change your directory to wherever your dataset is stored
os.chdir("E:\\") # Change this to your directory or path where you have
downloaded the dataset.
#Loading the dataset of the company for which prediction is required
df=pd.read_csv("BalmerLawrieColtd.csv",parse_dates=['Date'])
print(df.head(1))
print(df.columns)

Out[*]:
   Unnamed: 0      Date    Open    High    Low   Close    WAP  No. of Shares  \
0           1 2017-12-29  278.85  279.15  272.6  274.55  276.1          19372
   No. of Trades  Total Turnover  Deliverable Quantity  \
0            504       5348670.0               10024.0

   % Deli. Qty to Traded Qty  Spread H-L   Spread C-O
0                      51.74        6.55         -4.3
Index([u'Unnamed: 0', u'Date', u'Open', u'High', u'Low', u'Close', u'WAP',
       u'No. of Shares', u'No. of Trades', u'Total Turnover',
       u'Deliverable Quantity', u'% Deli. Qty to Traded Qty', u'Spread H-L',
       u'Spread C-O'],
      dtype='object')
df.shape
Out[91]: (5911, 14)
```

I have up to now loaded the data and had a look at its shape, which is comprised of 5911 rows and 14 columns or features. There is a lot of extra data that we do not need for building our prototype model, and therefore I am going to remove them and select only those features that are required for our model building exercise in Listing 16-5.

Listing 16-5. Selecting Only the Relevant Columns for Our Prototype Model

```
#Selecting only relevant columns required for prediction
cols=['Date','Open','Close']
df=df[cols]

print(df.columns)
print(df.head(5))
Index([u'Date', u'Open', u'Close'], dtype='object')
Date Open Close
0 2017-12-29 278.85 274.55
1 2017-12-28 276.75 276.15
2 2017-12-27 276.40 275.45
3 2017-12-26 269.00 268.10
4 2017-12-22 269.60 270.10
```

We can see from the result of the code in Listing 16-5 that it has only the relevant data that we want. Let us now proceed to the next step on checking empty rows in the data set in Listing 16-6.

Listing 16-6. Checking for Data Clean-Up

```
# Checking data if Cleaning up data is required
df.isnull().any()
#df=df.dropna()
#df=df.replace("NA",0)
df.dtypes
Out[96]:
Date datetime64[ns]
Open float64
Close float64
dtype: object
```

As can be seen from Listing 16-6 we do not have any clean-up to do as there are no empty rows. This is the advantage of selecting a good source for your data set. Quandl. com is a good source for stock market data worldwide. Let us now quickly visualize the data by plotting it in Listing 16-7. We visualize the data in Figure 16-2 below.

Listing 16-7. Plotting the data

```
#Sorting up data to plot historically ascending values in graph
df = df.sort_values(by='Date',ascending=True)

#Plotting the price of stock over the years
#What story does it tell?
import matplotlib.pyplot as plt
plt.plot(df['Date'],df['Close'])
```

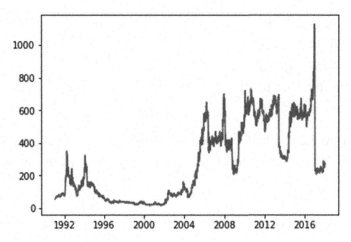

Figure 16-2. *Visualizing the data*

We see that this particular stock, Balmer Lawrie Co. Ltd., peaked in 2016 and was its highest ever price before dropping to a low. Next we plot the graph to check data for the last year and last month to see if we notice something unusual about its price movement given in Listing 16-8 and Figure 16-3.

Listing 16-8. Plotting data for last year and a month

```
#Now plot only for last one year and last 1 month
df['Date'].dt.year==2017
mask=(df['Date'] > '2017-1-1') & (df['Date'] <= '2017-12-31')
print(df.loc[mask])
df2017=df.loc[mask]
print(df2017.head(5))
plt.plot(df2017['Date'],df2017['Close'])
```

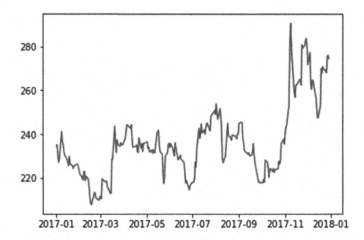

Figure 16-3. *Visulizing 1 year's worth of data*

We can see that this stock peaked around the month of November and December and then slightly went up in January, 2018 as well. Otherwise there were some quarterly results peaks that we see around March through June and then again in August to September of 2017.

Now let us look at the 1 month's worth of data and see if it shows us any peculiarities (Listing 16-9 and Figure 16-4).

Listing 16-9. Plotting 1 month stock data

```
#Plotting last 1 month data on stock
mask=(df['Date'] > '2017-11-17') & (df['Date'] <= '2017-12-26')
print(df.loc[mask])
dfnovdec2017=df.loc[mask]
print(dfnovdec2017.head(5))
plt.plot(dfnovdec2017['Date'],dfnovdec2017['Close'])
```

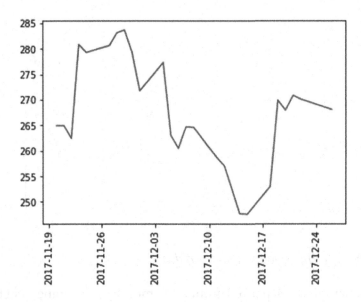

Figure 16-4. *Visualizing 1 month's worth of stock data*

We can see in the graph that the stock peaked just after November 26, 2017 and was at its lowest in between December 10, 2017 and December 17, 2017. While we could find out the reasons why the stocks went down through searching for news about the stock on dividends, quarterly results, share buyback news, or share split news, etc., that is something that you can do when you present the results to your clients, who will definitely be interested in knowing the reason for such peaks and troughs. However, for the purpose of this solution, I am going to skip this step and go straight to the next step of calculating simple moving average for the stock for 1 year in Listing 16-10 and Figure 16-5.

Listing 16-10. Calculating Simple Moving Average of the Stock

```
#Now calculating the Simple Moving Average of the Stock
#Simple Moving Average One Year
df2017['SMA'] = df2017['Close'].rolling(window=20).mean()
df2017.head(25)
df2017[['SMA','Close']].plot().
```

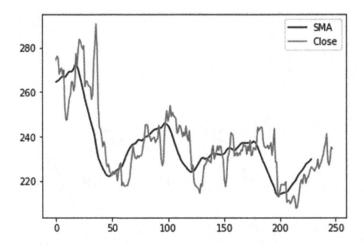

Figure 16-5. *Plotting stock price with simple moving average*

You will notice that the simple moving average follows the stock very carefully and sometimes does not fit very tightly with the price movement curve. For example, in between points 0 and 50 on the x-axis, the blue line of SMA goes well below the actual price line. You can see this again in between x-axis points 100 and 150, and again in between x-axis points in between 150 and 200. SMA is also known as a technical indicator, and I have used a rolling window of 20 days, which is defined in the part of code df2017['SMA'] = df2017['Close'].rolling(**window=20**).mean() while defining the mean or the average of the closing price. Now we come to the center part of this model building, where I ask whether the opening and closing prices follow each other very well. This is depicted in Figure 16-6.

```
#Does the Open and Closing price of the stock follow very well?
df2017[['Open','Close']].plot()
```

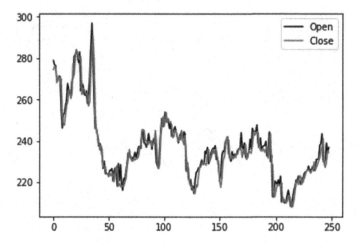

Figure 16-6. *Do opening and closing prices of the stock follow each other well?*

Yes, visually there seems to be a very good relationship between the opening and closing prices of the selected stock Balmer Lawries Co. Ltd. However, in a few places near the x-axis tick of 50 and between the x-axis ticks of 100 and 150, we find that there is a gap between opening and closing prices, and they have not followed themselves very closely in 2017. Let us check this by doing a correlation between them in Table 16-1.

```
df2017.corr()
Out[104]:

In [105]:
```

Table 16-1. *Checking Correlation Between the Columns*

	Open	Close	SMA
Open	1	0.962507	0.799758
Close	0.962507	1	0.788695
SMA	0.799758	0.788695	1

We can see that there is a strong correlation of 0.96 between the Open and Close columns. So yes, there is a great possibility of making a model for prediction of the stock price. The correlation for SMA is not relevant there, as it is a derived column and not something we can use for prediction purposes. This is also reflected in the correlation of 0.79 between opening price and SMA and correlation of 0.788 between closing price and SMA.

Now let us also look at SMA for a month before we move on to creating our new column for making predictions in Figure 16-7. Visualize SMA for 1 month.

Listing 16-11. Calculating Moving Average for One Month

```
#Simple Moving Average One Month
dfnovdec2017['SMA'] = dfnovdec2017['Close'].rolling(window=2).mean()
dfnovdec2017.head(25)
dfnovdec2017[['SMA','Close']].plot()
```

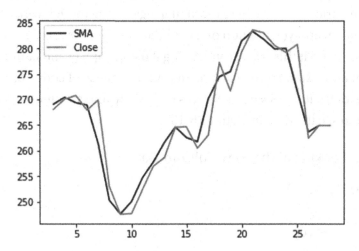

Figure 16-7. *Visualize SMA for 1 month*

The SMA for 1 month with a rolling window of 2 gives us the average for 1 month. dfnovdec2017['SMA'] = dfnovdec2017['Close'].rolling(window=2).mean(). It is this setting that enables us to get data for November and December 2017—approximately 30 days of data. Now in Listing 16-12, I am going to show you one way of creating a column NextDayOpen, which we looked at in Answer 5 earlier.

Listing 16-12. Creating NextDayOpen column for Prediction

```
#Now creating NextDayOpen column for prediction
ln=len(df)
lnop=len(df['Open'])
print(lnop)
ii=0
df['NextDayOpen']=df['Open']
df['NextDayOpen']=0
```

```
for i in range(0,ln-1):
    print("Open Price: ",df['Open'][i])
    if i!=0:
        ii=i-1
    df['NextDayOpen'][ii]=df['Open'][i]
    print(df['NextDayOpen'][ii])
```

You will notice that I have used a for loop to go through each row in the dataframe and then it goes into a for loop where the NextDayOpen column is updated from the previous opening price. This is where the actual logic of the model works. You can do the same through an apply() function or a lambda function; however, my roots in other languages make me do it this way. I think doing it using apply() and lambda() functions is more efficient and faster. So you can create your own piece of code here if you wish using these functions. It takes a while for this to be done and so after the new column is updated we get to see the data in Listing 16-13.

Listing 16-13. Looking at the New Column Data.

```
 ('Open Price: ', 70.0)
70
('Open Price: ', 65.0)
65
('Open Price: ', 67.5)
67
('Open Price: ', 65.0)
65
('Open Price: ', 65.0)
65
('Open Price: ', 60.0)
60
rint(df['NextDayOpen'].head())
5910 0
5909 0
5908 60
5907 65
5906 65
Name: NextDayOpen, dtype: int64
```

We see that the data has been updated in the NextDayOpen column and is ready for us to build the regression model.

Now we check the correlation between the Closing price and NextDayOpen to see if there is any relationship to build our model.

Listing 16-14. Checking Correlation between columns

```
#Now checking if there is any correlation
dfnew=df[['Close','NextDayOpen']]
print(dfnew.head(5))
dfnew.corr()
Out[110]:

In [111]:
```

Table 16-2. *Correlation Between NextDayOpen and Close Columns*

	Close	NextDayOpen
Close	1	0.997021
NextDayOpen	997021	1.000000

As we can see there is definitely a good correlation between the next day open prices and the closing price of this stock. So let us go ahead and build a prediction model using linear regression method in Listing 16-15.

Listing 16-15. Linear Regression Model Creation and Stock Price Prediction

```
#Now Creating the Prediction model as correlation is very high
#Importing the libraries
from sklearn import cross_validation
from sklearn.utils import shuffle
from sklearn import linear_model
from sklearn.metrics import mean_squared_error, r2_score

#Creating the features and target dataframes
price=dfnew['Close']
print(price)
```

```
print(dfnew.columns)
features=dfnew[['NextDayOpen']]
#Shuffling the data
price=shuffle(price, random_state=0)
features=shuffle(features,random_state=0)

#Dividing data into Train and Test
X_train, X_test, y_train, y_test= cross_validation.train_test_
split(features,price,test_size=0.2, random_state=0)

#Linear Regression on Sensex data
reg= linear_model.LinearRegression()
X_train.shape
reg.fit(X_train, y_train)
regDT.fit(X_train, y_train)
y_pred= reg.predict(X_test)
y_pred= regDT.predict(X_test)

print("Coefficients: ", reg.coef_)


#Mean squared error
print("mean squared error:  ",mean_squared_error(y_test,y_pred))

#Variance score
print("Variance score: ",   r2_score(y_test, y_pred))

#STANDARD DEVIATION
standarddev=price.std()

#Predict based on Opening BSE Sensex Index and Opening Volume
#In the predict function below enter the first parameter Open for BSE and
2nd Volume in Crores
sensexClosePredict=reg.predict([[269.05]])
#175 is the standard deviation of the Diff between Open and Close of sensex
so this range
print("Stock Likely to Open at: ",sensexClosePredict , "(+-11)")
print("Stock Open between: ",sensexClosePredict+standarddev , " & " ,
sensexClosePredict-standarddev)
```

5910 55.00
5909 60.00
5908 75.00
5907 70.00
5906 72.50
5905 75.00
5904 74.00
5903 75.00
5902 74.00
5901 72.50
5900 72.50
5899 72.50
5898 72.50
5897 72.50
5896 72.50
5895 72.50
5894 67.00
5893 72.50
5892 74.00
5891 75.00
5890 75.00
5889 75.00
5888 75.00
5887 75.00
5886 75.00
5885 75.00
5884 75.00
5883 72.50
5882 75.00
5881 75.00
...
29 262.95
28 264.95
27 264.95
26 262.45

```
25 280.85
24 279.30
23 280.65
22 283.15
21 283.70
20 279.35
19 271.75
18 277.35
17 263.05
16 260.50
15 264.70
14 264.60
13 258.65
12 257.00
11 252.40
10 247.65
9 247.55
8 252.95
7 269.90
6 267.95
5 270.85
4 270.10
3 268.10
2 275.45
1 276.15
0 274.55
Name: Close, Length: 5911, dtype: float64
Index([u'Close', u'NextDayOpen'], dtype='object')
('Coefficients: ', array([0.98986882]))
('mean squared error: ', 313.02619408516466)
('Variance score: ', 0.994126802384695)
('Stock Likely to Open at: ', array([269.34940985]), '(+-11)')
('Stock Open between: ', array([500.67339591]), ' & ',
array([38.02542379]))
```

In the first part, as usual I import the common scale and shuffle linear model, mean squared error, and R2 score. After this I create features and target dataframes—the target dataframe being price that contains the closing price of the stock. The features dataframe contains the next day open column after stock. After having done that, I have shuffled the data in the price and features dataframes, and in the next step I divide the data and split it into train and test data set. After this, I instantiate the linear regression model and then I fit the x train and y train and then make the Sensex predictions based on the x test using the predict method. So now we have predictions from our model based on the linear regression technique, and we can look at the regression coefficient next, and we get a regression coefficient of 0.989 ('Coefficients:', array([0.98986882])). After this, I look at the mean squared error and then the variance score, and then look at the standard deviation for this data set. The reason for looking at standard deviation is because in the stock market price data set, standard deviation is used to measure the volatility of the stock. And this is a commentary to use a range that is plus and minus of the standard deviation applied on the prediction given by our model. So now how do you predict once we have our model ready? It is simple—using the predict method, I input the last closing price of the stock of the last day, and the model then gives you the likely opening that it is going to see the next day. Remember that using this method we cannot be too sure or accurate, and hence we are going to use the standard deviation to predict a range in which the stock is likely to move. So in the last line, predicting the stock price will open between the plus and the minus standard is how we make a prediction based on this model. That concludes the solution for this case study. Let us now move on to the next case study.

CASE STUDY 2: Detecting Financial Statements Fraud

This last case study of this book is a discussion-based case study, and hence I will be discussing the possible solution for the questions discussed here. I will, however, urge you to apply the techniques and the process that I have discussed throughout the book to develop a complete solution. This will help prepare you for real-life applications in the area of finance. The case study has been modeled on a practical problem that I had received from a client some years back while working on a project. The data set, however, is fictitious and is not taken from any organization or agency whatsoever.

I was traveling from Indore to Mumbai after a client visit and sitting in the passengers lounge when I received a frantic call from a past client, Mr. Goriz, who seemed disturbed over the phone as he was explaining to me that he had lost a lot of money in the stock market due to his fund manager's mistake in selecting a company that was called a mid-cap multi-bagger stock but had turned turtle. He asked me if it was possible to predict and find out if a company was a fraud by looking at its financial statements. I explained to him that it was possible; however, it required more discussion in detail and could not be done over phone. So we arranged to meet Mr. Goriz at his office in Mumbai the following month.

After this conversation I did a bit of research and found out more about the company and did note that until a few months ago, there were no signs in the market about this company going toward bankruptcy. There was some bad news about the rising debt with the company, but apart from that it was a shock to the market when this company collapsed and filed for bankruptcy. It later turned out that there was massive siphoning of funds done by the founders, and that was the main reason why this had happened.

Mr. Goriz was an international investor and depended on his fund managers to make investments in companies in emerging economies like India. That is what he had done to his investments with this failed company.

When I met him next, Mr. Goriz explained to me that he had lost a sum of close to $59 million of his personal funds in this so called mid-cap multi-bagger stock. He asked me if there was a possibility to predict if a company was doing fraudulent activities based on their previous financial data that they filed with the exchanges for investors like him using machine learning techniques. I explained to him that there was various research work done on this and that there were PhD theses done to develop formulas to do this; however, there was not a single model in production yet. Moreover, there was a company like LexusNexus that used its own proprietary technique for detecting frauds. However, I was sure from my own sources it was not machine learning. Mr. Goriz said he had large investments in other economies like Africa and the Middle East and wanted me to develop a universal model for him that would help him in detecting such fraudulent companies worldwide.

The requirements were very clear indeed, and I was set up to carry out something that had not been done before using machine learning.

Questions for the Case Study

Question 1:

What do you think is the central problem in this case study?

Question 2:

Do you think it is feasible to build a machine learning system using past financial statements to predict if a company is going to go bankrupt?

Question 3:

If you were to build this model, what would be your approach to predicting bankruptcy using past financial statements data?

Question 4:

What data set would you need to build this model?

Question 5:

What is your recommended Python-based solution for building this model?

Discussion on Solution to the Case Study:

Let us now discuss the questions of this case study in more detail. The purpose of this discussion is to give you insight into the problem at hand and the various options available to solve this problem. Again please remember this is a solution that I applied that I thought was best; however, you may come up with a better and more efficient approach to solving this problem, which is totally okay since that is the purpose of bringing forward these case studies.

Answer 1

This is a situation where an investor has invested into a company on the advice of a third-party fund manager who did not do much research into the functioning of the company and its founders, and so the investor got trapped in the act where the promoters siphoned off funds to other operations or accounts abroad.

Answer 2

Yes, in my opinion it is very possible to build a model based on past financial statements by the company. There is enough research available such as by Johan Perols (2010) in *Financial Statement Fraud Detection: An Analysis of Statistical and Machine Learning Algorithms. Auditing A Journal of Practice & Theory*. Another piece of research that helps explain how this can be done is by R. Meenatkshi and K. Sivaranjani in *A Comparative Study on Fraud Detection in Financial Statement using Data Mining Technique*, taken from https://www.ijcsmc.com/docs/papers/July2016/V5I7201659.pdf.

This research is enough to get started with building a machine learning system to detect financial statement frauds.

Question 3

My approach, as with building any predictive model, would start with looking at data sources for getting financial statements. There are many such sources available on the web; however, issues like copyright violations can creep in if not dealt with while selecting your source for data. There are paid services on Quandl.com that are premium services and are paid, but they do promise better accuracy. So the decision would have to made whether to buy data of companies from a source like Quandl.com or to get it free through web scraping, which may need a careful evaluation on whether any copyright violation was happening or not.

Once the data is acquired using whichever source that is fit for the project, we then go to the data clean-up stage looking for accuracy in data and for any missing values that may be there. A premium paid service is most likely to have clean data and not require much manipulation, like missing value treatment, etc.

After this we will need to select the features and target variable for our prediction model. In our case, we will need a field to tell the machine if a financial statement row is a fraud or not—something like 1 for fraud and 0 for no fraud. Once we have this supervised learning data, we can then split it into training and test data sets and use classifier algorithms to come up with a prediction model. Since our target variable is simply 1 or 0 for fraud or no fraud, respectively, the situation it makes it easier to use classifier algorithms like Naïve Bayes, logistic regression, or decision trees classifiers—to name just a few.

Question 4

I will need a sample data set, such as the one given In Table 16-3 for a company like Balmer Lawrie Co. Ltd.

Table 16-3. *Sample Balance Sheet of a Company*

Balance Sheet of Balmer Lawrie and Company	----- in Rs. Cr. ----------				
	Mar 18	Mar-17	Mar-16	Mar-15	Mar-14
	12 mths	12 mths	12 mths	12 mths	12 mths
EQUITIES AND LIABILITIES					
SHAREHOLDER'S FUNDS					
Equity Share Capital	114	114	28.5	28.5	28.5
Total Share Capital	114	114	28.5	28.5	28.5
Reserves and Surplus	1,141.86	1,051.99	1,036.44	874.56	791.14
Total Reserves and Surplus	1,141.86	1,051.99	1,036.44	874.56	791.14
Total Shareholders Funds	1,255.86	1,165.99	1,064.94	903.06	819.64
NON-CURRENT LIABILITIES					
Long-Term Borrowings	11.16	0	0	0	0
Deferred Tax Liabilities [Net]	8.19	0	0	0	0
Other Long-Term Liabilities	0.57	0.26	0.27	41.91	34.18
Long-Term Provisions	37.77	55.79	65.42	0.01	0.04
Total Non-Current Liabilities	57.69	56.05	65.69	41.92	34.22
CURRENT LIABILITIES					
Short-Term Borrowings	3.74	0	0	0	0
Trade Payables	322.79	307.12	224.29	217.71	264.57
Other Current Liabilities	206.72	244.46	230.06	174.6	201.9
Short-Term Provisions	5.04	19.91	7.93	112.27	118.05
Total Current Liabilities	538.3	571.48	462.28	504.58	584.53
Total Capital And Liabilities	1,851.85	1,793.52	1,592.91	1,449.56	1,438.40

(*continued*)

Table 16-3. (*continued*)

Balance Sheet of Balmer Lawrie and Company	----- in Rs. Cr. ----------				
ASSETS					
NON-CURRENT ASSETS					
Tangible Assets	394.8	382.67	379.16	393.17	273.28
Intangible Assets	5.27	13.19	14.1	13.67	17.01
Capital Work-In-Progress	13.25	23.31	7.26	4.3	73.79
Intangible Assets Under Development	0	0	0	0.17	0
Other Assets	1.14	0.62	0.95	0	0
Fixed Assets	414.45	419.79	401.47	411.32	364.09
Non-Current Investments	138.41	87.38	57.5	57.4	57.39
Deferred Tax Assets [Net]	0	8.02	4.96	1.71	4.35
Long-Term Loans and Advances	4.28	4.85	5.07	15.09	14.27
Other Non-Current Assets	40.35	42.16	39.52	0	0
Total Non-Current Assets	597.49	562.2	508.52	485.53	440.1
CURRENT ASSETS					
Inventories	136.63	151.7	119.76	130.1	141.72
Trade Receivables	271.27	281.61	230.33	365.13	410.69
Cash and Cash Equivalents	480.67	508.65	443.7	361.29	346.86
Short-Term Loans and Advances	24.67	4.39	8.51	84.38	75.1
Other Current Assets	341.11	284.97	282.09	23.13	23.92
Total Current Assets	1,254.36	1,231.32	1,084.39	964.03	998.29
Total Assets	1,851.85	1,793.52	1,592.91	1,449.56	1,438.40

(*continued*)

Table 16-3. (*continued*)

Balance Sheet of Balmer Lawrie and Company	----- in Rs. Cr. ----------				

OTHER ADDITIONAL INFORMATION

CONTINGENT LIABILITIES, COMMITMENTS

Contingent Liabilities	211.06		213.15	54.45	214.32	326.74

CIF VALUE OF IMPORTS

Raw Materials	16.51		14.27	36.82	84.64	42.83
Stores, Spares, and Loose Tools	1.36		1.23	1.52	0.25	0.18
Trade/Other Goods	0.75		0	0	0	0
Capital Goods	1.24		0.19	0.12	0.11	42.33

EXPENDITURE IN FOREIGN EXCHANGE

Expenditure in Foreign Currency	172.29		173.45	172.64	178.25	106.69

REMITTANCES IN FOREIGN CURRENCIES FOR DIVIDENDS

Dividend Remittance in Foreign Currency	-		-	-	-	-

EARNINGS IN FOREIGN EXCHANGE

FOB Value of Goods	19.27		11.2	104.64	13.5	15
Other Earnings	81.56		84.92	-	112.24	23.78

BONUS DETAILS

Bonus Equity Share Capital	104.49		104.49	18.99	18.99	18.99

NON-CURRENT INVESTMENTS

Non-Current Investments Quoted Market Value	-		-	-	0	0
Non-Current Investments Unquoted Book Value	138.41		87.38	57.4	57.4	57.39

(*continued*)

Table 16-3. (*continued*)

Balance Sheet of Balmer Lawrie and Company	----- in Rs. Cr. ---------				
CURRENT INVESTMENTS					
Current Investments Quoted Market Value	-	-	-	-	-
Current Investments Unquoted Book Value	-	-	-	-	-

Source: MoneyControl.com https://www.moneycontrol.com/financials/ *balmerlawriecompany/balance-sheetVI/BLC#BLC*

Question 5

I am leaving it to the reader to build the Python-based model. However, it should not be difficult for you to create one, given that I have shared with you the research papers that will help you get the formulae required for detecting fraud. I have also shared with you a sample format of a financial statement that you will need to build such a data set.

With this I conclude this last case study of this book. I hope you enjoyed it as much as I enjoyed sharing with you some of the practical problems that clients face in their businesses in the area of finance.

End Notes

Perols, Johan. "Financial Statement Fraud Detection: An Analysis of Statistical and Machine Learning Algorithms." *Auditing A Journal of Practice & Theory*. 2010;30:2.

Meenatkshi R. and Sivaranjani K. *A Comparative Study on Fraud Detection in Financial Statement using Data Mining Technique*, taken from https://www.ijcsmc.com/docs/papers/July2016/V5I7201659.pdf.

## CHAPTER 17

Pitfalls to Avoid with Machine Learning in Finance

This chapter is about pitfalls that an organization can encounter while using machine learning technology in the finance sector. Throughout the finance section, we have looked at some of the challenges that this sector faces; however, in this chapter we are going to look at the two pitfalls that any organization wanting to implement machine learning for its financial operations can avoid. The two pitfalls are extremely important for this sector, and the financial experts I surveyed were also equivocal in ascertaining that these pitfalls were the major ones an organization should avoid in order to be successful. The two pitfalls are:

- The Regulatory pitfall

- Data Privacy pitfall

Let us now look in detail how these pitfalls can affect the implementation of any new technology in the finance domain and also some ways in which we can avoid them.

The Regulatory Pitfall

The financial sector, unlike healthcare and retail, is the backbone of the economy and is the lubrication on which the entire economy runs. The healthcare, retail, and other sectors like energy all depend on the financial sector for their operations. Since this sector is all-encompassing and it is not possible to think of having any business or personal transactions without it, it becomes imperative that it has the maximum regulation that a government can provide.

© Puneet Mathur 2019
P. Mathur, *Machine Learning Applications Using Python*, https://doi.org/10.1007/978-1-4842-3787-8_17

A scope of lawful and administrative instruments affect exchange financing (and money-related administrations all the more extensively): the major foundational directions (or large-scale prudential controls) that incorporate a scope of measures intended to distinguish and alleviate dangers to the solidness of the monetary and financial framework all in all; prudential controls (or small-scale prudential directions) that incorporate measures worried about the dependability of individual money-related organizations; and non-prudential controls that cover other parts of money-related administrations control.

For setting, the Basel III Accord created by the Basel Council on Keeping Money Supervision is a case of fundamental or macro-prudential directions planned with the steadiness of the financial framework at the top of the priority list. While it is, to a great extent, "delicate law," Basel III has had a huge effect on worldwide financial direction. What's more, it has assumed a critical job in the global back scene. However, by all accounts, it not the only vehicle.

For example, the euro territory financial segment is confronting challenges on all sides from new innovations, from new market players, and from new guidelines of the government. Those difficulties, seeing that they prompt rivalry and development, are sound. They are the means by which a well-working business sector economy works.

More tightly hostile to tax evasion and countering the government is more hostile to tax evasion and is countering fear mongering financial controls expanded prudential fraud detection and money laundering regulations are creating straightforward controls; and an upgraded requirement condition for financial administrations, including through financial and exchange sanctions, have changed the scene of government-driven mediation in the arrangement of money-related administrations. Changes in the reporter managing an account system do not just affect exchange financing streams but in addition influence the "operational administrations for exchange," or the whole administration's structure around settlements, installments, and accumulations. Any new introduction of technology needs to be vetted through these new rules, regulations, and laws that are spinning up as a result of fast law making.

To begin with, imaginative new methodologies are required, including using innovation, to help change the exchange fund investment. Non-bank financing arrangements, alongside models that make impetus for paperless exchanges, advance online exchange report administration, and move forward different advances (e.g., appropriated record innovation), could change the manner in which the exchange-back business is led while limiting the impact of CBR withdrawal. There is now a progressing shift in the utilization of customary bank-intermediated exchange-back instruments toward between-organization models and production network funds.

Further, as organizations turn out to be progressively comfortable with their exchanging accomplices, their requirement for hazard supporting may diminish and their utilization of exchange fund instruments may turn out to be more particular. The approach of digitalization is likewise liable to prompt new choices in the market and urge bank-intermediated funds to work in a more savvy and straightforward way. Non-bank money-related administrations could likewise give options in contrast to conventional bank financing, making it less demanding for SMEs and different partners to go to genuinely necessary monetary administrations and add to the fourth industrial revolution.

It should be noted that work should be possible at the national level in any country, be it in the US, Europe, Asia, or any other region, to reinforce the administrative and due steadiness limits of nearby (respondent) banks, including their capacity to distinguish, screen, relieve, and counteract money-related wrongdoing, as well as follow new prudential directions in a cost-effective way. For a new technological startup, this is extremely important.

In the European Union, the regulatory framework consists of the MiFID Order 2004/39/EC, which gives a bound-together system to securities: it incorporates speculation firms, Multilateral Exchanging Offices (MTF), Controlled Markets (i.e., trades), and budgetary instruments (transferable securities, cash showcase instruments, units in aggregate speculation endeavors and subsidiaries, barring bonds, and securitized obligation).

The Order is alluded to as "Level 1" because of its method of selection together by the EU Parliament and the Board sets the standards. It should be transposed. It is supplemented by "Level 2" writings comprised of executing measures. These writings have been embraced by the part states without including the EU Parliament: Mandate 2006/73/EC, which should be transposed, and Commission Control 1287/2006, which is appropriate in the part states without transposition.

In correlation with the United States, the rulemaking powers given to controlled trades by MiFID are more restricted, and they are centered around the arrangement of what's more reasonable, methodical exchange, the affirmation of budgetary instruments to exchange, and the entrance to the controlled exchanges (articles 39, 40, and 42 of the MiFID Directive). EU-managed trades don't have any forces to control the conduct of speculation firms that are their members, either in customer-facing areas (such as best execution, information, or speculation guidance) or market-facing zones (e.g., straightforwardness for orders executed off trade). Directed trades have restricted powers even vis-à-vis their guarantors, who get the bland idea to exchange on a Directed Market by recording their plan with their supervisor.

The US securities directions and oversight are sorted out in three unique layers, described in the next section.

Government Laws and an Administrative Controller, the Securities and Trade Commission (SEC)

The Securities and Trade Commission (SEC) is in charge of ensuring financial specialists and keeping up the trustworthiness of securities markets. A few government statutes direct securities, and the authentic pattern has been to move controls from the states to the federal level. The SEC may issue rules deciphering the securities laws passed by Congress (e.g., Reg ATS for Elective Exchanging Frameworks, Reg NMS for value markets). Moreover, the SEC audits any tenets proposed by self-regulatory organizations (SROs) and has last say about whether those rules are in keeping with the Securities Exchange Act of 1934. In any case, there are restrictions to the SEC's oversight: the SEC does not direct the essential government security advertise (as government securities, Treasury and Bolstered Oversight are absolved from securities registration) but it doesnt do so in the auxiliary market; it doesn't control product fates and alternatives (Ware Fates Exchanging Commission oversight), and it has just constrained oversight over the OTC subordinate market. Civil bonds are managed by an SRO under the oversight of the SEC. The SEC additionally does not control offers of securities by business banks (managing an account controller's oversight); the business banks can go about as securities merchant and merchants without having to enroll with the SEC under constrained exclusions allowed by the GrammLeach Bliley Act (GLBAct).

States Laws and Controllers

In the United States, states enroll and direct agent merchants and speculation guides that are not enlisted with the SEC, including venture guides overseeing less than 25 million US dollars. They are seized by and must depend on the SEC rules (Section15(h)of the Trade Act). They tend to center around fighting misrepresentation inside their fringes, and they track complaints. State law authorities can seek criminal prosecutions, while the SEC is constrained to common and regulatory activities and alluding criminal matters to the Equity Department. So singular states regularly team up with the SEC and SROs to control the securities industry inside state fringes.

Self-Regulatory Organization

Self-regulatory organizations (SROs) set standards and administer business loans for their individuals. Their tenets supplement the SEC's principles and government laws, despite the fact that they may have distinctive specifics and accentuation. Any laws that SROs adopt must be reviewed and, in some cases, approved by the SEC, which has extreme authority over them. Precedents of SROs include national trades (e.g., the NYSE, Chicago Atmosphere Trade, Nasdaq Stock Market), and national securities affiliations (the present one of which, the Monetary Industry Administrative Specialist FINRA was made in 2007 as the after-effect of a merger between the National Relationship of Securities Merchants [NASD] and the control, implementation, and discretion elements of the NYSE). For city securities, a particular SRO called the Metropolitan Securities Rulemaking Board is in charge of embracing speculator security rules and overseeing representative merchants and banks that guarantee, exchange, and offer expense-excluded securities, school reserve funds, designs, and different kinds of civil securities.

The purpose of looking at some of the regulations in the two most dominant economies in the world, the European Union and the US, was not to scare or confuse you about the implementation of machine learning. It was meant to make you aware that financial regulations are very complex and detailed, and doing anything in this field requires proper knowledge of these rules and regulations.

A recent rise of unregulated currencies has occurred, which is known as cryptocurrencies. These currencies are legal tenders in countries like the US and the European Union, as well as many others. However, they are still banned in countries like India, Bolivia, etc. The technology that allows use of these non-regulated currencies is blockchain, which works on the principle of peer-to-peer networking for authenticating monetary transactions. If you wish to implement machine learning for cryptocurrencies, then you need to be aware of the regulations on whether there is a total ban in the country or only for banking purposes. Visit this website for more updated information: [1; https://en.wikipedia.org/wiki/Legality_of_bitcoin_by_country_or_territory]. In the coming years, however, there is going to be a change in attitude toward cryptocurrencies, when popular beliefs make people confident to trade in these systems.

The Data Privacy Pitfall

Now let us move toward the next pitfall—that of data privacy. Data privacy law has been pioneered by the European Union. This regulation is known as the GDPR (Global Data Privacy Regulation) Act.

Data privacy, by plan and as a matter of course, implies that business procedures that handle individual information must be outlined and worked with remembering the standards and shields to ensure information is protected (e.g., utilizing pseudonymization or full anonymization where suitable). A business should utilize the most astounding conceivable protection settings of course, so the information isn't accessible openly without unequivocal, educated assent, and can't be utilized to distinguish a subject without extra data gained independently. No personal information might be prepared except if it is done under a legitimate premise indicated by the direction or except if the information controller or processor has gotten an unambiguous and individualized certification of assent from the information subject. The information subject has the privilege to deny this assent at any time.

The security of information of US occupants is controlled by laws established on both the national and the state levels. There is no single main information security enactment in the US. Government statutes are fundamentally gone for particular divisions, as depicted all the more completely underneath, while state statutes are more centered around ensuring the security privileges of individual shoppers. The privilege to security is a precedent-based right that has been consolidated into the state constitutions of numerous states and into the laws at both the state and federal levels. Laws securing information and buyer protection depend on the rule that an individual has a desire for security except if that desire has been reduced or dispensed with by statute, or revelation. Information security and security statutes in the US are ordered to ensure the privacy of people living in the US or one of its states. Government laws apply to ensure occupants are protected, all things considered. State laws are intended to secure their inhabitants.

We have so far looked at the financial regulations and data privacy laws around the world. Now let us look at a few applications of machine learning that will require the compliance of such laws before such services are rolled out.

Use of facial recognition to make offers of financial products to customers who walk into a bank is noble; however, it raises issues of ethics—mainly that the same technology can be used to do surveillance of people. For example, is an organization permitted to capture facial data and analyze it for its advantage without the knowledge of the people walking onto its premises? Who inside the organization ensures that the data collected for its customers is not used for any other purpose than for which it is being collected? How are you as an organization going to ensure that there is no racial discrimination done by your app for targeting such offers? All this needs clarity for such an application to be successful in the long run.

You as an organization create an application that makes cryptocurrency transactions based on machine learning predictions with regard to the best times to buy and sell currencies. How are you, as a payment system gatekeeper, going to ensure that the payments made through your system are not used for money laundering? How do you ensure there is no terrorist activity funding happening through your system? If you can't answer those questions with certainty, then you are likely to run across the regulations that we discussed earlier and likely to be stalled for non-compliance of law.

You design an app that uses people's social media accounts to create financial profiles. This app could take social media updates and scan them for any hints of financial transactions, such as making payments, making purchases, taking loans from a bank, using a micro-credit facility, etc. How are you going to ensure that this profile of a user is going to be used for ethical purposes and not for unethical purposes? You may argue that this is public data, but as per law you cannot blackmail or threaten somebody if you know they have made a financial transaction. That is unethical and unlawful. How are you going to ensure the data collected by your app does not fall into the wrong hands, like those of hackers?

Your mobile app uses retina iris scans to authenticate financial transactions. How are you going to ensure that if the customer loses their mobile phone, the biometric data about the customer stored in the app is not going to fall in the wrong hands?.

Your financial app provides financial services products like insurance, credit cards, and loans based on a customer profile and analyzing it using machine learning to predict which service the customer would require now. However, this customer information that you store goes through various insurance companies' servers, a credit card company's network, and a loan processing company's databases. How are you going to ensure that you comply with the data privacy laws and ensure that all the parties involved in this transaction are held liable for a data breach?

You have a micro-credit application that gives out small loans to its users in several countries. There has been a data breach in a particular country where the data has been stolen by a hacker and leaked on the dark net. Do you know what you need to do in order to comply with the data privacy and protection laws? Do you inform all the people in that country where the breach has happened, or do you inform everyone who is using the system? These are some of the questions you will need to be prepared to deal with when you build, create, and run such a service.

Your app stores financial profiles of individuals in a central database. This profile is not visible to the user. Nor is there a provision in your application to access it. However, the customer requests to see their financial profile that you have built around them. Is your application compliant with data protection and privacy laws? GDPR prohibits such applications and its uses and imposes a heavy sanction and fine for such malafide uses. You need to be aware of all this while building an app like this. You also need to inform the user on what you do with their financial profile, such as you use machine learning algorithms to predict their financial needs in the future. You need to let your user know about this in order to comply with data privacy and protection laws.

Your financial application stores stock market transactions data and uses it to analyze the next best move through machine learning algorithms and recommend the stock pick for the customer. Your customer tomorrow decides to part ways and not do business with you and your application. In other words, they want to terminate your services. In that case, while terminating the services, do you give them an option to delete their data or keep it with you? If you do not give them this option, you may be at risk of not complying with data privacy and protection laws.

These are some of the scenarios that I have presented to you so that you can understand how complex the world of financial technology implementation is given the various laws and regulations around it in almost all countries around the world.

With this, we come to the end of this chapter. I have enjoyed presenting these case studies and applications that I gathered over the years from my interactions with various customers and clients, taking care not to reveal the real-world data but keeping the spirit of the business alive in the fictitious data that was given in each of the cases. This book has met its purpose if you are able to apply at least one application of machine learning and gain from it. I urge you to build upon the applications and use your own expertise to expand the implementation of technology that is required by business stakeholders.

End Note

[1]   Legality of Bitcoin by Territory, https://en.wikipedia.org/
      wiki/Legality_of_bitcoin_by_country_or_territory

## CHAPTER 18

Monetizing Finance Machine Learning

In this chapter, I am going to put forward some innovative ideas that can be monetized using machine learning in the financial world. I will also show you some examples where a similar approach has been used and has succeeded. For some of them, there may not be an example now, as they are more future-looking.

The three areas for monetizing are the following:

- Connected banks

- Fly-in financial markets

- Financial asset exchange

In a way, as I will explain further, the concepts of connected retail stores and connected warehouses are linked to each other. We will, however, look at them separately to understand them in greater detail and then see how they can work together.

Connected Bank

In order for us to understand what I mean by connected banks, as we did with connected retail stores, let us understand what a connected bank is not first.

- A connected bank is not about just extending digital capabilities to your existing brick and mortar bank.

- A connected bank network is not just about having customers that use digital product technology of the bank.

363

© Puneet Mathur 2019
P. Mathur, *Machine Learning Applications Using Python*, https://doi.org/10.1007/978-1-4842-3787-8_18

- A connected bank network is not just having digital profiles of customers.

- A connected bank network is not just using machine learning for your existing bank customer data and offering them the bank's products.

After looking at what a connected banks network is not, let us now look what a connected bank network should be and whether we have any examples to emulate or learn from. Let us look at a diagram in Figure 18-1 of a current connected bank network in any country.

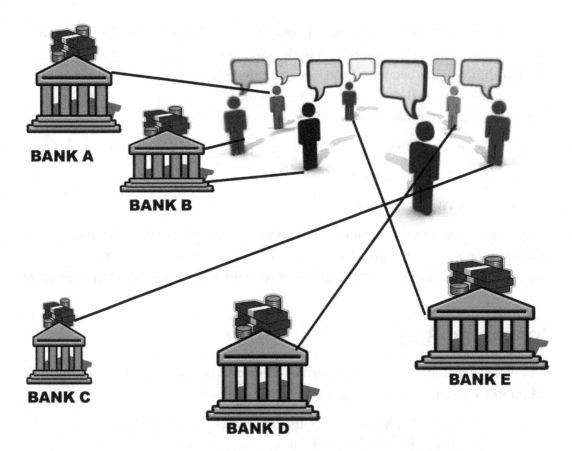

Figure 18-1. *Current connected banks network diagram*

In this example diagram of current connected banks, we see that each customer is connected with the bank either through a digital or brick and mortar network. Here, the key points to note are that Bank A, Bank B, Bank C, Bank D, and Bank E are tightly connected to their customers for transactions like credit cards, savings, bank accounts, loans, insurance, and other payments. However, these banks cannot access data on a customer of another bank. For example, if Bank E has a customer and that bank customer wants to open an account with Bank A, then that customer has to give all the information, documents, and other such know-your-customer requirements to the new bank as well. This is an overhead for each of the banks, as they have to independently verify and store information about a customer. The banks do not talk to each other, and hence they do not know about the historical information or the other banks networks about a customer. For example, a customer with Bank D may have a credit card account with them, whereas they may have a loan account with Bank B. Bank B will not have access to the customer's historical payment information, which resides in the Bank D network. Essentially the banks are dealing with customers in the dark, without knowing their financial history. For example, if a person defaults on credit cards frequently with Bank D, then the lender at Bank B can flag this person as a repeated defaulter and take corrective action. It is not possible to do so in the current network. Bank networks operate in silos, and they essentially do not talk to each other. You may argue that there are credit profiling agencies that provide credit profiles of a person—however, this is not just about credit profiling but also having access to data that gives insights into a person's savings habits or purchase cycles and things like that. By having such file load networks, the banks lose out on critical information that can help them engage with their customers better by predicting their needs, such as loan, insurance, etc.

That is why the current Digital Network of the bank is not sufficient to address all the needs of its customers and is inadequate to serve them. By creating a connected bank network, they can share information about personal banking and corporate banking customers and apply data mining to find out any hidden patterns on customers pending customer credit, etc.

Let us look at how our connected bank network will work in Figure 18-2. In this example we see that the square of banking is the same for the customer, where each customer is connected with their own banks for their own financial needs; however, there is another central customer profile database that is now available for each bank, and this central customer profile database allows the bank to access the profile of a customer after getting their permission. Let us look at how the transaction will happen in this hyperconnected environment.

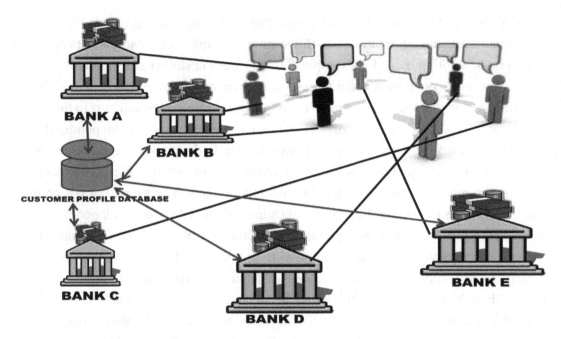

Figure 18-2. *Truly connected bank network*

Let us look at a customer of Bank C, who has been a customer of this bank for a housing loan for the last 15 years. However, the customer gets an offer from Bank A about the renewal of an insurance policy, wherein Bank A is giving this customer a better offer based on its customer profile database, where it can see that the customer has an insurance policy with another bank. Although there is competition between the banks, it is the customer who is also getting a better offer and is in a position to shift their products from one bank to another if they like the new offer. This kind of a unique scenario can only happen if we have this hyperconnected customer profile database that is centrally controlled by an agency like the central bank of a country. It can not only have personal individual customers but also corporate customers who have large financial loans and business accounts with other banks. In this hyperconnected scenario, that corporate customer's financial history is no longer a secret for the prospective bank who is about to give a loan to another corporate customer. Not just the payment history but all the financial transactions, including loan repayment credit facilities, among other things, become accessible by creation of this centrally controlled database. Although the banks lose by sharing information in terms of competitiveness, this goes a long way in introducing transparency throughout the banking system. Transparency in financial transactions brings with it a great benefit to the bankers by allowing them to read out bad clients from good ones. In this hyperconnected world, the customer gains by sharing data across banks because they do not have to provide the same data or different data again and again and then get a centralized identity in the hyperconnected banking network. The biggest challenge in implementing this kind of hyperconnected banking involves data privacy where an individual customer financial profile is shared across the different network. Customers consent to sharing of their personal or corporate financial profile is an absolute must before implementing such a system. Security in such a centralized system is also of immense importance.

Another hurdle that can be faced while implementing this kind of hyperconnected system is that of establishing identity of a person or a corporation. Issuing unique identity numbers or using existing identity documents, such as social security number, National identification number, or tax identification number, would definitely be a challenge for implementing it country to country. This is certainly not a small challenge because not many countries have National identification number for its citizens and corporations. However, in countries like the US or India, it should not put a big problem because there National identity for individuals and businesses is already set.

Fly-In Financial Markets

This is also a futuristic innovative idea; however, financial industry should start preparing for it now in order to take advantage of technological development taking place in the recent times. In this innovative use-case, the main motto of the bank becomes "Come to you!" This use-case is similar to the fly-in retail store; however, the function of a fly-in bank is entirely different. The bank flies to the customer due to the fact that there are heavy traffic jams and schedule work overload, which customer faces and hence does not find the time to go to the bank. From dispersing cash in remote areas to use of drones to deliver financial products like credit cards or debit cards to customers' doorsteps to serving customers Amazon for insurance damage claims, this innovation holds a lot of promise. The replacement of humans in some of these remote operations is inevitable.

The start of fly-in financial services market can be made independently by using social media platforms to survey and take feedback on the needs of individuals living in a particular community or locality. Geographically this tagging of surveys and then creating community-based finances and then creating the right offer to two doors people buy advertising of UV beforehand and letting them know of a financial services event in their area is what is going to be very common in the future. Bankers are increasingly going to use this route to reach out and engage with the customers who are already busy with their lives. So the bank decides to come to you and offer you financial products and services as per your needs. Things like the security of such a fly-in bank by humans or by IT are questions that the country and the communities that they are planning to target will need to answer. Figure 18-3 depicts such a scenario.

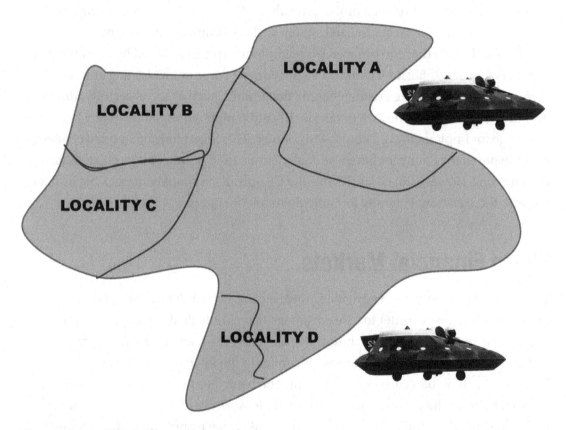

Figure 18-3. *Fly-in financial markets*

In Figure 18-3 we can see there are four notional localities in the city, and there are fly-in financial markets hovering over a locality before putting itself in a community place location. Getting financial institutions into the organizing such events would be costly affair for the company that organizes it, and hence they would like to have sponsors from various financial companies like banks and other financial institutions that would like to sell their products to the prospective customers and talk to a particular community or a locality. Division of localities and their geographic distribution for such an offline financial market is something that will evolve with time as the service is launched. The companies that organize such events will eventually target communities better performing than the ones where they get poor results in terms of financial services sales. Financial institutions would be able to have their own fly-in autonomous vehicles that would have machine learning capabilities to generate such events by serving the users and gaging their names before organizing such events. The entire process of organizing events to understanding the needs of customers and then creation of suitable products will be fairly automated in this whole process. There would be certain areas where human intervention might be required and that is where the machine learning model would take input from humans in order to fine-tune the final product offering to its potential customers.

Financial Asset Exchange

This is a concept whose time I feel has arrived. In order to understand that fully we need to understand how the financial asset-based transactions happen in today's times. An asset [1; https://fbs.com/glossary/financial-asset-29] typically is something of value to an individual. Money-related resources are elusive fluid resources—for example, bank stores, securities, and stocks, the expense of which is gotten from a legally binding case of what they speak to, as opposed to property or items they are not unmistakable physical resources separated from the records' paper.

Normal kinds of money-related resources incorporate authentications, securities, stocks, and bank stores.

A testament of store (CD) is an understanding between a financial specialist and a bank in which the speculator consents to keep a set measure of cash saved in the bank in return for an ensured loan cost. The bank may offer a higher measure of premium installment since the cash is to stay immaculate for a set timeframe. On the off chance that the speculator pulls back the CD before the finish of the agreement terms, he or she will miss out on the intrigue installments and be liable to monetary punishments.

Another well-known kind of monetary resource is securities, which are normally sold by organizations or government, keeping in mind the end goal to enable reserves to here and now extends. A security is an authoritative archive that states how much cash the financial specialist has loaned the borrower and when it should be paid back (in addition to premium) and the bond's development date.

Stocks are the main sort of money-related resources that don't have a settled after consummation date. Putting resources into stocks provides for contributors a responsibility for organization and offer in the organization's benefits and misfortunes. Stocks can be kept for any period of time until the point when the investor chooses to pitch it to another financial specialist. In spite of the way that financial records and bank accounts allude to fluid resources, they have a more constrained rate of profitability. In the meantime, CDs and currency showcase accounts confine withdrawals for a considerable length of time or years. At the point when financing costs fall, callable CDs are frequently called, and speculators confront moving their cash to conceivably bring down wage ventures.

Dispersing segments of your cash among various sorts of ventures could profit on the off chance that some of them don't have the right stuff. Each kind of asset has its own potential rewards and risks.

The current context of the financial assets are largely intangible, and they do not have a physical presence such as a document that certifies the ownership title of a person to that type of asset. There are drawbacks in this classification of financial assets and we are going to look at some of them now.

Table 18-1. *Classification of Asset class*

Asset class	Types
Intangible	Stocks, Bonds, Deposits, cypto currencies. Copyrights, Patents
Tangible	Lands, Houses, Vehicles, Buildings, High-end Mobile phones, High-end Electronic Devices, Robots, Drones, Machineries.

In Table 18-1, we can see intangible and tangible types. Tangible types of assets are those that we can touch and feel as humans. Variable types of assets are the ones that cannot be touched or felt by the senses. It is a simple categorization and this is fairly easy to understand. There is no single asset exchange that exists for somebody who is owning an asset like stocks and bonds, deposits, or cryptocurrencies to exchange them not just among the intangible assets but also with the tangible assets.

Let us look at an example that will make it clear as to what I am trying to say with regards to the asset exchange that we are talking about. Let's say a person holds a patent and they want to convert it into cash. Such a facility where they can go to sell their patents and get cash in return does not exist. Similarly there is no such exchange where somebody could go and offer their cash deposits and convert by buying copyrights from a particular person who owns them. Let's come to the second class of tangible assets, where we see a person on a high-end mobile phone and they would like to convert it in exchange rate for an electronic device in return. The change of asset class from an a device like a mobile phone or a drone or a machinery and the customer would like to exchange it with a land or a house. This type of asset exchange is very innovative and surely does not exist anywhere in the world.

Buying and selling of engines for sale in intangible assets is not there even today The concept here is to remove this differentiation of a financial asset in terms of intangible and tangible values, and I will give you an example where such an exchange can be built with the use of blockchain technology and machine learning to evaluate the current market price of an asset belonging to any asset class. Let us look at an example. If Paul is worth 2 million dollars and wants to buy a house in a particular city, then in the current scenario he needs to first sell the stock in the stock exchange and then buy the house by going to that particular city and hunting for it. However, in case the best new innovative financial asset exchange system comes into play, then the person who wants to buy a house directly goes to the financial asset exchange and offers start for a house in a particular locality or community inside the city. Such an asset exchange will make the life of people extremely fast as far as financial transactions are concerned. Similarly a person owning machineries or robots can exchange their things for stuff or cash deposits. I will call this financial services system of an asset exchange come into existence.

Although financial assets exchanges look very simple in operation, they are the biggest hurdle or roadblock in the financial regulations any country. There is a strong need among the consumers who do not have the time to go to each individual market to buy and sell products, and they want easy asset exchanges that take care of all this conversion for them. The financial regulators will need to understand this name and come out with solid regulations that check money laundering and fraud transactions when they happen using this kind of the universal asset exchange.

The ability to establish a market value for each of the tangible and intangible assets needs a message data set input into a machine learning system, which will then use prediction models to predict the future growth in the assets value in comparison to what it is right now. This will help the decision maker or the buyer to avoid an inappropriate decision by looking at its intrinsic value, the current offered market value, and the predicted market value for that financial asset. The unique selling proposition for this kind of exchange will be the use of machine learning to predict the future price of such tangible and intangible assets. So we have seen the last innovative concept that offers to alter the way financial assets are going to be evaluated, bought, and sold in the future. To start, a company can create an asset exchange between intangible assets that are easier to exchange and create another financial asset exchange for the tangible products. It can then later look to create and merge both the financial asset exchanges after all the regulatory compliances have been met.

End Note

[1]   Financial Asset, `https://fbs.com/glossary/financial-asset-29`

Index

A

B

C

© Puneet Mathur 2019
P. Mathur, *Machine Learning Applications Using Python*, https://doi.org/10.1007/978-1-4842-3787-8

S